The Working Class in American History

A list of books in the series The Working Class in American History appears at the end of the book.

Gender at Work

Most, however, had thought only for the future, asking, "Recken everting'ull shut down now?" or, "When u soldiers all come back tudu rightful jobs, somebody's gonna be laid off." The woman with the cactus, her husband behind her on the stoop, bandages still on his eyes, said, "I don't guess a woman can ever find a job, now"; and in her voice, as in all the other voices, Gertie could hear no rejoicing, no lifting of the heart that all the planned killing and wounding of men were finished. Rather it was as if the people had lived on blood, and now that the bleeding was ended, they were worried about their future food.

Harriette Arnow, *The Dollmaker*

Gender at Work

The Dynamics of Job Segregation by Sex during World War II

Ruth Milkman

UNIVERSITY OF ILLINOIS PRESS
Urbana and Chicago

© 1987 by Ruth Milkman
Manufactured in the United States of America
1   2   3   4   5   C   P   5   4   3   2   1

This book is printed on acid-free paper.

The quotation in the epigraph is taken from
The Dollmaker by Harriet Arnow (Macmillan Press, 1954).

Library of Congress Cataloging-in-Publication Data

Milkman, Ruth, 1954–
  Gender at work.

  (The working class in American history)
  Includes bibliographical references.
  Includes index.
  1. Sexual division of labor—United States—
History—20th century.   2. Women—Employment—United
States—History—20th century.   3. Women in trade-
unions—United States—History—20th century.   I. Title.
II. Series.
  HD6060.65U5M55   1987   331.4′0973   86-7001
  ISBN 0-252-01352-2 (cloth; alk. paper)
  ISBN 0-252-01357-3 (paper; alk. paper)

for my parents

Contents

Illustrations

Tables

Preface

In the late 1970s, when I began work on this book, more women were working outside the home than ever before. A new generation of feminists had challenged the age-old inequality between women and men. There were laws banning sex discrimination. And yet, most women still worked in poorly paid, low-status, stereotypically "female" jobs. Job segregation struck me as fundamental to gender inequality. It kept women's wages low and maintained their economic dependence on men.

The consequences of segregation were clear to me, but the explanation for its resilience was more elusive. A study of World War II seemed relevant. The one apparent exception to the longstanding pattern of segregation was the massive integration of women into "men's jobs" in wartime industry. Yet after the war, sex segregation had been quickly reconstructed. By examining that historical process, I hoped to gain some insight into the dynamics of segregation and the reasons for its long-term persistence.

Inevitably, I began with certain preconceptions—most of which I had to abandon along the way. I began with the presumption that sex segregation was broken down during the war; instead, I found extensive evidence of wartime segregation in the very industries where the influx of women was greatest. I started out viewing women's entry into "men's jobs" during the war as a feminist achievement; I soon realized that women war workers themselves were not much interested in proving they were men's equals, but simply in earning good pay on the home front—which was really an extension of domesticity, rather than a challenge to it.

There were other surprises of a different order. I began with the view that organized labor played the primary role in shaping the sexual division of labor, but I soon became convinced that the predominant influence was that of management. Initially, I wanted to compare the auto and electrical workers' unions in order to explore the differences between Socialist and Communist union leadership, but I concluded that the contrast between women's experiences in the two unions was due to other factors. And although I had intended to examine the war experience itself in order to explain the postwar pattern of job segregation, I found that to make sense out of the war and the years that followed it, I had to look at the prewar period in detail. Through such twists and turns, the book gradually assumed its present shape.

The text had its inception as a dissertation at the University of California at Berkeley. Michael Burawoy, a model thesis director, offered thoughtful guidance, rigorous criticism, and unfailing support at every stage of the project. David Brody and Michael Rogin also provided valuable help, carefully reviewing successive drafts of the text and offering many bibliographic suggestions. In addition, Karen Anderson, Nancy Gabin, Ruth Meyerowitz, and Ronald Schatz, all of whom were engaged in closely related research, generously shared their unpublished work and led me to many sources that I would otherwise never have discovered. I was also fortunate to have the financial assistance of the Danforth Foundation, the Mabelle McLeod Lewis Memorial Fund, the Social Science Research Council, and the Woodrow Wilson National Fellowship Foundation.

Many individuals who played a part in the historical events traced in this book took the time to share their memories of the 1930s and 1940s with me. Although few of these oral interviews are cited directly in the text, they influenced my thinking a great deal. My thanks to Erwin and Estar Baur, Andrew Court, Edward Cushman, Malcolm Denise, Edith Fox, the late Jesse Glaberman, Martin Glaberman, Ronald Haughton, the late Ruth Young Jandreau, Mildred Jeffrey, Clarence Johnson, Clark Kerr, Kathleen Lowrie, Frank MacIntosch, Al Nash, Carnegie Pardue, the late Stephanie Prociuk, James Robson, Hilda and Larry Rogin, Brendan Sexton, Edith Van Horn, Morley Walker, Mariana Wells, and B. J. Widick.

I received extensive help from the staffs of many libraries and archives around the country. Dione Miles at the Wayne State University Archives of Labor History and Mark McColloch at the UE Archives at the University of Pittsburgh deserve special thanks. Nat Spero, at the UE's research department, was also very helpful and allowed me to copy materials from his office files. I was less fortunate, however, in gaining access to corporate archival records. Although some fragmentary materials relevant to my project were available in the Ford Archives, most of the accessions on labor issues, although listed in the card catalog, have been "transferred to the company's internal archives," to which I was refused access. General Motors and Westinghouse also rebuffed my repeated inquiries regarding such records. (Westinghouse, however, did inform me that it keeps its historical records in an abandoned salt mine near the East Pittsburgh plant.) I was admitted to the General Electric library in Schenectady, but found no primary data of the type I sought. Fortunately, I was able to gather some data on management from the National Archives, because of the government's extensive role in the wartime economy.

I am deeply indebted to the many friends and colleagues who read earlier drafts of the book and guided me in making revisions. Carmen Sirianni offered extraordinarily careful and incisive criticisms and helped me to resolve an important ambiguity in an earlier formulation of the argument. Fred Block, the late Bert Cochran, Nelson Lichtenstein, Mark McColloch, Ronnie Steinberg, Alan Wolfe, and two anonymous peer reviewers read the entire draft text and provided many useful comments and criticisms. Thanks are also due to the editorial boards of *Feminist Studies* and *Politics and Society,* both of which published portions of the text in article form and offered critical suggestions along the way. Others who read portions of the manuscript at various stages and offered valuable help include Ava Baron, Eileen Boris, Steve Fraser, Nancy Gabin, Marty Glaberman, Clara Lilyblade, David Matza, Karen Skold, Judith Stacey, and Erik Wright. I am especially indebted to David Brody, who was involved with the project from its inception, and who also served as an exemplary editor in the final stages of rewriting.

Finally, my deepest appreciation goes to Nathan Laks, whose unfailing love, good sense, patience, and support sustained me during the long revision process.

New York, N.Y.
October 1985

1 Introduction

World War II was a major turning point in the history of America's working women. Wartime mobilization swept aside the traditional sexual division of labor, and women entered "men's jobs" in basic industry on a massive scale. Women showed that they were fully capable of performing such work. Yet after the war, they were forced back into traditionally female occupations, or out of the labor market altogether. This was no mere temporary setback. On the contrary, the pattern set after the war has persisted to the present. Although the number of women workers has increased rapidly in recent decades, the vast majority are confined to "pink-collar" jobs, while men continue to predominate in the better-paid manufacturing jobs from which women were expelled during the demobilization.

·The defeminization of basic industry after the war raises a number of difficult questions. First, it seems to defy the logic of profitability inherent in the capitalist system—particularly because women's labor has always been cheaper than men's. Having discovered that women could be successfully substituted for men in industrial jobs, why should employers have insisted on returning to the prewar pattern of sex-segregated work? Second, why did women war workers not protest their expulsion from primary manufacturing jobs—or, if they did, why was their resistance so ineffective? Finally, what about the role of the unions? The Congress of Industrial Organizations (CIO), which had organized the mass-production industries during the late 1930s, was strongly opposed to employment discrimination on the basis of race or sex. Why did the industrial unions fail to protect women's wartime employment gains? This book explores these critical questions through a detailed analysis of two key industries, auto and electrical manufacturing.

Both industries were at the center of the dramatic transformation in the sexual division of labor that took place during the 1940s. At the peak of wartime employment, women constituted one-third of the production workers in the automotive industry and half of those in electrical manufacturing.[1] These industries also confronted two of the strongest unions in the labor movement. At the war's end, the United Automobile Workers (UAW) was the largest union in the United States, with one million members, 28 percent of whom were female. The United Electrical Workers (UE) was the third largest union in the CIO and the largest of the labor organizations in which the Communist Party enjoyed substantial influence during this period. In 1945, 40 percent of the seven hundred thousand UE members were women.[2] Both the UAW and the UE took relatively advanced positions on women's issues, and both were deeply involved in conflicts with management over the sexual division of labor at the war's end.

The exclusion of women from the "men's jobs" that they had performed during the war is a specific case of a much more fundamental paradox. Throughout the history of capitalism, the incorporation of women into wage labor seemed to hold the promise of equality between the sexes. As "impersonal" market relations spread into more and more spheres of life, industrial capitalism was expected by friend and foe alike to develop a sex-blind division of labor. Both Marx and Weber predicted this in the nineteenth century, and many social commentators have echoed their arguments since. In recent years, the view that increased female employment will lead to gender equality has won new adherents against the background of the dramatic postwar expansion of the female work force and the resurgence of feminism.[3]

However, the economic and political forces that were expected to undermine the sexual division of labor have not done so. Profit-maximizing capitalist firms should have continually substituted cheap female labor for its more costly male equivalent, eliminating sex differentials in wages; yet this has not occurred. And the emergence of capitalist democracies and ideologies promoting individual rights, which produced female suffrage and the female citizen, should have led long since to a sustained political assault on so blatant a barrier to individual achievement as sex-exclusive employment practices. Organized labor and the feminist movement have indeed challenged sex discrimination at many points in the history of capitalism. And the contemporary women's movement has done much to undermine the *legitimacy* of gender inequality at work. Yet the position of women in the labor market has undergone remarkably little change. The starkest indicator of this is the gender gap in earnings: full-time, year-round women workers today earn, on average, 62 cents for every dollar paid to their male counterparts—a ratio that has not changed significantly for half a century.[4]

The real problem is not "discrimination" in the sense that women are paid 62 percent of what men receive for the same work—although such practices are not unknown. Most of the pay gap is due to the concentration of women in poorly paid, low status occupations. Pervasive stereotypes designate such jobs as "women's work," while more desirable positions are reserved for men. The specific jobs performed by men and women sometimes change, because the occupational structure is always in motion, with new positions constantly being created and old ones destroyed. But job segregation itself has been continually maintained and reproduced throughout the history of capitalism.[5] Like the earnings gap, the extent of segregation has been remarkably consistent over time. Today, just as at the turn of the century, women are concentrated in relatively few occupations, clearly labeled "women's work."[6]

How can this pattern of segregation be explained? What sorts of struggles have taken place over it—and with what results? Insofar as these questions have been explored at all, attention has focused on the dynamics of capitalism, or of patriarchal capitalism, at the most general level. For example, some argue that segregation is a "divide and rule" strategy on the part of capital. The attempts to develop a theoretical account of segregation (discussed below) offer valuable insights, but leave many issues unresolved. This book explores the problem at a different level, examining the history of sex segregation and the struggles around it through two industry case studies.[7]

An industry-specific, historical approach to job segregation by sex has several advantages. The first involves the structural inertia characteristic of sex-typing. Once a job is labeled "male" or "female," the demand for labor to fill it is sex-specific, barring disruptions of labor supply or a restructuring of the labor process. Once sex-typing takes root in an industry or occupation, it is extremely difficult to dislodge. From that time on, in day-to-day managerial practice, "traditions" of sex-typing guide employment decisions. To understand these traditions requires a historical investigation of the formation of the labor market for the specific type of work involved. The appropriate unit of analysis here is the industry or occupation, not the labor market as a whole.

A second advantage to an industry-specific strategy for exploring job segregation is the opportunity for systematic comparative analysis. Examining the similarities and differences between industries helps isolate the factors that produce distinct patterns of employment by sex. Auto and electrical manufacturing make an especially illuminating comparison. Despite their parallel development into large, concentrated industries early in the twentieth century, they always had different patterns of female employment. Women were a higher proportion of production workers in electrical manufacturing than in any other durable goods industry—about one-third of the total in peacetime. In auto, by contrast, women never accounted for even a tenth of the production work force until World War II. As is demonstrated in chapter 2, electrical manufacturing's extensive employment of women reflected its relative labor intensity as well as the distinct nature of its labor process. And, as shown in later chapters, the

contrasting sexual divisions of labor in auto and electrical manufacturing produced different types of struggles over women's position in these two industries during the crucial mid-1940s.

A final advantage of an industry-specific, comparative approach is that it
exposes the limits of deterministic theories of job segregation by sex. Both
the theories of Marxist-feminists who have analyzed women's work, and those
of radical economists who view sex segregation as part of labor market segmentation, reduce the sexual division of labor to structural features of the
larger society.[8] The analysis here, while borrowing insights from these theories, rejects their determinism, stressing instead the historically specific
economic, political, and social factors that shape patterns of employment by
sex. Before turning to the historical comparison, however, it is worth looking
more closely at the theories themselves.

Theoretical Perspectives on Job Segregation

Marxist-feminists took up the problem of job segregation as part of an effort
to develop a theory of women's subordination in capitalist society. The first
analyses centered on the connection between women's position in the family
and in the work force, and argued that job segregation derives indirectly from
domestic life. Preserving a family arrangement in which women perform unpaid housework is in the interest of capital, the argument runs, because it
minimizes the costs of maintaining and reproducing the labor power (or ability
to work) of family members. It follows that capital also benefits from confining
women to jobs that pay low wages, because this ensures their economic de-
pendency on husbands or fathers for whom they perform unpaid housework.
In this view, it is the sexual division of labor within the family that constitutes
women as cheap, expendable labor.[9]

The early Marxist-feminists also saw "women's work" outside the home as
modeled on domestic labor. In industries like food and clothing, for example,
female wage-earners produce goods once manufactured by women at home;
as secretaries, teachers, waitresses, and health-care workers, women perform
the wifely and motherly tasks of schedule management, socializing children,
cleaning up, caring for the ill, and so on. Whatever their jobs, women workers
are ideologically defined not as workers, but as *women* who happen to be
working. The early Marxist-feminists understood job segregation as the institutional expression of this ideology, keeping women in low-paying jobs and
economically dependent on men and ensuring their continued service as unpaid family workers.[10]

Although this view of the interdependence between the sexual division of
labor at home and at work offers insight into the general functions of sex

segregation, it does not explain why *particular* jobs are labeled "female" or "male." Instead, it accepts sex-stereotyping at face value, as if the analogies between domestic labor and women's work outside the home were an explanation for women's location in the paid work force. However, because housework consists of an infinite variety of tasks, such analogies can be extended arbitrarily to virtually any job that women happen to be doing. During World War II, when industrial jobs previously considered quintessentially masculine were transferred to women, the work involved was suddenly proclaimed to resemble housework.[11] This kind of occupational sex-labeling obscures rather than reveals the reasons for the specific location of women in the work force. Confusion on this point is a serious limitation of the early Marxist-feminist literature.

Theories of labor market segmentation have done more to explain why particular jobs are allocated to certain types of workers—if not to women specifically, then to the larger population of "secondary" workers. In this view, there is a correspondence between the sexual division of labor and the cleavage between stable, high-paying "primary" jobs in oligopolistic firms and "secondary" jobs, with high turnover and low wages, in the competitive sector of the economy. In one influential formulation of segmentation theory, the primary sector is itself divided into two parts: the predominantly white and male "independent primary" group of professional, managerial, and technical jobs; and the racially and sexually mixed semi-skilled, blue- and white-collar "subordinate primary" segment.[12]

One basic problem is that this approach treats women, racial minorities, and other forms of cheap labor in an undifferentiated way. Sex segregation is seen as one of several "divisions" among workers in advanced capitalism. The critical link between the family and women's paid work—ultimately the unique feature of women's relationship to the labor market (and the major focus of the early Marxist-feminist discussion)—is simply absent. The strength of the segmentation literature is its insight into the way in which different economic constraints operate within each sector of the economy. But the typology of labor markets suggested (independent primary, subordinate primary, and secondary markets) is far too simple, and the empirical propositions are often inaccurate. For example, the auto and electrical manufacturing industries fall into identical categories according to this literature. Yet, as is demonstrated in chapter 2, they have always had sharply contrasting sexual divisions of labor.[13]

The presumptions of segmentation theory about the interests of different classes and genders in (or against) a sexually segregated labor market are also problematic. The *raison d'etre* for sex segregation (as well as other types of segmentation), in this view, is capital's continual effort to "divide and conquer the workforce."[14] Workers (both male and female), conversely, are presumed to have an interest in opposing segregation in favor of class unity. Thus "interests" are determined by the class structure, not historically formed.

It is certainly plausible to argue that capital has a class interest in a divided labor force. However, on the level of the firm, sex segregation conflicts with capital's interest in profit maximization—at least in firms employing male workers. Treating male and female labor as noninterchangeable (the operating principle of segregation) limits the possibility of substituting cheap female labor for the more costly labor of men. As long as female labor is cheaper, this also limits profits.

One way to explain such apparently irrational firm-level behavior is to view the ideology of sex-typing, which figured so prominently in the early Marxist-feminist literature, as a means of enforcing the *collective* (or class) interest of capital in job segregation on individual capitals, despite their short-term interest in substitution. But segmentation theory misses this aspect of the problem entirely, simply conflating the class interest of capital with the interests of individual employers. Analysis of the specific economic and political constraints facing employers in various industries could generate a fuller, more adequate typology of labor markets. The variability in patterns of employment by sex in different industries might reflect different resolutions of the conflict between the collective and individual interests of capital, depending on specific historical conditions.

Labor market segmentation theory not only takes the interest of capital in sex segregation as given, but also does the same with the interests of workers. As Heidi Hartmann has pointed out in a pathbreaking contribution to the Marxist-feminist literature, segmentation theory presumes that male workers have an interest in class unity, and therefore in opposing job segregation by sex. On the contrary, Hartmann argues, "as men" male workers have a material interest in perpetuating segregation, because it enforces low wages for women and keeps them dependent on and subordinate to men, both at work and at home. In her view, the interests of male workers do not conflict with, but rather reinforce, the interest of capital in sex segregation.[15] For Hartmann, moreover, job segregation is not only part of the capitalist mode of production, but also a product of a separate, coexisting system of male domination, patriarchy, that preceded capitalism and is theoretically irreducible to it.[16]

Hartmann suggests not only that men have an interest in job segregation "as men," but also that they have historically had greater organizational resources than women—for example, male-dominated labor unions, which have frequently exhibited hostility toward women workers. This introduces a dimension conspicuously absent in the segmentation literature. While the power of labor organizations to influence hiring and placement policies has been quite limited in U.S. labor history, their relationship to sex segregation must be systematically addressed. In this respect Hartmann's theory is a major advance.

However, her argument shares some defects with the labor market segmentation theory she so insightfully criticizes. Just as that perspective ignores the conflict between the class interests of capital and the interests of individual employers, Hartmann ignores the conflict between male workers' class and gender interests—perhaps because she is reacting to a theory in which gender interest is totally invisible. Hartmann correctly identifies the dominant historical pattern of male workers' (and unions') hostility toward women workers. But in some instances, men have actively fought against gender inequality on the basis of self-interest, as is illustrated extensively in later chapters of this book. It would seem far more fruitful to examine the conditions under which male workers' class interests have prevailed over their gender interests, and the conditions under which the opposite has occurred, than to invoke the interests of "men as men" to explain the dominant historical trend.

All of these theories are useful in suggesting the overall functions of sex segregation for capitalism (and in Hartmann's case for patriarchy as well). But they do far less well in explaining the specific location of "women's" and "men's" jobs in particular firms or industries. At this point, indeed, they all lapse into determinism. For the early Marxist-feminists, the domestic division of labor determines women's location in wage work. For the segmentationists, dualism in the marketplace determines the sexual division of labor. And finally, for Hartmann, patriarchal power, manifest in such organizational forms as exclusionary unionism, determines "woman's place" in the labor market.[17]

Industrial Structure and the Sexual Division of Labor

The designation of jobs as "male" or "female" is a more complex and historically contingent process than any of these theories acknowledges. None of them pays sufficient attention to the effect of industrial structure on the sexual division of labor and on the struggles that take place over "woman's place" in the labor market. The comparative case-study analysis in the following chapters will demonstrate that an industry's pattern of employment by sex reflects the economic, political, and social constraints that are operative when that industry's labor market initially forms. An industry's location in the competitive or monopoly sector, the factor stressed in the segmentation literature, is but one of many such constraints. Others include the labor intensity of the industry, the available supplies of female and male labor, and their relative costs. An additional factor is the actual or anticipated political impact of the employer's choice of a labor force. For example, resistance of male workers to female substitution might dissuade employers from hiring women.

The formative period is critical, because an industry's pattern of employment by sex, once established, quickly gains all the weight of tradition and becomes extraordinarily inflexible.[18] Employers show surprisingly little interest in tampering with it, even to enhance profitability. Workers, too—both male and female—tend to accept the sexual division of labor, once established, as "natural." Such is the power of the ideology of sex-typing.

On those infrequent occasions when workers do challenge the prevailing definition of women's position, the existing sexual division of labor in the industry defines the political terrain. Where the labor force is predominantly male, conflict generally centers around the issue of exclusion, or hiring discrimination. Where female representation is substantial, however, conflict focuses instead on the boundaries between women's and men's work *within* the industry. Here the prospects for workers demanding gender equality—especially the elimination of sex differentials in pay—are relatively favorable. Not only does the presence of women workers with an immediate interest in parity galvanize such demands, but fear of female substitution, which would lose all its appeal for management if wage differentials were eliminated, also encourages male workers to support them.

The impact of industrial structure on the sexual division of jobs and on struggles between labor and management over women's position is illustrated in the historical comparison of auto and electrical manufacturing in the following chapters. The primary focus is on the dramatic changes that took place in the 1940s. But the significance of the war and postwar transformations can only be understood against the background of the initial definition of "women's work" in each industry in the prewar era.

In chapter 2, accordingly, the early history of the auto and electrical manufacturing industries is examined, and an explanation for their contrasting patterns of female employment is developed. Although both emerged in the same period as highly concentrated, mass-production industries, electrical manufacturing employed a much higher proportion of women from the outset than did auto. This is because of the relatively high labor intensity of electrical manufacturing, and its heavy reliance on piecework as a means of control over workers. In contrast, automotive management used the moving assembly line together with *high* wages to control labor, so that women workers—whose main appeal was their "cheapness"—remained marginal.

Having thus crystallized early in the twentieth century, the sexual division of labor in both industries proved extraordinarily stable. As shown in chapter 3, this was so even during the Great Depression of the 1930s, when one might have expected the profitability crisis to lead both auto and electrical manufacturing firms to replace male workers with cheaper female labor on a massive scale. Instead, the economic contraction helped to stabilize the patterns of sex segregation previously established in each industry. Nor did the rise of industrial unionism, which transformed so many other aspects of auto and electrical workers' situation, alter the sexual division of labor. The experience of the 1930s graphically demonstrates the hegemony of the ideology of sex-typing over management as well as the difficulty of building sustained opposition to it among workers.

Against this background, the impact of the economic mobilization for World War II on the sexual division of labor in auto and electrical manufacturing is traced in chapter 4. Contrary to the presumption of most commentators that sex segregation was broken down during the war, this chapter shows that *new* patterns of segregation were established "for the duration" within previously male sectors. Rosie the Riveter did a "man's job," but more often than not she worked in a predominantly female department or job classification. The boundaries between women's and men's work shifted their location, but were not eliminated. Indeed, the wartime experience is an extreme example of how job segregation by sex can be reproduced in the face of dramatic economic changes.

While segregation persisted during the war, the disruption of the prewar sexual division of labor was nevertheless extensive. The presence of women in "men's jobs" precipitated major struggles between management and the young CIO unions in both auto and electrical manufacturing, the subject of chapter 5. In both industries, the unions were primarily concerned with what would happen once the military conflict was over. Would the sexual division of labor be permanently altered? On what terms should women be permitted to replace men, even temporarily, in view of the potential postwar consequences? In the auto industry, the union demanded equal pay for equal work, arguing that virtually all the war jobs being done by women were really "men's jobs" (and thus deserved "men's pay"), because men had been the vast majority of prewar auto workers. But this approach was not viable in the electrical industry, which had always had large numbers of women in its work force. The UE was thus led to a more radical approach to the issue. It ultimately questioned the basis for differential evaluations of female and male labor, even when men and women did not do "equal work," and demanded "equal pay for jobs of comparable worth." Thus, their contrasting historical patterns of employment by sex produced distinct forms of struggle in these two industries.

In both, the equal pay struggles were primarily directed at protecting the wages of "men's jobs" in the face of wartime female substitution. Accordingly, management and *male* workers were the protagonists in these struggles. Although women workers benefited from equal pay, they were marginal to the union efforts to win it, especially in the auto industry. But the war also brought dramatic changes to the unions themselves as women workers flooded their ranks. The changing role of women in the UAW and the UE is surveyed in chapter 6. To win the allegiance of the new recruits, many of whom became union members automatically under special wartime "maintenance-of-membership" agreements, the unions hired unprecedented numbers of women organizers and staffers. Female union activism also flourished at the rank-and-file level during the war, generating new campaigns for gender equality in industry. By the war's end, women were much more involved in union-management conflicts over the sexual division of labor than in the mobilization period, although still less so than their male co-workers.

In both the auto and electrical industries, women workers were laid off in massive numbers immediately after the war. And as consumer goods production resumed, employers refused to rehire women in "men's jobs," even when this violated union seniority rules. Women were almost entirely excluded from postwar employment in the auto industry, except in the few jobs that had always been considered "women's work." In electrical manufacturing, too, women were eliminated from the "men's jobs" that they had performed during the war, although here the effect was much less dramatic because there were so many traditionally female jobs in the industry. In chapter 7, the logic of management's postwar reconstruction of the prewar sexual division of labor is explained—in terms of industry structure, on the one hand, and in relation to the political constraints which existed at the war's end, on the other.

Women workers in both the auto and the electrical industries protested against the restoration of the prewar sexual division of labor, but their efforts were generally ineffective. These protest actions and the reasons for their failure are analyzed in chapter 8. Both the forms of struggle and the obstacles to success were quite different in the two industries. In auto, where the main issue was the violation of women war workers' seniority rights, a major problem was male workers' collusion with management in excluding women from postwar jobs. Because fear of unemployment was widespread, it was difficult to mobilize male auto workers to protest against sex discrimination in seniority at the war's end. They saw their interest as best served by a male monopoly over the bulk of jobs in the industry. In electrical manufacturing, however, the same fear of unemployment instead led men to define their interest as the elimination of sex discrimination in wages, in order to reduce the likelihood of female substitution. Thus the electrical workers' union carried on its fight for equal pay for comparable worth into the demobilization period. Here the problem was not lack of unity between men and women (as in the auto industry), but the union's postwar weakness and internal division. In both industries, then, although for different reasons, historical circumstances were unfavorable to efforts to maintain women's wartime gains.

The implications of the events of the 1940s for women workers today are explored in chapter 9. Of course, no direct extrapolation is possible. The war and immediate postwar years were highly unusual ones both for women workers and for the labor movement. The CIO unions were at the peak of their militance and strength, and the war mobilization not only created a dramatic rupture with the previous sexual division of labor but also brought women into the central strongholds of industrial unionism. Even under these unusually favorable circumstances, women workers' protests failed to prevent the reconstruction of a postwar world of sex-segregated work modeled along prewar lines. Yet the 1940s experience remains relevant today, both for understanding the persistence of segregation and for confronting the challenge of dismantling it.

2 Fordism and Feminization: The Sexual Division of Labor and the Development of the Labor Process in Auto and Electrical Manufacturing

The electrical products and automobile industries grew from tiny fledglings into giants of mass production during the early twentieth century. Each elaborated a distinctive pattern of female employment reflecting its particular mode of managerial control. Automobile manufacturing developed as a high-wage, capital-intensive industry based on the use of the moving assembly line. In this "Fordist" system (named for its premier practitioner, Henry Ford), employers had relatively little incentive to substitute female labor for its more expensive male equivalent. Electrical manufacturing was far more labor-intensive, however, relying not on machinery but on elaborately constructed piecework systems to ensure control over labor—conditions that encouraged extensive employment of women and girls.

As early as 1910, more than one-third of the operatives and laborers in the electrical industry were female, compared to less than 3 percent in auto. The gap narrowed somewhat after 1910, but electrical manufacturing consistently employed a much greater proportion of women than auto (Table 1). Originally, however, the electrical manufacturing labor force had been almost entirely male. In 1880, the U.S. Bureau of Labor found only seventy-two women engaged in the manufacture of "electrical apparatus and supplies," a mere 5 percent of the young industry's work force.[1] According to Elizabeth Baker, "When Edison established his first factory at Menlo Park in 1880 only men were employed to make lamps—specialists who knew both the method of manipulating glass and wire and the basic theory upon which the lamp was constructed. It was largely handwork, and costly. Then, by a series of steps, the work was so greatly simplified, minutely divided, and consolidated that it could be performed by machines tended by women. [By 1910], a surprising 80 out of every 100 makers of electrical lamps were women and girls."[2]

Table 1. Female Employment in the Auto and Electrical Manufacturing Industries, 1910 to 1958—Selected Years

	Auto			Electrical		
Year	Total Employment	Number of Women	Women as % of Total	Total Employment	Number of Women	Women as % of Total
1910[a]	41,516	1,014	2.4%	33,654	12,093	35.9%
1920[a]	231,462	15,644	6.8	85,249	29,751	34.9
1930[a]	321,214	23,182	7.2	143,220	47,439	33.1
1939[b]	447,000	29,500	6.6	295,900	100,300	33.9
1940[b]	533,300	30,400	5.7	334,200	107,600	32.2
1944[c]	746,000	185,000	24.8	778,000	380,400	48.9
1945[c]	705,800	158,100	22.4	730,900	347,200	47.5
1946[c]	646,300	61,400	9.5	460,900	181,600	39.4
1950[d]	707,000	70,700	10.0	817,100	310,500	38.0
1958[e]	624,000	62,400	10.0	1,095,200	394,300	36.0

Sources:
a. Janet M. Hooks, *Women's Occupations through Seven Decades,* U.S. Department of Labor, Women's Bureau, Bulletin no. 218 (1947), 221-22, 237; operatives and laborers.
b. U.S. Department of Labor, Bureau of Labor Statistics, *Women in Factories,* mimeographed (1947), 6-7; production workers; figures for the month of October of each year.
c. Ibid., figures for the month of April of each year.
d. U.S. Department of Labor, Bureau of Labor Statistics, *Women Employees in Manufacturing Industries* (1957), 16-17; production and nonproduction workers, figures for the month of April of each year.
e. U.S. Department of Labor, Bureau of Labor Statistics, *Women Employees in Manufacturing Industries* (1958), 16-17; production and nonproduction workers; figures for the month of April of each year.

De-skilling and feminization occurred not only in the lamp industry, but also in other branches of electrical manufacturing (although to a lesser extent). At the National Recovery Administration (NRA) Electrical Code hearings in 1933, Charles Keaveney described the changes that had taken place at General Electric's huge Schenectady plant, where he had worked for eight years before becoming an official of the International Brotherhood of Electrical Workers. This plant, GE's largest and the company's headquarters, produced heavy industrial equipment such as generators, turbines, and machine apparatus, as well as refrigerators. Keaveney testified that:

> Some 14 or 15 years ago, to turn out a certain amount of a given apparatus might require, for example, some five or six or ten all around mechanics who would be capable of performing work on any part of that operation. . . . Those men have been replaced by five or six, or seven or eight specialists, who perform only work on each individual part of the operation. . . . The work of women employed in the industry . . . is work that, over a period of fifteen years to my knowledge, has been gradually taken away from the male worker. That has been one of the battles in the electric industry, of women replacing

men on the same class of work on a lower rate of wages, work that men formerly
did for years, the winding of armatures and winding of coils, and other inci-
dental parts going to it.[3]

At plants like GE-Schenectady, producing primarily capital goods, much of
the work was tailored to special orders, and skilled workers were still required
in considerable numbers. The proportion of women employed varied considerably among the electrical industry's many subdivisions. Women were less
than 20 percent of the workers making industrial apparatus, for example, but
more than three-fourths of those making lamps (Table 2). But feminization
and job fragmentation apparently went hand in hand throughout the industry.
Moreover, de-skilling, which was occurring in many industries during this
period, made especially rapid progress in electrical manufacturing. In part,
this was because the industry expanded so rapidly that its skilled workers were
not directly displaced but instead ascended within the ranks. And in the absence of strong craft traditions in this technologically revolutionary industry,
resistance to job fragmentation was minimal.[4]

The increased employment of women that accompanied de-skilling in electrical manufacturing did *not* take place in automotive manufacturing, despite
many similarities between the two industries. Auto, too, was a newcomer to

Table 2.   Female Employment in Electrical Manufacturing, by Industry
Subdivision, 1939, Manufacturing Wage-Earners Only

Industry Subdivision	All Workers	Percentage of Industry	Women Workers	Women as % of Total
Electric lamps	10,698	3.7%	8,269	77.3%
Radios, radio tubes, and phono-graphs	55,422	19.1	30,013	54.2
Communication equipment	38,680	13.3	16,130	41.7
Electrical measuring instruments	7,524	2.6	2,603	34.6
Wiring devices and supplies	15,764	5.4	4,853	30.8
Insulated wire and cable	17,583	6.1	5,396	30.7
Automotive electrical equipment	18,941	6.5	5,696	30.1
Electrical appliances	20,702	7.1	5,767	27.9
Electrical products, n.e.c.	6,461	2.2	1,742	27.0
Generating, distribution, and indus-trial apparatus	74,827	25.8	13,932	18.6
Batteries, storage and primary	17,858	6.2	3,194	17.9
Carbon products	3,493	1.2	481	13.8
X-ray and therapeutic apparatus and electronic tubes	2,019	0.7	146	7.2
Total: All Subdivisions	289,972	100.0	98,222	33.9

Source: U.S. Department of Commerce, Bureau of the Census, *Census of Manufactures: 1939,*
vol. 1, Statistics by Subject, 70-87. Percentages computed by the author.

the industrial scene and had no strong craft traditions. In both industries, the vast majority of jobs were easily learned and unusually monotonous. Both subjected workers to previously undreamed of speed-ups—by means of piece-work in electrical manufacturing and by manipulating the pace of the moving assembly line in auto. Before the rise of the CIO in the late 1930s, most workers in both industries lacked the benefits of unionization. The demand for labor in both was highly seasonal and unusually sensitive to the vagaries of the business cycle. Even in the peak season and in good years, turnover rates were alarmingly high in both industries.

Electrical and auto manufacturing shared other traits as well. Both came of age in the transition from competitive to monopoly capitalism and quickly joined the ranks of the nation's most concentrated industries. Both industries garnered a vastly disproportionate share of the nation's rapidly expanding consumer markets. Both offered novel wares, and indeed, neither electrical products nor automobiles had been manufactured in the preindustrial house-hold by either women or men. While the large representation of women in nondurable goods industries like textile, clothing, and food manufacturing was often accounted for as a movement of women's work from the home to the factory, no one could suggest such an explanation for the high proportion of women among electrical manufacturing workers.

It was not a historic link to domestic labor but instead the "light" character of women's work that was said to distinguish it from men's. "We employ in the electrical manufacturing industry a very large number of persons engaged at very light minor operations," the president of the Reliance Electric and Engineering Company declared at the NRA Electrical Code hearing in July of 1933. "It merely requires dexterity of the fingers. . . . the operator can be seated at his or her work, and I want to distinguish very carefully between that class of work and what is usually recognized as the unskilled manual labor, which . . . requires heavy physical effort and strain. We also have that class, but we have this other class of light labor, in which either boys or girls or men or women can be employed, but at the present time it is largely girls and women."[5]

So it was that employers themselves accounted for the sexual division of labor between the electrical and auto industries, as well as that within each one. Both industries had rigidly sex-segregated job structures, conforming to the pattern found throughout the economy. But while sex segregation itself has been a constant feature of virtually all industries throughout the history of capitalism, the specific content of occupational sex-labeling, or what I call the *idiom* of sex-typing, is highly variable. In pink-collar service and clerical jobs, skills and capacities presumed to be developed by women in the family context, such as nurturance, solicitousness to emotional and sexual needs, and skill in providing personal services, are the central reference point of the idiom. In the manufacturing sector, sex-typing speaks a different language, rooted not in women's family role but in their real or imagined physical characteristics and capacities. No one pretends that being nurturant or knowing how to make a good cup of coffee are important qualifications for "female" factory jobs. Here the idiom centers on such qualities as manual dexterity, attention to detail, ability to tolerate monotony, and, above all, women's relative lack of physical strength.

Did the electrical industry by its physical nature include more "light" jobs than auto? It probably did. In the lamp industry, which relied almost exclusively on female labor, it is undeniable that women's work was light and "delicate."[6] But in other branches of the industry, the idiomatic equation of women's work and light work did not correspond to the actual situation. Charles Keaveney, conceding that the lamp industry was different, testified that in large electrical apparatus factories like the GE-Schenectady plant where he worked, "90 percent of the work of women employed in the industry is not light work."[7] He suggested that women had been substituted for men because they commanded lower wages, not because the work was light.

Elizabeth Butler's classic study of women workers in Pittsburgh in the first decade of the century confirms Keaveney's suggestion that many "women's jobs" in electrical manufacturing were physically strenuous. Observing the huge East Pittsburgh Westinghouse plant, where 650 women were among the 10,000 workers manufacturing coils, armatures, transformers, and motors, she wrote:

> Most of the women are employed at coil winding. The machine process is simple and easily learned, as each girl simply starts the machine and holds in her hands coil and tape, while the rapid revolutions of the wheels bind both together. The power action is so strong that the operator sways backward and forward and is often forced to exert considerable physical strength to keep the tape in place. In a Pittsburgh firm where women are employed only for hand taping, and the machine taping is done by men, the superintendent said that he would never allow women to operate machines, as the pull of the power demands too much strength in keeping the winding right. A different practice is followed at East Pittsburgh [Westinghouse], and if any coil is wound imperfectly at these power machines, the girl operator is required to rewind it without pay.[8]

The variation in firms' definition of heavy and light work suggests the inadequacy of the idiomatic equation of women's work and light work for explaining the sexual division of labor in durable-goods manufacturing.[9]

Like Keaveney, Butler suggested that electrical firms like GE and Westinghouse employed women on these strenuous jobs largely because they were a cheaper form of labor. Men, she observed, "are never put on the same kind of work for which women are employed, unless there is a rush order and their what the girls are paid, it would be a costly policy for the firm to permit the men ordinarily to undertake any of the girls' work."[10] Yet if cost were the only consideration, one would expect all the men to eventually be replaced by women, except in jobs requiring such great skill or physical strength as to be more efficiently performed by men, even at higher pay. This is essentially what had occurred in the lamp manufacturing branch of the electrical industry. Why was feminization so limited in the other branches—and why did it not proceed even to that degree in the automobile industry?

In auto, that most modern of industries in the early twentieth century, mechanization and streamlined production had largely eliminated the need for workers capable of great physical exertion. "The rank and file of men come to us unskilled," wrote Henry Ford in 1922. "They do not have to be able-bodied men. We have jobs that require great physical strength—although they are rapidly lessening; we have other jobs that require no strength whatsoever—jobs which, as far as strength is concerned, might be attended to by a child of three."[11] And Charles Reitell observed in a 1924 essay on the auto industry that, "Quickly—overnight as it were—the machine, gigantic, complex and intricate, has removed the need of muscle and brawn. As Frederick W. Taylor puts it, 'The Gorilla types are no more needed.' Instead we have a greater demand for nervous and mental activities such as watchfulness, quick judgments, dexterity, guidance, ability, and lastly a nervous endurance to carry through dull, monotonous, fatiguing rhythmic operations."[12]

These were precisely the characteristics of jobs best suited to women, according to the prevailing idiom. So one might expect automotive management's incentive to maximize the use of female labor to be very great indeed. Yet women were a tiny minority of the industry's labor force until World War II. They were employed mostly in parts plants, where they performed tasks more akin to electrical manufacturing than to the rest of the auto industry, and in the "cut-and-sew" (upholstery) departments of body plants. Although women were occasionally substituted for men, and at lower pay, the auto firms showed no serious interest in large-scale feminization.[13] A 1925 survey by the U.S. Bureau of Labor Statistics (BLS) found women in only 22 of 110 job classifications, and they made up only 2.4 percent of the industry's work force (parts plants were not included). Fully 68 percent of the women were employed in just four job classifications, and nearly one-half of these (32 percent of the total) were sewing-machine operators.[14]

The idiom of sex-typing in auto was the same as in electrical manufacturing. Thus one commentator asserted that women were especially well represented in auto parts plants "since they are adept at assembly of light units."[15] The idiom focused not only on women's lesser physical strength, but also elevated more dubious presumptions about the mechanical capacities of men and women to the level of organizational principles. Women were said to excel in

1-2. Women upholstering automobile seats, Hudson Motor Car Co., Detroit, April 1927. (National Archives)

women to the level of organizational principles. Women were said to excel in monotonous tasks requiring manual dexterity and attention to detail. "In finishing, polishing, and upholstery, where much hand work is required," a 1929 account suggested, women "are considered fast workers, as well as on inspection work, trimming, stock and tool-crib work, and thread machine operation."[16]

Yet, as in electrical manufacturing, the boundaries between men's and women's work in auto varied both regionally and among individual firms. If jobs were clearly identifiable as more suitable for one gender than the other, geography should not have affected either the proportion of women in the industry or their distribution through its occupational classifications. But the 1925 BLS survey found that women were less than 1 percent of the auto workers in Illinois, Wisconsin, Pennsylvania, and New York, while they made up between 2.5 and 3 percent of those in Indiana, New Jersey, Ohio, and Michigan. The survey also found regional differences in women's representation in particular jobs. For example, in Indiana, 10 percent of the "top builders" (automobile roof assemblers) were women, but in Ohio, where women comprised the same overall proportion of workers in the industry, there were no females among the five hundred top builders employed. Female punch operators were numerous in Michigan and New Jersey, while this was an exclusively male occupation in the six other states surveyed.[17]

There were also interfirm variations in female employment in the auto industry, despite an overall similarity in the organization of production across firms. General Motors employed relatively few women except in its parts plants. Ford also employed fewer women than most other auto firms in the pre-World War II period. Only 250 women were on the factory rolls at the Ford Highland Park plant in 1914, out of a total of 15,000 workers. (Henry Ford disapproved of female employment altogether and once claimed that women who worked outside the home "did so in order to buy fancy clothes.") But Chrysler and several smaller auto and auto parts companies employed a relatively high proportion of women in the prewar years, although men were still the majority of the work force.[18]

In general, the jobs that women did in a particular auto plant came to be viewed as requiring a feminine touch, even though elsewhere the identical operation might be seen as intrinsically suited to men. In 1926, the *Wall Street Journal* reported that women crane operators at the Hudson Motor Company, who lifted motors and carried them to the chassis, "were more sensitive and accurate than men," while elsewhere, according to the BLS survey conducted the previous year, this was an exclusively male occupation.[19]

Despite all the variations, in each instance the idiom of sex-typing was adapted to rationalize the specific boundaries between women's and men's work. This is not to say that employers did not genuinely believe in the definitions of women's work that the idiom embodied. They did, and they made hiring and placement decisions accordingly.[20] Thus, the fact that managers themselves considered a wider range of jobs in electrical manufacturing than in auto to be "light" jobs suitable for women is part of the explanation for the difference in the degree of feminization in the two industries.

But this is only a starting point for analysis. The crucial question is why the idiomatic construction of the sexual division of labor developed so differently in the two industries, giving rise to such managerial beliefs. The answer lies in the industries' contrasting managerial strategies for control over labor and the way the labor process was organized in each case.

For a commentator like Richard Edwards, both auto and electrical manufacturing in this period exemplify the shift from "simple" control, where close personal supervision ensured production, to the advanced form of management he calls "technical control," where "machinery itself directed the labor process and set the pace."[21] However, because he collapses the Fordist revolution (the use of the moving assembly line) and the broader development of mass production, Edwards's framework cannot explain the contrasting sexual divisions of labor that developed in the electrical and auto industries.

In electrical manufacturing, piecework and incentive pay schemes were the primary means of controlling labor (in the sense of ensuring the transformation of labor power into labor). By the 1920s, 75 to 90 percent of the production workers employed by GE and Westinghouse were paid on an incentive basis.[22] As in other mass-production industries, the introduction of machinery led to de-skilling in electrical manufacturing and helped lower production costs. Yet the industry remained quite labor-intensive despite mechanization, so that cost-cutting efforts continued to focus on manipulating wage payment systems in order to increase the speed of work. The early development of the lamp industry illustrates this well:

> From the time that the first commercially useable incandescent lamp was invented by Edison until the development of the tantalum lamp there was practically no change in the nature of the raw materials, or in their cost, although during this period the cost of the lamps was very greatly reduced. This reduction has been possible only because of the increased rapidity with which the lamps could be produced and the consequent decrease in the labor cost of production. A part of this increase in the speed of production . . . is due to the simplification of process and the introduction of machines which relieve the operator of some parts of the work, but by far the greater part of the present speed is due to the increase in the working speed of the operators. . . . In few industries . . . has there been such unremitting attention to this feature or such highly developed methods devised for securing this result as in the electric lamp industry, due, it would seem, to the very large proportion of the total cost formed by wages.

These methods are four in number: First, the establishment of a minimum output, below which the employees dare not fall for fear of discharge. . . . Second, the payment of higher piece rates for increased production. . . . Third, . . . giving bonuses for all production above a certain standard. Fourth . . . one of the most skilled and willing workers is made the "leader" of a group. She acts as a pacemaker, and is urged to her best efforts to increase both her own production and that of her group by being paid 5 percent more than the average of the entire group.[23]

Precisely because machinery did not, by itself, exert sufficient control over labor in their industry, the electrical companies experimented with many other methods, among them Taylor's scientific management with its emphasis on piecework and associated speed-up schemes. Later on, an electrical company, Western Electric, would pioneer in developing the "human relations" school of management. Gerard Swope of GE had laid the groundwork for this in the 1920s in his experiments with corporate "welfarism," with which his name became synonymous. And Westinghouse took the lead in developing "job analysis" schemes, which systematically set pay rates in relation to job content—and also according to the sex of the worker. GE also developed job evaluation systems quite early.[24]

Even as they endorsed these managerial innovations, which promised to improve workers' output, electrical manufacturing firms also reduced wage costs directly by employing cheap labor. In the Northeast and Midwest, where the industry's early operations were concentrated, that meant hiring large numbers of women and girls.[25] This strategy produced substantial savings. Westinghouse had special "women's keysheets" (lists of pay rates for various job classifications) with piece rates substantially lower than those on the parallel "men's keysheets" for jobs that the company itself considered comparable in skill and responsibility. The 1937 keysheets for the East Pittsburgh Westinghouse plant had women's rates ranging from 40 to 59 cents per hour, while men started at 46 cents and rose to as much as $1. The lowest nonlearner male rate was only 1 cent below the maximum female rate. Similarly, the GE job evaluation manual explicitly stated that "for female operators, the value [wage rate] shall be two-thirds of the value for male workers" for jobs of similar content, and until 1945 the GE rate sheets directly designated jobs as men's or women's.[26]

The association between piecework and extensive female employment was not unique to electrical manufacturing. Older industries that relied on "sweated" female and child labor, such as garment manufacturing, had similar practices. But the electrical case suggests that the standard interpretation of the link between women and piecework may be misleading. Perhaps David Montgomery's suggestion that there was "a widespread belief among employers that simple piecework . . . was the best pay system for immigrants, and above all, for immigrant women," implies the wrong line of causality.[27] In electrical manufacturing at least, reliance on piecework may have facilitated women's employment, rather than the reverse.

In sharp contrast, the auto industry relied only marginally on piecework or on cheap labor. Here the supreme lever of control was the high wages made possible by the Fordist revolution, which dramatically reduced labor costs as a component of total production costs. The industry quickly gained a reputation for good pay after Ford's 1914 announcement of the famous "Five-Dollar Day." Ford was then the largest firm in the industry and had pioneered in the development of control over labor through the use of the moving assembly line. This innovation, along with the high wages that it made possible, spread rapidly throughout the industry. Ford had done away with incentive pay "the moment moving belt lines came into being," according to Keith Sward.[28] "The Flivver King," as Henry Ford was known, boasted that he had no use for the bureaucratic job classification schemes instituted by the electrical manufacturers. He scoffed at "scientific management" as well and spoke proudly of how piecework had been completely eliminated from his operations. (At General Motors, too, most workers were paid flat-time wages by the mid-1930s.) "Machinery," said Ford, "is the new Messiah."[29]

It was, indeed, Ford's mechanization that rendered piecework obsolete. As one auto industry observer pointed out in 1924:

> The development of a uniform, standard production turned out by machines, whose capacity per day is measurable, lays the basis for paying on a standard production basis. This differs from the ordinary piecework. . . . Measured production tied up with adjustments in the pay envelope means that management needs little else to induce the worker to productive effort. The worker soon realizes that he is a link in a long chain of operations, which link, if it does not function properly, is quickly noticed by management and by other workers.[30]

Under these conditions, high wages became a sensible industry policy. Indeed, pay rates in auto were high relative to other manufacturing industries. In 1925, the average hourly earnings of male auto workers was 73 cents, while skilled male electrical workers averaged only 67 cents an hour, and unskilled men averaged only 45 cents.[31] Even during the depression, when wage cuts were endemic throughout the economy, the weekly earnings of auto workers were 24 percent higher than the comparable average for all manufacturing.[32]

Even female wages were high in auto relative to the other jobs available to women. But women auto workers earned substantially less than men, generally about two-thirds as much (on an hourly basis) in the pre-World War II era.[33] Nevertheless, auto industry management did not seek to depress wage costs by substituting women for men. Very few women were employed in the industry at all, and most of them were concentrated in auto-parts manufacturing. Interestingly, in this branch of the industry, machine pacing was used far less extensively, and piece rates remained the predominant form of wage payment as late as 1950.[34] The auto-parts industry was also relatively competitive, with some notorious sweatshop operations like Briggs's, where women were used more extensively, and where wage rates were reported as low as 4 cents per hour in the 1930s.[35] But this was atypical. The predominant policy of the major auto firms was to pay high wages in exchange for subordination to the machine-paced organization of production.

With dramatically lowered turnover rates and speeded-up production, Ford workers produced more per dollar paid in wages after the introduction of the Five-Dollar Day than before. Ford himself justifiably called it "one of the finest cost-cutting moves we ever made."[36] That comment captures the essence of the management strategy that became a model for the auto industry as a whole.

Once high wages had become the key to control over labor, Ford was able to take up the popular banner of the "family wage" (a male wage sufficient to support a dependent wife and children), an ideal with great appeal to working-class communities in the prewar period. He wrote in his autobiography:

> If only the man himself were concerned, the cost of his maintenance and the profit he ought to have would be a simple matter. But he is not just an individual. He is a citizen, contributing to the welfare of the nation. He is a householder. He is perhaps a father with children who must be reared to usefulness on what he is able to earn. . . . The man does the work in the shop, but his wife does the work in the home. The shop must pay them both. . . . Otherwise, we have the hideous prospect of little children and their mothers being forced out to work.[37]

This wage policy was also used to justify excluding those few females who did work for the firm from the much-lauded Five-Dollar Day. Ford himself told the U.S. Commission on Industrial Relations in 1916 that only a tenth of the women in his employ received the $5 minimum.[38] Unmarried men under twenty-two and married men not supporting their dependents, living away from home, or pursuing divorces were also paid less than $5. Those otherwise eligible men who were discovered by the infamous Ford "Sociology Department" to be "living unworthily" could also be excluded. In effect, nearly one-third of the company's workers earned less than $5 a day, and Ford's average wage in the first four years of the Five-Dollar Day era was not much higher than his competitors' in and around Detroit.[39]

The popular myth of the prosperous auto worker deviated from reality in other respects as well. The industry was both highly seasonal and extremely vulnerable to the ups and downs of the business cycle. Employment was thus

3. Women working in the small parts department, Ford Motor Co., Highland Park, Michigan, c. 1912. (Wayne State University Labor Archives)

4. "Ladies in White perform the delicate job of assembling the elements that go into electron tubes," Western Electric Co., Allentown, Pennsylvania, n.d. (National Archives)

very unstable despite high hourly wages. And the industry's reputation for high wages attracted so many men to Detroit that employed workers were continually threatened with displacement into the large pool of unemployed in the local labor market. The auto firms deliberately advertised for more workers than they actually intended to employ and regularly sent recruiting agents to the South and West to ensure that the Detroit labor market was constantly flooded with surplus workers. Any worker who failed to be sufficiently compliant thus faced the threat of immediate replacement.[40]

While some men migrated to Michigan's auto production centers with their families, large numbers of single men were also attracted to the area. In Flint, about fifty miles from Detroit and with an economy even more dominated by the auto industry than the "Motor City" itself, men were overrepresented in the prewar population. Single women, like their male counterparts, migrated in large numbers in search of well-paid auto production jobs, but far fewer of them could hope to secure employment. One Flint plant reported that of 3,338 women who applied for work in 1925, only 271 were hired. Women who were gainfully employed in Michigan's auto-dominated labor markets, other than the few fortunate enough to find factory jobs in the car or parts industries, were concentrated in "traditional" women's jobs such as saleswork, waitressing, or laundry work.[41]

Electrical contrasted sharply with auto manufacturing in its relation to labor supply. It was quite decentralized, with even the largest plants located in relatively small cities and towns. This reflected the industry's labor-intensity and the concomitant pressure to depress wage levels. While the auto companies recruited immigrants to Detroit and its environs, where the industry was overwhelmingly concentrated, the electrical firms chose to migrate to low-wage areas, where they sought out women and girls for employment. This was especially true of the smaller firms and of the segments of the industry that required the fewest skilled workers, such as lamp and radio tube manufacturing. But even the giant electrical firms paid the "community wage"—that is, they surveyed (sometimes selectively) wages in a given locality and set their rates accordingly. At the NRA hearings on the industry code in 1933, when the National Electrical Manufacturers' Association proposed that they be permitted to pay lower minimum wages in cities with populations under two hundred thousand, the labor union officials present pointed out that virtually all the large plants in the industry were in cities that size or smaller.[42]

Low wages and manipulation of piece rates secured control over labor in electrical manufacturing. The typical policy was clearly articulated by one superintendent in a lamp plant who, when asked how he was able to maintain rapid production, said, "We keep the piece rate so low that they have to keep right at it in order to make a living."[43] The industry's heavy reliance on female labor served primarily to depress the wage bill. It also helped exert control over male labor, for whom the threat of female substitution was omnipresent. In auto, this function was served by the pool of unemployed *men* that the industry's firms deliberately maintained in the local labor market. But in auto, with its high wages, there was no need for female substitution, at least outside the parts branch of the industry.

If employing women in lieu of men made good sense in the electrical industry, where wages made up a high proportion of production costs, favoring young female workers was even more expedient. In the radio industry, for example, employers regularly advertised for young girls, and women themselves realized that the plants favored the youthful. "You have to be young and strong to get a job there," one explained to a government investigator.[44] To ensure high turnover rates and to maintain a youthful work force, there were formal and informal bans on employing married women during the prewar years—although the electrical firms, being heavily dependent on working-class daughters, were in no position to endorse the ideology of the "family wage" as did Henry Ford.[45]

The different labor processes and modes of managerial control in the auto and electrical industries thus produced a sharp contrast in the extent of women's representation in each. However, the basic principles by which management organized the sexual division of labor within each industry were otherwise quite similar. The extent of feminization appears to vary—not only between these two industries, but also throughout the economy—considerably more than do managerial policies toward women. In both auto and electrical factories, as elsewhere, jobs were strictly sex-segregated.[46] Employers explicitly designated the positions that they sought to fill as "women's jobs," "men's jobs," or (sometimes) "boys' jobs." The subtlety with which these categories would be recast in later years, when such blatant forms of discrimination were challenged, was entirely absent in the early part of the century. In both the auto and electrical industries, the sex-labeling of jobs was explicit, routine, and legitimate.

Once they were established, moreover, the distinctive patterns of employment by sex that developed in each of these industries would be extremely difficult to alter, even when the specific conditions that produced them were no longer present. Employers and workers alike came to view the sexual division of labor as a "natural" and permanent feature of the labor process. The ideology of sex-typing reigned supreme even in the face of the dramatic economic and political crises that shook both industries in the 1930s.

3   The Great Depression and the Triumph of Unionization

Two key changes occurred in the 1930s that might have been expected to alter the sexual division of labor in industry. The deep economic crisis led many contemporaries to fear that employers would replace male workers with cheaper female labor in order to reduce wage costs. Yet this occurred surprisingly little during the depression. Some incidents of female substitution were reported, but the overall effect of the economic downturn was to *stabilize* the previously established sexual division of labor, even in the hard-hit auto and electrical industries.

The 1930s brought not only changed economic conditions but also a political transformation to mass-production industry. In both auto and electrical manufacturing, strong, socially progressive unions that profoundly altered labor relations were organized in the second half of the decade. Committed to opposing discrimination, the new industrial unions organized women factory workers alongside men. However, women's concerns were a low priority, even for the electrical workers' union, a large part of whose membership was female. Both the UE and the UAW advocated equal pay for equal work for women, but their main goal was to remove the economic advantage to employers of women's lower pay and thus prevent female substitution. The practical result was to stabilize the existing pattern of job segregation by sex, whereby women and men did not do "equal work." The institutionalization of seniority systems for layoffs and rehiring also had a stabilizing influence. Thus the sexual division of labor persisted unchanged in the 1930s, despite the rise of industrial unionism and the extraordinary economic situation.

The Impact of the Great Depression

The depression breathed new life into the ideological dictum "a woman's place is in the home." It had been undermined in the teens and twenties with the growth of female labor-force participation and the achievement of women's suffrage, but in the 1930s it enjoyed a resurgence. Some contemporaries went so far as to suggest that women's flocking into the work force in the pre-depression years had caused the scarcity of jobs. Married women who worked outside their homes drew special censure, as the "family wage" ideal (a male wage sufficient to support an entire family) gained new popularity. A 1936 Gallup poll found that 82 percent of Americans believed that employers should discriminate against married women. Both private industry and public-sector agencies did so in the 1930s to a greater extent than ever before.[1]

Despite this ideological backlash, women were generally less affected than men by the economic contraction in their role as paid workers. In 1930, women's unemployment rate was lower than men's, because employment levels in "female" occupations dropped less than in predominantly male occupations. Specifically, unemployment rates were lower for clerical and service occupations, which primarily employed women, than in the manufacturing sector, where men were more concentrated. And despite the strong cultural sanctions that surfaced with the unemployment emergency against female employment, those women who could keep their jobs did so. More than ever, they needed any income they could get, especially if the household's male breadwinner (if there was one) was unemployed or threatened with unemployment. Ironically, the rigidity of job segregation by sex protected many women from unemployment during the 1930s, for even unemployed men were disinclined to do "women's work," and employers remained reluctant to hire them for it.[2]

Women employed in the manufacturing sector were far more likely to lose their jobs than their white-collar counterparts, however. In durable goods industries like auto and electrical manufacturing, which were especially hard hit by the economic crisis, workers of both sexes were extremely vulnerable to unemployment. Between 1929 and 1933, the number of electrical workers was cut by almost one-half, falling from 343,000 to 164,000. The decline in auto was equally steep, from 447,000 to 244,000 over the same four-year period.[3] Wages in both industries also fell precipitously in the early 1930s, and worker complaints of rate cuts and speed-ups reached fever pitch. The average hourly earnings of auto factory workers dropped from 75 cents in 1928 to 56 cents by early 1933. The Ford Motor Company's minimum wage (for qualified workers) dropped from $7 per day in 1929 to $4 in late 1931, while average hourly wages at Ford's River Rouge plant went from 92 cents in 1929 to only 59 cents in 1933. Wages also fell sharply in electrical manufacturing, from an average of 65 cents per hour in 1930 to 57 cents in 1933. Female electrical workers' earnings dropped even more, from 44 to 36 cents over the same three-year period. These figures actually understate the decline in employment and earnings, because the length of the work week was also reduced substantially in both industries.[4]

Unemployment statistics for the 1930s are notoriously poor, but the available data suggest an interesting contrast between auto and electrical manufacturing. The 1930 census recorded an unemployment rate for male auto workers nearly double women's, while in the electrical industry women's rate was slightly higher than men's. (The overall unemployment rates for the two industries were roughly similar, with a slightly higher percentage out of work in auto.) Women's unemployment was probably underreported, but that cannot explain the contrast between the two industries. The 1937 special unemployment census, using enumeration methods radically different from those used in 1930, found an unemployment rate for female auto workers slightly higher than men's, while in the electrical industry, women's rate was nearly twice men's.[5] In the 1937 count, women's unemployment was high in both industries relative to the 1930 data. But the contrast between electrical and auto is consistent across both these (otherwise quite different) enumerations, with unemployment taking a greater toll on women in the electrical industry, where their employment opportunities had always been far greater than in auto before the depression.

The difference might at first appear to involve the sexual division of labor *within* each industry. Indeed, automobile sales plummeted during the 1930s, while demand for auto parts, the branch of the industry where women were most concentrated, remained strong. However, this hypothesis does not fit the electrical manufacturing case. Production levels in the segments of the industry where women were most highly concentrated (such as incandescent lamps, radios, and refrigerators) actually fell substantially less than in the predominantly male segments (capital goods), and yet women's unemployment rate was higher than men's.[6] What then explains the relatively high female unemployment in electrical manufacturing?

The answer lies in the personnel policies adopted by the electrical firms in the 1920s. Many of them had, of their own accord, instituted systematic criteria for layoffs, including seniority and "need" as well as ability. Women, on the average, had less seniority than men—particularly in the electrical industry with its disproportionately youthful female labor force. Taking need into account in allocating layoffs also tended to favor men. Married women as well as young single workers who could be supported by their families were quickly dismissed, whereas married men, especially those with families, were likely to be retained.[7]

This policy was one of the industry's broader corporate "welfare" programs, best known in connection with the name of Gerard Swope, then president of

General Electric, the nation's largest electrical firm. GE adopted life insurance, unemployment compensation, and pension plans in the 1920s, as did Westinghouse and other electrical companies. One motive was to reduce turnover, which had climbed to alarming levels during World War I, by increasing workers' incentives to stay with their employer. Concern with minimizing turnover, however, did not extend to women electrical workers, focusing instead on the better-paid and more extensively trained skilled men. Women were excluded from most of the welfare programs, and, indeed, turnover was tacitly encouraged among them (for example, by means of the policy of terminating their employment upon marriage), further depressing their wages.[8]

The welfare and employment security policies pioneered by the electrical firms were conspicuous by their absence in the auto industry in the pre-World War II era. A 1940 study by the Automobile Manufacturers' Association of twelve large member firms found that, although seven had life insurance plans for their workers, only one had a formal pension system, and none had unemployment insurance.[9] Although turnover was a serious problem in the auto industry, the proportion of highly skilled workers was lower than in electrical manufacturing. Employment levels also fluctuated wildly in auto, so that the potential costs of employment stabilization policies were enormous. Insofar as they did seek to reduce turnover, the auto manufacturers relied primarily on high wages. Thus, after the inauguration of the Five-Dollar Day, Ford reported a dramatic drop in turnover rates, to about 6 percent of the earlier level.[10] Turnover rose again later, but the auto firms still did not turn to welfare policies like those used in electrical manufacturing. Indeed, in the late 1920s, GE's Swope marveled that Ford could simply throw 120,000 men out of work for six weeks, with no unemployment pay, in order to retool for Model A production.[11]

Seniority would not become an explicit criterion for layoffs in auto until the UAW negotiated its first contracts in the late 1930s, so that during the early depression years employers were free to lay off whomever they chose. The employment records of GM's Fisher Body Pontiac Division show that long-service workers of both sexes were often laid off for "lack of cooperation" or "inefficiency," although there was a tendency to retain experienced workers. These records also show a May 1934 layoff in which married women were disproportionately affected, with "married" listed as the reason for their discharge. But long-service widowed and divorced women were also laid off at this time, along with many married men—while some married women were retained.[12]

The contrasting managerial policies of the auto and electrical industries, then, meant that women electrical workers were more likely to lose their jobs in the early 1930s. This was facilitated by the relative flexibility of the sexual division of labor in electrical manufacturing. Women and men worked in similar jobs far more frequently than they did in auto: Women did "light" coil and armature winding, men did "heavy" winding; women worked on "small" drill presses, men on "large" ones, and so on. Thus men could easily be transferred to jobs formerly done by women. In auto, however, "the definition of what was a woman's job and what was a man's job was so clear cut that there really seemed to be not this strong feeling of resistance against women" in the 1930s, recalled Dorothy Haener, an auto worker who later became a UAW official. "For instance, all the welding that was done on wire cloth was so small and tedious that they never put a man on that job."[13]

Rather than putting men on women's jobs, the depression might have been expected to lead employers to hire women on men's jobs to reduce wage costs. Female substitution had always been attractive to the electrical companies, and although seniority policies militated against this practice, it also grew increasingly tempting as the depression deepened. The NRA code hearings in both the auto and electrical industries elicited numerous complaints that women were displacing men because their customarily lower wages offered such substantial savings to employers. Nathan D. Sleames, a worker from the Muskegon Piston-Ring Shop laid off after seven years, complained that at his former place of work "they are printing great write ups in the daily paper how they are hireing and adding to their force but it is the wimmen & girls they have hired and there is nothing said about the men that are let go."[14] And the NRA's own study of the auto industry reported in January 1935 that, "It is quite apparent that there are many women now doing work that men did either a year ago or some years back. This seems especially true on cushions and on upholstery work where the job is essentially that of using tacks. It appears to be true also for any kind of machine operations, such as drilling machines, and presses of various kinds. This is the type of work which workers, both men and women, consider to be 'man's work.' "[15]

In electrical manufacturing, fear of female substitution was longstanding, but widespread unemployment made it particularly poignant in the 1930s. At the Lynn GE plant, workers complained in 1935 that they found in management's attitude the "inference . . . that if a woman can do a job, and does it, it then becomes a woman's job."[16] And Philco diluted "men's jobs" and employed women to perform the redefined tasks, claiming it could no longer compete with other radio manufacturers without taking this step. These were but two of the many reports of female substitution in the electrical industry.[17]

In both industries, increasing the proportion of women in the work force could effectively cut wage costs. Although the absolute decline in wages during the depression was probably greater for male workers because their pre-depression earnings had been relatively high, far more women were found working at substandard wages. When the NRA established a minimum wage of 43 cents per hour for the auto industry in 1933, women were disproportionately represented among those whose wages had to be raised. Although even during the depths of the depression the code-set minimum was actually lower than the prevailing wage level in the industry, General Motors had to increase the pay of 19 percent of its women employees at this time, whereas only 3 percent of male GM workers were affected. At Briggs, an auto industry sweatshop notorious for paying women as little as 4 cents an hour, the NRA code increased the wages of all 1,800 women workers, along with 23 percent, or 2,000, of the men.[18] Similarly, in the electrical industry, as AFL President William Green pointed out at the code hearing, "The minimum wage provided will do practically nothing to raise the earnings of men in the industry . . .the minimum wage does benefit only women, not men, heads of families. And it does not benefit women to the point where . . . it could be said they were receiving a wage that would maintain them in decency and comfort."[19]

There are no systematic data on the extent to which employers substituted women for men. In both industries the female percentage of operatives and laborers rose between 1930 and 1940. In auto, it rose from 7.2 to 10.5 percent over the decade—a greater increase than between 1920 and 1930. Similarly, in the electrical industry, the proportion of women grew from 33.1 to 40.7 percent between 1930 and 1940, while in the 1920s female representation had actually declined slightly.[20] But these changes were largely artifacts of depression shifts in product demand, which declined less in the heavily female auto parts and consumer electrical goods industry branches than in the predominantly male auto assembly and capital electrical goods branches.[21]

In general, the sexual division of labor in both industries remained surprisingly stable in the 1930s. The incentive for substituting female labor for male was surely more compelling under depression conditions than previously. But so was the ideology that condemned the employment of women, especially married women, while men were out of work. Management had faced these conflicting pressures before, but now both were intensified. Electrical firms often had refused to hire married women before the depression, and there is scattered evidence that employers in both auto and electrical manufacturing adopted this policy more consistently in the 1930s. But hiring younger, unmarried women was probably attractive to employers anyway, and in a situation where they could pick and choose, this did not necessarily preclude female substitution.

Working-class women themselves generally agreed with the prevailing sentiment that married women should not have jobs while male breadwinners were desperate for work, and they were often reluctant to replace men directly. "I refused to take a man's job which would have taken from him, his wife, and his children his weekly wage," said one single woman who had worked in an auto parts plant until she was laid off in 1931. Mrs. Helen Gage, who worked at the Packard Company, stated, "I, for one, would not give my job up to another woman, but I will give my job up to a man, as a man has more responsibilities than a woman."[22]

Yet, despite their favorable view of the "family wage" in the abstract, most women who worked in industry, married or not, did so because of economic necessity. And necessity was far more pressing in the 1930s than before, precisely because male unemployment was so widespread. "Forced to choose between the marriage license and a job," one contemporary noted, "many young women have managed without the license and are living in sin and secrecy with their life's partners and a double income."[23] At the GE plant in Decatur, Indiana, for example, women hid their marriages effectively for years. This was a common practice in the auto industry as well. "I have worked in plenty of shops in Detroit, and I have lied to get into them and I have lied to stay in there," acknowledged Irene Young when the issue arose at the UAW's 1940 convention. "I worked at Ford ten months and got there by saying I was a single woman." And Helen Gage pointed out, "I definitely know that married women would get divorced or separated in order to hold their job." Irene Young summarized the dilemma:

> I know most of the married women working in the plant would be darned glad to get out of it. . . . [But until] the men are guaranteed a sufficient hourly working wage to enable the women to raise their children in accordance with the decent living standards to which they are entitled, they will have a hard time solving the problem. . . . These women are wholeheartedly in favor of going back home and taking care of their families, but they don't intend doing it at the expense of having their children without proper food and shoes.[24]

The depression increased both women's need for employment and employers' need for low-wage labor. Thus, married women were more likely to work for pay in the 1930s than ever before, despite the backlash against this. While married women's employment could become a basis for opposition to conventional sex roles in more prosperous years, the "role reversals" of the 1930s occurred under such negative circumstances that nostalgia for the old roles was reinforced instead.[25] Thus the depression experience strengthened the ideology of "woman's place," and set limits on female substitution in industry. While employers sometimes did replace men with women during the 1930s, the stability of the sexual division of labor under the impact of the economic contraction seems more remarkable.

Women Workers and the Rise of Industrial Unionism

Industrial unionism swept the nation in the late 1930s, forever changing the lives of women and men in the auto and electrical industries. Unlike the AFL craft unions that had dominated the labor movement for the preceding half-century, the new CIO unions organized workers in mass-production industry regardless of skill, race, or sex. The craft unions saw skilled workers as their only constituency, and viewed women and other unskilled workers as "unorganizable." With some important exceptions, such as the garment and textile unions—which were actually organized on an industrial basis and together accounted for more than one-half of all female union members in 1920, when AFL membership was at its peak—the AFL unions had few female members, and many actively excluded women.[26]

After the formation of the CIO in 1935, the shift from craft to industrial unionism dramatically increased female (as well as male) unionization. By 1940, eight hundred thousand women were organized—a 300 percent increase over ten years earlier and double the 1920 figure.[27] But sex discrimination persisted within the revitalized labor movement. Women remained underrepresented among union leaders, especially at the top. And although most CIO activists—a group that included many Communists and Socialists— viewed industrial unionism as part of a larger program of social change, few had any special commitment to the elimination of sexual inequality. Those who did pursue this goal, most of them women active at the grass-roots level, faced enormous obstacles. Not only had women's right to work been newly questioned during the depression, but the organized women's movement was also at a low ebb and seriously divided.[28] Recruiting women was a low priority for the CIO, in part because few women were employed in the mass-production industries that were the main target of the organizing drives, and in part because of the widespread acceptance within the labor movement of the socially pervasive ideology of "woman's place."[29]

Still, the new unions did take in many women who were employed in manufacturing, and this opened up new possibilities, especially in industries where a substantial part of the labor force was female. There was an important difference between auto and electrical manufacturing in this respect. Of all the mass-production industries organized by the CIO, electrical manufacturing had by far the largest proportion of women in its work force. This meant that almost from the beginning, successful organizing required attention to the specific concerns of female workers. In the auto industry, by contrast, although women were organized along with everyone else, they were such a small minority that UAW organizers could achieve their goals without giving any special attention to women's needs.

Where women's concerns were directly addressed in the early years, in both the UAW and the UE, female organizers and activists took the initiative. But male union leaders encouraged such efforts in the UE much more than in the UAW, simply because women workers in the electrical industry were too numerous to be ignored. "If women could be attracted . . . to take a more active interest in our organization," wrote UE national secretary-treasurer Julius

Emspak to Bertha Scott and other female organizers in May 1936, "it would be of great organizational value."[30] Women's involvement was actively cultivated on the local level as well. Many UE locals established women's committees in the 1930s, including both Local 301, which represented workers at the GE headquarters plant in Schenectady, and Local 601 at the huge East Pittsburgh Westinghouse plant—two of the largest and most important locals in the union. Local 601's first constitution empowered the women's committee, made up of assistant shop stewards from each department in the plant, "to sit in on all standing committees and to offer suggestions so that the proper women's appeal shall be made in all the affairs of this union."[31]

During World War II, when its female membership expanded, the UAW would develop similar organizational forms and take more interest in women's concerns. But in the 1930s this was a low priority at best, except in locals with large female representation (primarily at parts plants).[32] Even in the UE, while the importance of recruiting women was recognized, the role of women in union leadership was circumscribed. "They knew they had to fight for the rights of women in the UE," recalls Mary Voltz, formerly a UE organizer based in St. Louis. But her personal experience was difficult. "I was not accepted by the other representatives of the UE," she remembers. "They were men. And they tried very hard to make me into an office clerk."[33]

It was not uncommon for women UE activists to be consigned to such positions. Even Margaret Darin, who was active in the East Pittsburgh Westinghouse local from its first days, attended the union's national conventions faithfully, and initiated the first UE women's conference, ended up as a specialist in the union's officework. Having served Local 601 as Recording Secretary and Executive Board member for several years, she visited various locals to teach them how to improve their record-keeping systems. And while Darin felt respected by the men in Local 601, when she became a business agent for a year in Lima, Ohio's Local 724, "some of them came up to me and said that . . . I had too much power for a woman."[34]

Before World War II, there was resistance in the UE to the idea of employing women organizers with specific responsibility for recruiting female workers. When a resolution was introduced at the union's 1939 convention calling for the employment of an International Woman Representative with such duties, the Committee on Resolutions recommended against it, arguing that organizers should be hired based on "ability regardless of sex." Those favoring the resolution argued that women would be more effective than men in approaching women workers, having a better understanding of their special needs and problems. "We have to show the girls in our shops that there is not a position in our organization that is not open to them," implored Ruth Young, who would later become the first female member of the UE's Executive Board. "In my local," she continued, "girls don't come to meetings because they feel the men have built the union and probably know how to make a point of order better than they do. If we go out of our way to educate these girls, I am sure these girls can and will show they are capable of leadership." The convention delegates were divided over the issue, and the resolution was ultimately referred to the union's Executive Board for further consideration.[35] That this debate took place at all in the 1930s distinguished the UE from the other CIO unions, but the electrical union's commitment to women remained limited.

There were external as well as internal obstacles to women's participation in the new industrial unions. For daughters and wives alike, family obligations and authority structures often constrained women's participation in union activity. As Ronald Schatz has shown, female activists in the early UE had personal lives unlike those of most women workers in the 1930s in that most were free of traditional family ties. Ruth Meyerowitz found the same to be true of women UAW activists in the 1940s.[36]

Despite these difficulties, women were active participants in building the CIO in the thirties, especially at the local level. In the auto industry, they were particularly active in organizing parts plants, where women workers were numerous.[37] In electrical manufacturing, women were active even in the largest factories. At the East Pittsburgh Westinghouse plant, for example, women signed up workers, became shop stewards and organizers, and held local women's conferences to discuss equalizing male and female wage rates and other concerns of special interest to women. Much of the work contributed by women was invisible and unacknowledged, however. As Margaret Darin recalled, "their activity in the union was overshadowed by the activity of the men that took the leadership role in it. Their role, in those early days, was a little bit clouded."[38] Women unionists would gain more prominence in the CIO during World War II. In the 1930s, however, their quiet participation provided them with skills and organizational commitments that would prove valuable when the war provided new opportunities for union leadership.

The process of unionization took different forms in the auto and electrical industries, and women's experience in the two unions was consequently quite different as well, beyond the fact of their greater numerical strength in the electrical workers' union. The UE and the UAW faced managements with sharply contrasting labor policies, and thus developed distinct organizational strategies. The UE worked within the company unions set up by the large electrical firms in the 1920s, while simultaneously building support among workers in the plants. In an industry that relied heavily on corporate welfarism, the UE trod an electoral path toward union recognition. There was resistance to the CIO from the electrical companies, of course, but there were few prolonged strikes. To gain a foothold, the UE often accepted the existing company union agreements in lieu of negotiated contracts.[39]

Conditions were quite different in the auto industry. Company unions were not established until after the passage of the Wagner Act (and then only as a means to circumvent it), and management was intransigent in opposing the CIO, spending millions on goon squads and industrial espionage. The corporate welfarism that flourished in the electrical industry was conspicuously absent in auto. Under these conditions, the UAW could win recognition only by means of protracted and often violent strikes, most importantly the wave of sit-downs that began with the famous Flint strike of 1936-37.[40]

Although women were a small minority of both workers and union activists in auto, they did participate in the organizing that culminated in the sit-downs. During the strikes themselves, however, union leaders discouraged women from joining men in the factory occupations. In the Flint strike, for example, the women working in the cut-and-sew department of GM's Fisher Body Plant No. 1 were told to leave the plant when the strike began. "The press and the radio were so eager to say there was sexual mingling," recalled Genora Johnson Dollinger, who led the Women's Emergency Brigade that played a critical role in strike support outside the occupied plants. "A few of them offered to stay, but they were asked, 'No, don't do it because we can't give General Motors any propaganda.' " This was the typical pattern in the auto sit-downs. In some cases, however, such as the January 1937 strike at the Detroit Bohn Aluminum plant, the women refused to leave.[41] And as the sit-down wave spread to retail stores, hotels, and cigar factories, many of Detroit's women workers joined in.[42]

Women's main role in the auto strikes themselves, however, was in the women's auxiliaries, many of which recruited women workers along with the wives and daughters of men in the plants. The Flint Women's Emergency Brigade is the best known and probably the most developed instance of this type of female support organization. It played a paramilitary role in protecting the occupied plants from the police in the "Battle of the Running Bulls." Women's auxiliaries won enormous praise throughout the CIO. "You gals who want to be free, just take a tip from me," the popular 1940 labor song "Union Maid" tellingly recommended. "Get you a man who's a union man and join the ladies' auxiliary."[43]

Although their activities were sometimes unconventional, the auxiliaries did not challenge the ideology of "woman's place." On the contrary, they extended women's family responsibilities into the public sphere.[44] However, some of the women who were auxiliary activists in the 1930s would become UAW members in the 1940s, when the wartime mobilization drew them into auto factory jobs.[45] Women in traditionally female service and sales jobs in and near Detroit who struck in the the 1930s were also pulled into the UAW during the war. So while the auto sit-downers themselves were men, women's

5. UAW Women's Auxiliary members from Detroit demonstrating support for General Motors sit-down strikers, Flint, Michigan, 1937. (Wayne State University Archives)

participation in the 1936-37 strike wave, whether in support of their male kin or on their own behalf, was important preparation for the war years, when women's leadership in the UAW would gain ground.

The situation was different in electrical manufacturing. Not only was women's representation in the work force far greater than in auto, but because the UE usually won recognition through elections, women also had a more ongoing role in the union-building process. Women's auxiliaries were important in the electrical union where there were long strikes, as at the Newton, Iowa, Maytag plant. But auxiliaries were marginal or nonexistent in most UE locals.[46] Female workers, however, were more fully involved in organizing the union and had more space to pursue issues of particular concern to women than their counterparts in the UAW.

The UE's top leadership gave women and women's issues more attention than most other CIO affiliates. But they were primarily interested in organizing the largest electrical plants, like GE's headquarters in Schenectady and East Pittsburgh Westinghouse. These factories, "the central fortresses of the industry," produced heavy industrial equipment and employed relatively few women. The overwhelmingly female Cleveland lamp division, in contrast, was the last part of GE to be organized.[47] This reflected the CIO's broader focus on the strategic core of American industry—a focus that reinforced the low priority accorded to organizing women.

The commitment of the new unions to the eradication of gender inequality was limited at best. Significantly, the inclusionary principle of industrial unionism was rarely extended to the substantial numbers of female clerical workers employed by the large manufacturing firms that were organized in the 1930s. In at least a few recorded instances, moreover, the CIO bargained away the contract rights of clerical workers and failed to resist wage cuts, layoffs, and speed-ups to which office workers were subsequently subjected.[48] But women production workers in industries like auto and electrical manufacturing benefited enormously from the CIO's breakthroughs in the late 1930s. In the auto industry, women's average hourly wages rose from 54 cents in 1936 to 65 cents two years later, while men's rose from 81 to 98 cents over that period. Wages in the electrical industry continued to lag behind those in auto, but now rose to the pre-unionization level of auto wages. Between July 1936 and July 1937, the wages of women production workers in electrical manufacturing rose 17 percent, to a 55 cent hourly average, while men's rose 15 percent, to 81 cents. These wage gains were maintained in both industries despite the economic downturn of 1937-38, and by 1941, the unions had won substantial additional increases.[49]

The institutionalization of seniority systems for layoff and rehiring was another major achievement of the CIO in the 1930s. This was particularly important in the auto industry, where job security guarantees constituted a radical break with past practice. Frequent abuses of the management-initiated seniority systems in electrical manufacturing during the depression made the issue a serious concern there too, but the overall principle had long since been established. At General Electric, in fact, the existing company policy on seniority was simply added to the union contract.[50]

Seniority systems gave women some protection from sexual harassment and favoritism for the first time. "I can think of some of the gals who actually had to sleep with some of these guys," recalled Sadie Rosenberg of UE Local 427, "and you'd expect the hands to creep as the foremen walked up and down the aisles. . . . I don't think it was ever completely eliminated, but certainly the situation improved during the period of the union's strength increasing and more and more women becoming part of the leadership in the shops." Similar reports came from the auto industry, where sexual harassment and favoritism had been widespread.[51]

But this was an indirect benefit of seniority. Its direct effects offered men significantly more protection than women. After the Flint strike, when GM agreed to make seniority the major criterion for layoffs and rehiring, management insisted that married men be given preference in the event of long-term reductions in employment. In addition, many companies had separate seniority lists for women (and sometimes married women), allowing management considerable flexibility in distributing layoffs between men and women by manipulating job classification by sex. In electrical manufacturing, despite the longstanding acceptance of the general concept, seniority did not become the predominant factor determining the order of layoffs until the end of World War II. Here again, men were favored over women, because "need" continued to be weighted very heavily, as it was before unionization.[52]

Not only did such longstanding "traditions" as sex differentials in wages and male and female job classifications persist into the union era, but they were also institutionalized in many local contracts. The new unions were primarily concerned with consolidating their organizational gains in the late 1930s, and that was difficult enough without taking on the burden of challenging gender inequality. Moreover, women were still considered—by unionists as well as management—to be temporary workers, whose needs were secondary to men's. Thus, a male picket line depicted in the *CIO News* displayed signs reading, "Restore Our Manhood: We Receive Girls' Wages."[53] The vast majority of workers (of both sexes), as well as union leaders, viewed women as family members first and workers second. Both the ideology of "woman's place" and the long-cherished "family wage" ideal were left unchallenged by the CIO in the 1930s.

At the same time, however, such unexamined assumptions about gender presented problems for the new unions. They conflicted with a central principle of industrial unionism: opposition to all forms of discrimination in industry.

The dilemma arose repeatedly as the CIO grappled with the question of married women's employment in the late 1930s. In the UAW, while some locals signed agreements sanctioning discrimination against married women in layoffs, most union leaders opposed this. They argued that although the family wage ideal was desirable, it was not a viable option at depression-era wage levels, and that the union should therefore resist discrimination against married women. "Some day," the vice president of UAW Local 2 wrote in 1939 in response to a letter from the wife of a member suggesting that married women be expelled from the plant, "I hope we will reach that economic ideal where the married woman will find her place in the home caring for children, which is God's greatest gift to women and her natural birthright."[54] In the meantime, the principle of nondiscrimination took precedence for most union leaders.

The issue of married women's employment aroused even more passion in the electrical workers' union, with its many women members. Faced with layoffs in the 1937-38 recession, UE locals were often divided over married women's seniority standing. The problem was intensified by the carryover into the union era of longstanding company policies barring married women's employment altogether. The issue did not break down neatly along sex lines, but split women workers themselves. "There was disagreement amongst the women," Margaret Darin recalled. "Oh, sure. Some felt that married women had a husband to take care of them, therefore why should they be taking jobs. It was a question of jobs."[55]

The issue was resolved differently in various UE locals. In Lynn, Massachusetts, GE's policy had always been not to hire married women. But after a protracted debate on the issue, Local 201 took the position that length of service should be the sole factor governing layoffs.[56] In the UE Westinghouse local in Mansfield, Ohio, however, the opposite position triumphed. There, married women had been subject to dismissal since the early 1930s, but management had enforced this policy selectively. The local union insisted that the company adhere to its official policy, and a clause to that effect was added to the contract. A U.S. Women's Bureau investigator found that the union had persuaded the firm to lay off married women, and further, that the union officers negotiated this without the concurrence of women union members.[57]

In GE's Decatur, Indiana, plant, when the policy of denying employment to married women directly impeded the recruitment of women into the UE, the local union there took up the issue. The process began when Emma Hebble, a married woman who had worked in the plant for many years while keeping her marriage secret, sued for divorce in 1940—thus bringing her marital status to management's attention—and was immediately dismissed. A union member, she appealed to the UE for help. At this point, the issue became critical for the union's organizing efforts. "The women will not attend open meetings," a Local 924 staffer reported. "It is known to us that several of the women are married, and because they are still employed we believe that they desire to continue as such." The Decatur plant employed ninety-two women, 30 percent of the total work force, but only five had joined the union by 1940.[58] Although the prohibition on married women's employment was often popular among workers, management could turn the policy to its own advantage in situations like this.

Local 901 in Fort Wayne, Indiana, unable to resolve the issue of married women's job rights, wrote to the UE national office for guidance in early 1938. "We realize there is considerable feeling as to what should be done in this matter," replied President James Carey. "We also know from past experience, if a local union can be used as a pawn by the company on a question such as this, the company is only too glad." But although acknowledging the divisiveness of the issue, the national office declined to take a firm stand, instead referring the matter to a conference of GE locals.[59] At the 1939 UE convention, however, a resolution in favor of "equal rights for married women" was adopted with no debate. The resolution noted that married women were only 6 percent of the nation's labor force, and suggested that discrimination against them "would serve as an opening wedge for discrimination against different groups and sections of our population."[60] Individual locals continued to do as they pleased in handling the issue, however.

It is striking that even in the UE and the UAW, two of the most democratic CIO unions and also among those most heavily influenced by Communists and Socialists, the impulse to pursue "women's issues" was so weak. Perhaps it would have been weaker still without the involvement of the Left.[61] But as it was, neither the UE nor the UAW even considered challenging the pervasive social ideology of "woman's place," or the overall sexual division of labor in industry in the 1930s. They did, however, struggle for "equal pay for equal work" for women, usually in response to management hiring women on "men's jobs." The equal pay issue became the focus of labor-management conflict over the sexual division of labor in both auto and electrical manufacturing in the late 1930s.

The New Unions and the Struggle for Equal Pay for Equal Work

Female substitution was a familiar problem long before the CIO appeared on the scene. But it was a particularly explosive issue in the depression decade, because it both increased male joblessness and threatened the wage standards of those still employed. The organizational victories of the CIO made substitution more attractive to management, but at the same time workers could resist it more effectively.

In electrical manufacturing, the potential for substitution was especially great because of the extensive representation of women in the industry and the flexibility of the sexual division of labor. Consequently, the UE took up the equal pay issue in many different settings. One example was the 1938 Philco strike, which began when the company—ironically the first electrical firm to have recognized the UE—suddenly announced plans to replace men with women in large numbers, along with an across-the-board wage cut. Philco was a radio manufacturer at the time of the strike, but the firm had previously produced storage batteries and had inherited a labor force with a greater proportion of men than most of its competitors. Management argued that large-scale female substitution was necessary in order for Philco to survive in the marketplace.[62]

The strike went on for six months, but was finally lost. At its end, the company had a majority of women on its payroll, whereas previously most of its employees had been men. For the men who remained, however, the strike settlement offered some protection. Philco agreed to designate certain jobs as exclusively male and to pay women the established men's rates if they were ever employed on these "men's jobs" in the future. As the U.S. Women's Bureau observed, here "the circumstances that led to equal pay were definitely the undercutting of men by women."[63] Equally significant, the strike settlement increased the rigidity of the sexual division of labor. Although the union failed to preserve the previous allocation of jobs between the sexes, it did extract guarantees against future substitution and effectively incorporated the sexual division of labor into collective bargaining.

The emergence of the equal pay issue at the East Pittsburgh Westinghouse plant was less dramatic than at Philco, but more typical. After gradually increasing the percentage of women in the plant's work force from 10.5 percent in mid-1938 to 12.7 percent in October 1939, management suddenly began hiring women on the second (night) shift, and UE Local 601 vehemently protested. Apparently the women workers sided with the men. "We women will not allow ourselves to be used as tools to cut wages and tear down the standard of living of Westinghouse employees," exclaimed Margaret Darin. Management agreed to take women off the second shift pending further negotiations, which then led to a compromise allowing women to work until 10 p.m.[64]

At this point, the local took up the demand of "equal pay for equal work regardless of sex." Local 601 business agent Charles Newell explained why in the *UE News*. "I am not suggesting that we should in any manner deprive women of the right to work," he wrote. "I am not even suggesting that we deprive married women of the right to work, but it is quite obvious that we will have to do something about the alarming situation of the men cooking and women going out to earn their livelihood. . . . If this [equal pay for equal work] is accomplished the main danger to the workers' wage standards brought about by women in industry will be eliminated."[65] When Westinghouse finally signed a contract with Local 601 in 1941, an equal pay for equal work clause was included.[66] As at Philco, the effect was to stabilize the sexual division of labor.

A third example of the emergence of the equal pay demand in the electrical industry in the late 1930s involved a Westinghouse plant in Lima, Ohio. In June 1939, management hired two hundred young *men* just out of high school on jobs formerly done by women. They worked as winders, punch press operators, and other "women's jobs." Because they were paid the "women's rate" of 30 cents per hour, the union dubbed them "girls without skirts." Then, when management placed some of them (at the same low pay rate) on jobs previously been done by men at a 50 cent or higher rate, the UE filed a grievance. In response, the boys were transferred back to "girls' work," still earning the minimum rate for *female* employees of 30 cents. When the union pointed out that this violated the company's own written policy of a minimum rate of 50 cents for males, management asserted that it regarded the young men "in every way as girls." As the *UE News* noted, "Rather than admit that they were slashing the agreed minimum, the company found it easier to change the sex of the new employees, and, by simply declaring it to be so, turn the young men into girls. . . . They were girls, but the laws regulating female labor in the state of Ohio did not apply to them when it came to night work. They were men, but were paid and treated like the girls in the plant." The company continued to insist that the boys were "permanent female employees," until finally the UE, in utter desperation, called for the abolition of "men's rates" and "women's rates" and again put forward the demand for "equal pay for equal work."[67]

Although atypical, this case renders the concerns underlying the equal pay issue transparent. That the threat of substitution here involved males who occupied positions normally assigned to females was inconsequential. The critical issue, just as at Philco and East Pittsburgh, was the substitution of low-paid for higher-paid labor. Given the fluidity of the sexual division of labor in the electrical industry and the longstanding legitimacy of sex differentials in wages, such substitution was a continuous threat. Indeed, it is striking that in all three of these equal pay controversies, no one questioned women's ability to perform the jobs involved. At Philco, the work was done by women at other radio firms; at East Pittsburgh, women already worked on the day shift in equivalent jobs; and at Lima too, the "girls without skirts" were presumed to be capable (if relatively inexperienced) workers.

There were also efforts in the electrical industry to narrow sex differentials in wages. The women's committee of UE Local 601, for example, pursued this goal at the East Pittsburgh Westinghouse plant, although with little success, for management proved intransigent on the issue. Local 601 did win a single keysheet in place of separate rate lists for men and women, but this was a purely formal change that left job segregation and the wage discrimination tied to it intact. As Margaret Darin pointed out bitterly in her union newspaper column, under the new system, "A job is classified and then after it is classified by some superman complex a decision is reached by the masterminds of industry as to whether this job is to be a man's job or a woman's job. If it is designated as a woman's job a 'W' is put next to the labor grade and 'presto chango' the rate is reduced by 15 cents. Yet this company claims to classify the job and not the person!"[68] During the war, efforts to narrow wage differentials between men's and women's jobs and to challenge the job classification system would be more fruitful. In the 1930s, though, the UE concentrated on holding the line against female substitution through equal pay.

The UAW also pressed for equal pay for equal work in the 1930s. But here, the sexual division of labor was more sharply defined than in electrical manufacturing, so that the otherwise quite similar struggles for equal pay generated debates between the UAW and management over women's capabilities. This is well illustrated by a 1941 case at the Briggs Mack Avenue plant in Detroit. UAW Local 212 filed a grievance protesting the placement of Anna Maltese on an electric motor operation, arguing that it was a "man's job." Maltese was being paid 80 cents an hour, more than she had earned previously, but less than the job had paid before. "This job is not one that is physically healthy for a woman to work on," the grievance read. "We request that a man be placed on the job at the pay rate of $1 per hour." Management's answer was that the operation was a "light" one "on which a woman can work without physical strain."[69]

It became obvious in the ensuing negotiations that the real issue was management's effort to cut the wage for this job. But because the union did not question the principle that women should be paid less than men, it had to argue that the job itself was inherently a "man's job," and hence "a dollar job"—whereas management insisted that it was a "girl's job." "We probably have girls around here who are doing other jobs that are the same," Briggs stated. When the union countered that a similar operation was done exclusively by men in the "upstairs" part of the plant, at the rate of $1 an hour, management replied that "there are a lot of those jobs upstairs that we would probably have girls on but we don't like to put a couple of women up there among all those men."[70]

At this point, threatened in effect with further substitution, the UAW representative switched tactics. "I'm not particular who you keep on the job—as long as you pay the proper rate," he said. "If you've got a girl out there who is tough enough to take it and wants to run this job, I've no objections." Management pointed out, "We're not having any trouble with the girl," to which the union representative replied, "No, but you're having trouble with the rate." The union was quite straightforward about the reasons for its intransigence on the issue. "I'm anxious from several points of view," the UAW representative stated, "to perhaps give another man a job at a regular man's rate—not only that it is going to protect our classifications upstairs."[71]

Because the auto industry paid women substantially more than they could earn in other fields of "women's work," they were less concerned with obtaining equal pay for equal work than one might expect. Laura Hayward, an A.C. Spark Plug worker and UAW activist in the early organizing drives in Flint, recalls no widespread feeling among women auto workers in the prewar years that they deserved pay equal to men's even on "men's jobs." "In those days we didn't think of it," she said. "Or, I don't know, I didn't think of it. Of course, I never did a job that would be a man's job."[72] In fact, most women auto workers never did a "man's job." And despite its apparent status as a "woman's issue," the equal pay demand was most often raised by men, who feared that their own wage rates would be endangered by female substitution, as in the Briggs case.

Women did take the initiative on the equal pay issue, however, at GM's Oldsmobile division. A group of twenty-nine women complained to the Michigan Department of Labor and Industry in 1937 that they were being paid less than men for doing similar work, in violation of Michigan's equal pay law. They took the case to court and won back pay. All twenty-nine did jobs that men also performed, but earned substantially less. Newly employed men earned the same hourly rate as women with many years' experience and quickly rose above the maximum female rate. Although usually wage discrimination against female auto workers coincided with job discrimination (and was indeed masked by the sex-typing of jobs), here "any differentiation urged as between the employment of men and women [by management] exists only in theory, rather than in fact; in form rather than in substance," concluded Federal Circuit Court Judge Charles Hayden.[73]

GM's defense was to claim that men and women did not do similar work in that certain practices and requirements were present in women's employment but not in men's. For example, the company claimed that women were prohibited from doing "heavy lifting." The court found, however, that both men and women had to do quite a lot of lifting and hauling of stock in order to keep up with production quotas. And although it was true that the bulk of jobs in the Oldsmobile plant were performed exclusively by men, in the three departments where the women complainants were employed, the jobs they did were also done by men.[74]

A particularly interesting aspect of this case is the way in which the company responded to the women's protest action. In September 1937, shortly after the women complained to the state agency and an investigation was launched, GM created a "Women's Division" in the plant and transferred all the women there. The work in the new division had previously been done by men and women working side by side, and indeed, many of the women did the same jobs that they had performed previously elsewhere in the plant. Management's response to the women's protest against wage discrimination was simply to segregate women and men so that job discrimination would coincide with the differentials in pay.[75]

This tactic was adopted too late, however, to persuade the court that women and men actually did distinct work. So GM offered a series of arguments to demonstrate that women labored under special conditions justifying their lower pay. They claimed that women had two fifteen-minute rest periods per shift that the men did not have, as required by law. The court noted that the women had to turn out the same amount of work as the men, and questioned whether the rest periods were actually enforced. Undaunted, GM highlighted other differences between the conditions of women and men employees. "In the women's toilet it appears that there was a hot plate, a sanitary cot, some old rocking chairs, and perhaps a mirror," the court noted. "It is urged by the defendant that this tended to distinguish the work of the women from that of the men but I am not impressed that the operation of this statute is to be avoided by any difference in the appointment of toilets."[76]

The objective of this equal pay lawsuit—simply to eliminate wage discrimination—distinguished it from the more frequent instances where the equal pay demand originated with men. At Briggs, for example, both management and the union accepted the legitimacy of both job segregation and sex differentials in wages, and the controversy focused on whether the operation involved was a "woman's job" or a "man's job." The overall structure of the sexual division of labor was thus taken as given, and indeed became a reference point for the ensuing debate—in which management took the position that women were perfectly capable of doing the job in question. In the GM case, by contrast, job segregation did not accompany wage discrimination, so that management was forced to directly defend sex differentials in pay for identical work.

The GM case was atypical, however. Most equal pay cases in both auto and electrical manufacturing in the prewar period were brought by the union (primarily on behalf of men), not by women acting through the courts. And most of the challenges were provoked by marginal alterations in an established system of sex segregation, typically through substitution of women for men. Their aim was to restore the previous situation, not to eliminate it. If that could not be achieved, the likely outcome was a renegotiated sexual division of labor buttressed by an equal pay for equal work provision, which guaranteed the new order greater stability than the old. Thus, the equal pay demands made by the CIO in the years before World War II, while challenging *particular* management initiatives affecting the sexual division of labor, unintentionally helped consolidate the *general* structure of gender inequality in industry.

Although the principle of nondiscrimination embedded in industrial unionism provided the basis for challenges to sex segregation and pay inequity, in
the 1930s the main impact of unionization was instead to reinforce the existing
pattern of female employment. This was true not only in regard to the struggles
over equal pay, but also more generally. Sex differentials in wages and separate
seniority systems, established by management in the preunion era, were now
institutionalized in many local contracts. The basic pattern of female employment in both auto and electrical manufacturing remained unchanged from the
nonunion era. It was not the political forces unleashed with unionization, but
the economic impact of World War II that exploded the traditional sexual
division of labor in industry.

4 Redefining "Women's Work": War Mobilization and the Sexual Division of Labor

The economic mobilization for World War II dramatically transformed women's relationship to the labor market. They poured by the millions into jobs previously done only by men. As military conscription reduced the ranks of available workers and war production generated rapid economic expansion, the labor surplus of the 1930s was quickly replaced by a labor shortage—especially a shortage of male labor. Suddenly there was deep uncertainty about where the boundaries between "men's" and "women's" work should be drawn. Not only were women integrated into "men's jobs" on an unprecedented scale, but also, with conversion to war production, many entirely new occupations emerged—with no clear sex labels.

The war is often viewed as a period when job segregation by sex was broken down, albeit temporarily. Yet what is most striking about the wartime transformation is the way *new* patterns of occupational segregation developed in the industries opened to women. The boundaries between "women's" and "men's" work changed location, rather than being eliminated. If the most remarkable aspect of the sexual division of labor in the depression was its stability in the face of dramatic economic and political change, the wartime experience highlights something even more fundamental: the reproduction of job segregation in the context of a huge influx of women into the work force and a massive upheaval in the division of labor.[1]

Rather than hiring women workers to fill openings as vacancies occurred, managers explicitly defined some war jobs as "suitable" for women, and others as "unsuitable," guided by a hastily revised idiom of sex-typing that adapted prewar traditions to the special demands of the war emergency. As married women and mothers joined the labor force in growing numbers during the war, occupational segregation and the sex-typing of war jobs helped to reconcile women's new economic position with their traditional family role. Wartime propaganda imagery of "woman's place" on the nation's production lines consistently portrayed women's war work as a temporary extension of domesticity. And jobs that had previously been viewed as quintessentially masculine were suddenly endowed with femininity and glamour for the duration. The war mobilization era not only illustrates the resilience of job segregation by sex, but also graphically demonstrates how idioms of sex-typing can be flexibly applied to whatever jobs women and men happen to be doing.

Women's Wartime Employment in Auto and Electrical Manufacturing

Although the wartime economic mobilization transformed the entire occupational structure, manufacturing was most dramatically affected. In 1940, on the eve of U.S. entry into the war, women factory workers made up only 20 percent of the female labor force, and most of them were employed in older, low-wage industries like textiles and clothing. In the war boom, however, the industries that had traditionally employed the fewest women drew on them most extensively (Table 3). Although women's employment grew by 50 percent between 1940 and 1944 in the economy as a whole, it increased by 140 percent in manufacturing. And in major war industries (metal-working, chemical, and rubber), women's employment rose 460 percent in that four-year period.[2]

Electrical manufacturing and auto were among the industries most affected:

Table 3. Women Production Workers in Manufacturing Industries as a Percentage of All Production Workers, 1940 to 1950—Selected Years

Industry	1940	1944	1946	1950
Iron and Steel	6.7%	22.3%	9.4%	5%
Electrical Machinery	32.2	49.1	39.1	39
Automobiles[a]	5.7	24.4	8.9	10
Textile Mill Products	43.0	51.4	46.7	43
Apparel	75.2	78.0	76.9	76
Chemicals	15.4	31.6	20.5	18
Rubber	25.4	35.1	23.9	27
All Manufacturing	24.1	33.2	26.6	27
Total Labor Force	28.0	36.0	31.0	33

Sources: 1940, 1944, and 1946 data are from U.S. Department of Labor, Bureau of Labor Statistics, Women in Factories, mimeographed (1947). 1950 data are from U.S. Department of Labor, Bureau of Labor Statistics, Women Employees in Manufacturing Industries (1957). All figures are for the month of October of the years indicated.

[a]In 1944, this industry did not produce automobiles, but instead tanks, aircraft, military vehicles, etc. This category, however, does not include all aircraft manufactured, but only that produced by automobile firms.

women's employment increased by 600 percent in auto and by 350 percent in electrical manufacturing in the mobilization period.[3] The curtailment of civilian production, the vast expansion of employment, and the conscription of prewar workers into the military compelled both industries to completely overhaul their production processes as well as their labor utilization policies. Employers' views about what kinds of work were and were not appropriate for women had to be drastically modified.

Between 1940 and 1944, the number of workers in electrical manufacturing grew more than twice as much as in the auto industry. The increase in women workers was also substantially greater in the electrical case. Even at the wartime employment peak, the proportion of women among auto production workers was far below the *prewar* proportion in electrical manufacturing, and only half of the wartime proportion in the latter (Table 4). Yet it would be a mistake to conclude from these data that the war mobilization was more disruptive to the sexual division of labor in the electrical industry than in auto. In fact, precisely the opposite was true.

The longstanding tradition of extensive female employment in electrical manufacturing made the process of incorporating women into "men's jobs" in that industry relatively smooth. In auto, however, neither management nor labor was accustomed to women's employment in production work, except in parts plants and a few small enclaves of assembly plants like the cut-and-sew or wiring departments. The introduction of women into the all-male preserves of the auto industry was therefore a dramatic break with past practice. In addition, the process of conversion to military production was far more disruptive to the *status quo ante* in auto than in electrical manufacturing. While consumer goods production was curtailed in both industries, the changeover

Table 4. Female and Total Employment in the Auto and Electrical Industries, 1940 to 1944—Production Workers Only

Month/Year		Automotive Industry			Electrical Manufacturing	
	Total Employees	Number of Women	Women as % of Total	Total Employees	Number of Women	Women as % of Total
Oct. 1940	533,300	30,400	5.7%	334,200	107,600	32.2%
April 1941	585,200	31,600	5.4	411,300	131,200	31.9
Oct. 1941	577,500	28,300	4.9	492,500	158,600	32.2
April 1942	429,200	20,600	4.8	520,900	174,500	33.5
Oct. 1942	576,000	69,700	12.1	618,900	222,800	36.0
April 1943	670,200	121,300	18.1	725,900	327,400	45.1
Oct. 1943	775,900	199,400	25.7	757,900	370,600	48.0
April 1944	746,000	185,000	24.8	778,000	380,400	48.9

Source: U.S. Department of Labor, Bureau of Labor Statistics, *Women in Factories,* mimeographed (1947), 6-7.

from car production to the manufacture of tanks, aircraft, and ordnance required more extensive retooling than conversion of the electrical industry involved. Electrical manufacturing was less capital-intensive to begin with, and there was far more overlap between its wartime and peacetime products.[4]

If incorporating female labor into the auto industry was relatively difficult, it was also avoided longer than in electrical manufacturing and other war industries, thanks to the major auto corporations' procrastination in converting their plants to military production. In the first half of 1942, when the rest of the nation already had a labor shortage, Michigan was grappling with severe "conversion unemployment." The problem was particularly pronounced among women auto workers.[5] Indeed, both the absolute number and the proportion of women among auto production workers dropped between April 1941 and April 1942 (Table 4). Not until late 1942, when conversion was complete and the prewar labor force had been reabsorbed into defense work, did the proportion of women in auto begin to rise.[6] While the slow conversion process initially delayed the influx of women into the industry, it also made for an especially sudden shift in the sexual division of labor. In April 1942, only one of every twenty auto production workers was female; eighteen months later, one out of every four workers in the industry's plants was a woman.

The growth in female employment was more gradual in the electrical industry. Initially, it seemed like a marginal change in an industry that had always employed large numbers of women, and everyone concerned adjusted relatively easily. A U.S. Women's Bureau survey in mid-1942 found that only 7 percent of the women employed in New Jersey's electrical plants were "substitutes" for men, with the vast majority of them employed in "occupations that have always been women's." And as late as July 1943, only 14 percent of the production jobs in the Erie GE plant were considered "men's jobs" being performed by women.[7] As the war-converted electrical industry expanded during the mobilization period, many of the new jobs that women filled closely resembled positions routinely occupied by females in the prewar years. Of course, the fact that women were also employed during the war in a range of jobs previously considered appropriate only for men did create tensions. But because female labor was a familiar presence in electrical manufacturing, and the sexual division of labor in the industry was relatively flexible, the wartime transition was much smoother there than in auto.

Although women were incorporated into electrical manufacturing more easily, and the wartime increase in total employment was much greater in that industry, the ratio of female to total employment increased far more in auto. This was primarily because of the geographical concentration characteristic of automotive production during this period. In 1939, the city of Detroit alone accounted for 48 percent of the nation's auto workers, and no other American city contributed more to the nation's military production during the war.

Michigan, with 4 percent of the U.S. population, obtained more than 10 percent of the war contracts awarded by the government. Most of the work was carried out in the Detroit area, where employment doubled between 1940 and 1943.[8] Not for nothing was the Motor City dubbed the "Arsenal of Democracy."

Before the war, the concentration of automotive production in the Detroit area had not facilitated women's employment in the industry. On the contrary, active company recruitment efforts and the industry's reputation for high wages had continuously attracted a surplus of male labor to the area.[9] But the war mobilization period was different. Not only were men being drafted into the military, but also the city's housing, transportation, and other facilities could not accommodate the population growth that would accompany a doubled *male* labor force. Such rapid expansion of infrastructural and community facilities would have been difficult at any time, but it was simply impossible with wartime restrictions on construction and rationing of scarce materials.

There was substantial wartime migration to Detroit, whose population grew by 15 percent between 1940 and 1943. Most of the newcomers came from southern states where well-paid war jobs were not available. Despite the community's inability to accommodate more in-migrants, employers continued to recruit workers in the South. As the situation deteriorated, families who came to the city found it impossible to secure housing, and many simply left after a few months.[10] Well before the problem reached this point, government officials recognized that the solution to the city's labor shortage was the employment of women who already lived in the area. In mid-1942, the War Production Board (WPB) threatened to withhold additional war contracts from Detroit manufacturers, and even to cancel existing contracts, if in-migration was not stemmed. The Detroit regional director of the WPB wrote to the Michigan Manufacturers' Association in July 1942, urging that the alternative to continued in-migration was "the recruiting of large numbers of women who do not ordinarily consider themselves a part of the industrial labor supply." As the WPB noted, "The recruitment of local women who are not now in the labor market is free from the disadvantages or limitations of the other methods of meeting the labor deficit. Local women workers will not require new housing, transportation or other facilities. They do not create a possible future relief burden. Each woman who is recruited will reduce the necessary in-migration correspondingly and thus reduce or eliminate the need for transferring contracts elsewhere." The same logic led the government to encourage employment of blacks as well as older and handicapped workers, groups that (like women) had always been shunned by most auto manufacturers.[11]

Ultimately the Detroit labor shortage would be met in exactly this way. But employers refused to go along with the plan until the supply of male labor had been exhausted. "As long as the employers can hire men," Ernest Kanzler, the head of the Detroit WPB, pointed out at a meeting on the labor supply problem held in June 1942, "they don't talk about hiring women." The automotive management representatives at the meeting agreed. "They are used to talking in terms of men," acknowledged H. J. Roesch, of the Briggs Manufacturing Company. "In our plant," said the Industrial Relations Manager of Packard, "we have 3,000 applications for women right now that we can't use. I doubt if there isn't a plant in Detroit with the same predicament."[12] It was not because auto industry employers were more flexible than their counterparts in electrical manufacturing, but because they were left with no choice in the matter that the wartime change in the sexual division of labor in auto was so much more extensive.

Although management recognized early on that unprecedented numbers of women would probably have to be employed in the auto industry during the war, they showed little interest in hiring women as long as the labor surplus created by conversion unemployment persisted. Initially, women war workers were employed only in jobs that had long before been established within the industry as "women's work." Although a U.S. Employment Service survey of war work in early 1942 found that women could capably perform the tasks required in 80 percent of the job classifications, UAW plants that employed women had, on average, women in only 28 percent of the classifications in July of that year. "The chief classifications on which they were employed," the UAW reported, "were assembly, inspection, drill press, punch press, sewing machines, filing, and packing." Such positions had often been filled by women before the war.[13]

Even as the labor supply dwindled, auto employers were loath to forsake their prewar hiring preferences for white males. Ultimately, the federal government intervened, setting male employment allocation ceilings and giving the War Manpower Commission (WMC) the power to enforce them. "Over our strenuous objections," Detroit WMC director Edward Cushman recalls, "the Ford Motor Company began hiring 17, 18 and 19 year-old men. And we kept drafting them!"[14]

The pressures that increased female representation in auto also led to growth in black employment during the war. In the industry's Detroit plants, black representation rose from about 4 percent of the work force in the prewar period to 15 percent in 1945. Before the war, auto employers (with the partial and eccentric exception of Ford) had refused to hire blacks. John L. Lovett, secretary of the Michigan Manufacturers' Association, believed that "Negroes do not have the 'speed and rhythm' to do this type of work," according to a 1941 government report. Lovett assured the investigator that "most Michigan employers have the same belief." As late as July 1943, after black employment had begun to increase in many automotive plants, employers complained that blacks "leave the job easily and are absent a lot."[15] Management's objections to hiring blacks, while cast in a different idiom, paralleled their opposition to female employment.

Employers in electrical manufacturing were even more resistant to hiring blacks—in contrast to their willingness to employ women in greater numbers during the war. In 1940, blacks made up less than 1 percent of the electrical manufacturing work force, and only 3 percent at the wartime employment peak. Those blacks who did get jobs in electrical plants during the war, significantly, were concentrated in areas with tight labor markets. A 1943 government report on the radio and radar industry, which had a higher proportion of blacks than other branches of electrical manufacturing at the time, noted that "very few firms expect to increase their employment of nonwhites significantly unless forced to by greatly increased labor stringencies or by compulsory labor market controls." Because government intervention focused on "congested" war production areas like Detroit, the geographical decentralization of the electrical industry saved it from the political pressures that increased black employment in auto.[16]

In addition to the geographical factor, the low level of black employment in wartime electrical manufacturing was related to the extensive participation of white women in the industry. "Those industries which delayed longest the employment of Negroes," Robert Weaver pointed out in his authoritative 1946 study, *Negro Labor*, "were usually light and clean manufacturing. They were the industries in which women (white) were used in the largest proportions."[17] The electrical manufacturers relied primarily on the reserves of white female labor to meet their requirements, and introduced blacks only in localities where they had no alternative. In auto, on the other hand, management wanted neither women nor black workers so long as white men were available; but black men were often preferred over white women for unskilled "heavy" jobs.

The least favored group of workers in both industries was black women. "The [black] men are o.k. on unskilled jobs," reported one government representative in mid-1943, summarizing the attitude of auto industry employers toward black workers, "but the women are a drug on the market." In Detroit, Geraldine Bledsoe of the U.S. Employment Service complained publicly in October 1942 that more than one thousand black women had completed vocational training courses, "and yet they go day after day to the plants and are turned down." By mid-1943 the WMC estimated that twenty-eight thousand black women were available for war work in Detroit, but most war plants would employ them only as janitors, matrons, and government inspectors. Auto manufacturers began to hire black women in substantial numbers only after all other sources of labor had been fully exhausted.[18] No data are available on the sex breakdown among the small group of blacks employed in electrical manufacturing during the war, but the much larger number of "women's jobs" in this industry may have made for less disparity between women and men. By

1950, black representation among women electrical workers was slightly greater than among men.[19]

Redefining "Women's Work" in Wartime Industry

Conversion to war production involved redefinition of the entire employment structure. Some civilian automobile production jobs were also necessary for the production of tanks, aircraft, engines, and ordnance; other war jobs were completely new. The changeover to war production in electrical manufacturing was less dramatic, but also involved shifts in the character and distribution of jobs. Thus, many of the war jobs that had to be filled (in both industries) were not clearly labeled as "women's" or "men's" work, at least at first. Such ambiguities in sex-typing had occasionally been experienced before (with changes in the job structure resulting from technological innovations, for example), but the scale of the problem during the war was totally unprecedented.

While the government had actively pressured some firms to hire women, it made no effort whatsoever to influence their placement within industry once management complied. The U.S. Employment Service routinely filled employer job openings that called for specific numbers of women and men. Although ceilings were imposed on the number of men who could be allocated to each plant, employers had a free hand in placing women and men in particular jobs within this constraint.[20] Although the unions sometimes contested the sexual division of labor after the fact, the initial job assignments were left entirely to management.

Women were not evenly distributed through the various jobs available in the war plants, but were hired into specific classifications that management deemed "suitable" for women and were excluded from other jobs. Some employers conducted special surveys to determine the sexual division of labor in a plant; probably more often such decisions were made informally by individual supervisors.[21] Although data on the distribution of women through job classifications in the wartime auto and electrical industries are sketchy, there is no mistaking the persistence of segregation by sex. A 1943 survey of the auto industry's Detroit plants, for example, found more than one-half of the women workers clustered in only five of seventy-two job classifications. Only 11 percent of the men were employed in these five occupations.[22]

Jobs were also highly segregated in the electrical industry during the war. A 1942 study of electrical appliance plants (most of which had already been converted to military production when surveyed) found women, who were 30 percent of the workers, in only twenty-one job classifications, whereas men were spread across seventy-two of them. Nearly half of the women (47 percent) were employed in a single job category, and 68 percent were clustered in four

6. "A group of women who used to turn out automobile parts turning out armor-piercing shell cores in a Chrysler Ordnance Plant," Detroit, n.d. (National Archives)

7. Women working on bomber parts at a De Soto plant, Detroit, 1942. (Wayne State University Labor Archives)

occupations. Only 16 percent of the men were in these four job classifications.[23] Another study of radio, radio equipment, and phonograph plants, conducted in early 1945, told the same story. Women were 58 percent of the workers surveyed, but half of them were found in four occupations, although these four categories accounted for only 6 percent of the male minority.[24]

Job segregation by sex was explicitly acknowledged in many war plants: Jobs were formally labeled "male" and "female." The two largest electrical firms, GE and Westinghouse, continued this practice until the end of the war. And in 45 percent of the auto plants with sexually mixed work forces responding to a survey conducted in mid-1944 by the UAW Women's Bureau, jobs were formally categorized as "male" or "female."[25] Available records suggest that sex segregation also existed elsewhere, even if it was not formally acknowledged. A case in point is the Ford River Rouge plant. The available data do not offer a very detailed breakdown, yet a great deal of segregation is apparent. In December 1943, when women's employment in the industry was at its wartime peak, women made up 16 percent of the Rouge work force. More than one-half of the job groups listed in the company's internal "factory count" included women, but 62 percent of the women workers were clustered in just 20 of the 416 job categories. And nearly two-thirds of the occupational groups were at least 90 percent male.[26]

Segregation appears to be a constant across both industries during the war years. However, in both industries there was considerable plant-to-plant variation in patterns of employment by sex. In the Detroit area, for example, there was a wide range in the proportion of women employed, even among plants manufacturing the same products. In April 1943, women were 29 percent of the workers at the GM Cadillac plant, which was producing engine parts, but women made up 59 percent of the work force at the Excello Corporation's Detroit plant, which made the same product. Similarly, although women were only 2 percent of the workers at Continental Motors, they were 27 percent of those at the Jefferson Avenue plant of the Hudson Motor Car Company. Both plants made aircraft motors.[27] In the electrical industry, too, there was considerable variation of this sort, even among plants owned by the same company and producing similar goods. For example, in 1945, within the division of GE that manufactured electrical apparatus, women made up 16 percent of the workers at the Erie, Pennsylvania, plant, 27 percent of those at Schenectady, 39 percent at Fort Wayne, Indiana, and 56 percent at West Lynn.[28]

Whatever the sexual division of labor happened to be at a given point in time, management always seemed to insist that there was no alternative. When a War Department representative visited an airplane plant where large numbers of women were employed, he was told that the best welder in the plant was a woman. "Their supervisors told me that their work is fine, even better than that of the men who were formerly on those jobs," he reported. "In another plant in the same area, I remarked on the absence of women and was told that women just can't do those jobs—the very same jobs. It is true, they can't do that type of work—as long as the employer refuses to hire and train them."[29]

Although the specifics varied, everywhere management was quick to offer a rationale for the concentration of women in some jobs and their exclusion from others, just as it had in the prewar era. "Womanpower differs from manpower as oil fuel differs from coal," proclaimed the trade journal *Automotive War Production* in October 1943, "and an understanding of the characteristics of the energy involved was needed for obtaining best results." Although it was now applied to a larger and quite different set of jobs, the basic characterization of women's abilities and limitations was familiar. As *Automotive War Production* put it:

> On certain kinds of operations—the very ones requiring high manipulative skill—women were found to be a whole lot quicker and more efficient than men. Engineering womanpower means realizing fully that women are not only different from men in such things as lifting power and arm reach—but in many other ways that pertain to their physiological and their social functions. To understand these things does not mean to exclude women from *the jobs for which they are peculiarly adapted,* and where they can help to win this war. It merely means using them as women, and not as men.[30]

The idiom of women's war work in the electrical industry closely paralleled that in auto. "Nearly every Westinghouse plant employs women, especially for jobs that require dexterity with tiny parts," reported an article in *Factory Management and Maintenance* in March 1942.

> At the East Pittsburgh plant, for instance, women tape coils. The thickness of each coil must be identical to within close limits, so the job requires feminine patience and deft fingers.
>
> Another job that calls for unlimited patience is the inspection of moving parts of electric instruments . . . .
>
> Thirty-one pieces are assembled into a thermostat control for refrigerators at the Mansfield works. Westinghouse finds that women can handle these minute parts, and are willing to perform the highly repetitive operations that this type of assembly requires.[31]

Repeatedly stressed, especially in auto, was the lesser physical strength of the average woman worker. "Woman isn't just a 'smaller man,'" *Automotive War Production* pointed out. "Compensations in production processes must be made to allow for the fact that the average woman is only 35 percent muscle in comparison to the average man's 41 percent. Moreover, industrial studies have shown that only 54 percent of woman's weight is strength, as against man's 87 percent, and that the hand squeeze of the average woman exerts only 48 pounds of pressure, against man's 81 pounds."[32]

Accompanying the characterization of women's work as "light" was an emphasis on cleanliness. "Women can satisfactorily fill all or most jobs performed by men, subject only to the limitations of strength and physical requirements," a meeting of the National Association of Manufacturers concluded in March 1942. "However . . . jobs of a particularly 'dirty' character, jobs that subject women to heat process or are of a 'wet' nature should not be filled by women . . . despite the fact that women could, if required, perform them."[33]

The emphasis in the idiom of sex-typing on the physical limitations of women workers had a dual character. It not only justified the sexual division of labor, but it also served as the basis for increased mechanization and work simplification. "To adjust women's jobs to such [physical] differences, automotive plants have added more mechanical aids such as conveyors, chain hoists, and load lifters," reported *Automotive War Production*. A study by Constance Green found job dilution of this sort widespread in electrical firms and other war industries in the Connecticut Valley as well. "Where ten men had done ten complete jobs, now . . . eight women and two, three, or possibly four men together would do the ten split-up jobs," she noted. "Most often men set up machines, ground or adjusted tools, and generally 'serviced' the women who acted exclusively as machine operators."[34]

Although production technology was already quite advanced in both auto and electrical manufacturing, the pace of development accelerated during the war period. Management attributed this to its desire to make jobs easier for women, but the labor shortage and the opportunity to introduce new technology at government expense under war contracts were at least as important. However, the idiom that constructed women as "delicate" and, although poorly suited to "heavy" work, amenable to monotonous jobs, was now marshaled to justify the use of new technology and work "simplification." At Vultee Aircraft, for example, a manager explained:

> It definitely was in Vultee's favor that the hiring of women was started when production jobs were being simplified to meet the needs of fast, quantity production. . . . Special jigs were added to hold small tools, such as drills, so that women could concentrate on employing more effectively their proven capacity for repetitive operations requiring high digital dexterity.
>
> Unlike the man whom she replaced, she as a woman, had the capacity to withstand the monotony of even more simplified repetitive operations. To have suspended the air wrench from a counterbalanced support for him would have served merely to heighten his boredom with the job. As for the woman who replaced him, she now handles two such counterbalanced, air-driven wrenches, one in each hand.[35]

Of course, such changes led to greater efficiency regardless of the sex of the workers. But the potential for resistance to job dilution was substantially undercut by the claim, cast in the patriotic idiom of "production for victory," that the changes were necessary in order to facilitate women's employment. The significance of this is suggested by the fact that more than one-half the plants employing women in "men's jobs" that the Conference Board surveyed in 1943 had "simplified" the operations involved.[36]

There was a contradiction in the management literature on women's war work. It simultaneously stressed the fact that "women are being trained in skills that were considered exclusively in man's domain" and their special suitability for "delicate war jobs."[37] These two seemingly conflicting kinds of statements were reconciled through analogies between "women's work" at home and in the war plants. "Note the similarity between squeezing orange juice and the operation of a small drill press," the Sperry Gyroscope Company urged in a recruitment pamphlet. "Anyone can peel potatoes," it went on. "Burring and filing are almost as easy." An automotive industry publication praised women workers at the Ford Motor Company's Willow Run bomber plant in similar terms. "The ladies have shown they can operate drill presses as well as egg beaters," it proclaimed. "Why should men, who from childhood on never so much as sewed on buttons," inquired one manager, "be expected to handle delicate instruments better than women who have plied embroidery needles, knitting needles and darning needles all their lives?"[38] The newsreel *Glamour Girls of '43* pursued the same theme:

> Instead of cutting the lines of a dress, this woman cuts the pattern of aircraft parts. Instead of baking cake, this woman is cooking gears to reduce the tension in the gears after use. . . .
> They are taking to welding as if the rod were a needle and the metal a length of cloth to be sewn. After a short apprenticeship, this woman can operate a drill press just as easily as a juice extractor in her own kitchen. And a lathe will hold no more terrors for her than an electric washing machine.[39]

In this manner, virtually any job could be labeled "women's work."

Glamour was a related theme in the idiom through which women's war work was demarcated as female. As if calculated to assure women—and men—that war work need not involve a loss of femininity, depictions of women's new work roles were overlaid with allusions to their stylish dress and attractive appearance. "A pretty young inspector in blue slacks pushes a gauge—a cylindrical plug with a diamond-pointed push-button on its side—through the shaft's hollow chamber," was a typical rendition.[40] Such statements, like the housework analogies, effectively reconciled woman's position in what were previously "men's jobs" with traditional images of femininity.

Ultimately, what lay behind the mixed message that war jobs were at once "men's" and "women's" jobs was an unambiguous point: Women *could* do "men's work," but they were only expected to do it temporarily. The ideolog-

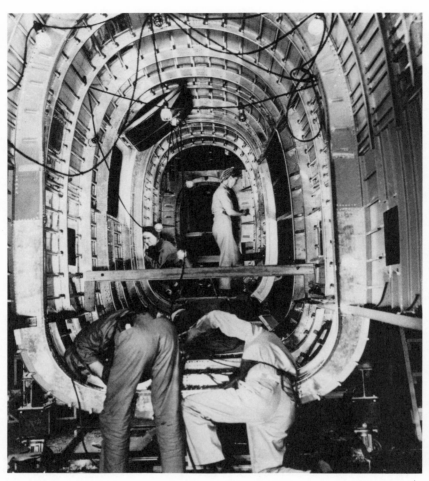

8. Women installing structural parts in the tail fuselage of a Consolidated transport plane on the West Coast, n.d. (National Archives)

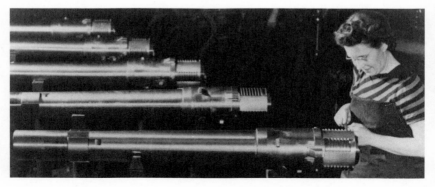

9. Evelyn Adkins filing threads on a 75mm Pack Howitzer, General Electric Co., Erie, Pennsylvania, March 1943. (United Electrical Workers)

ical definition of women's war work explicitly included the provision that they would gracefully withdraw from their "men's jobs" when the war ended and the rightful owners returned. Women, as everyone knew, were in heavy industry "for the duration." This theme would become much more prominent after the war, but it was a constant undercurrent from the outset.

Before the war, too, women had been stereotyped as temporary workers, and occupational sex-typing had helped to ensure that employed women would continue to view themselves as women first, workers second. Now this took on new importance, because the reserves of "womanpower" war industries drew on included married women, even mothers of young children, in unprecedented numbers. A study by the Automotive Council for War Production noted that of twelve thousand women employed during the war by one large automotive firm in Detroit, 68 percent were married, and 40 percent had children. And a 1943 WPB study found that 40 percent of the one hundred fifty thousand women war workers employed in Detroit were mothers. "With the existing prejudice against employing women over forty, the overwhelming majority of these women workers are young mothers with children under 16."[41]

This was the group of women least likely to have been employed in the prewar years. "In this time of pressure for added labor supply," the U.S. Women's Bureau reported, "the married women for the first time in this country's history exceeded single women in the employed group."[42] Married women were especially numerous in the auto industry, probably because of the vigorous effort to recruit local female labor in Detroit. Although comparable data are not available for the electrical industry, the major companies did lift their longstanding restrictions on the employment of married women during the war mobilization.[43]

Some firms made deliberate efforts to recruit the wives and daughters of men whom they had employed before the war. A 1942 study by Princeton University's Industrial Relations Section reported on the reasons given by employers for this policy: "(1) It increases the local labor supply without affecting housing requirements; (2) it brings in new employees who are already acquainted with the company and who are likely to be as satisfactory employees as their male relatives; and (3) it may help to minimize postwar readjustment since wives of employed men are not looking for permanent employment."[44] Similarly, the Detroit Vickers aircraft plant had a policy of hiring "members of men's families who have gone to forces so that when these men come back there will be less of a problem in getting the women out of the jobs to give them back to the men."[45]

The dramatic rise in married women's employment during the war raised the longstanding tension between women's commitment to marriage and family and their status as individual members of the paid work force to a qualitatively different level. Before the war, the bulk of the female labor force was comprised of unmarried women; young wives with no children; and self-supporting widowed, divorced, and separated women. When married women and mothers went to work during the war, the occupational sex-typing that linked women's roles in the family and in paid work, far from disintegrating, was infused with new energy.

The wartime idiom of sex segregation combined such prewar themes as women's dexterity and lack of physical strength with an emphasis on the value of women's multivaried experience doing housework and an unrelenting glamourization of their new work roles. That "woman's place" in wartime industry was defined so quickly and effectively owed much to the power of this sex-typing. Although the initiative came from management, neither unions nor rank-and-file workers—of either gender—offered much resistance to the *general* principle of differentiation of jobs into "female" and "male" categories. Nor was the ideology of "woman's place" in the war effort ever frontally challenged. There was a great deal of conflict, however, over the location of the boundaries between the female and male labor markets in wartime industry, and over wage differentials between these newly constituted markets, and this is the subject of chapter 5.

5 Wartime Labor Struggles over the Position of Women in Industry

The industrial unions took far more interest in the sexual division of labor during World War II than before. In the late 1930s, the fledgling CIO unions had been preoccupied with consolidating their organizational gains, and seldom had attempted to influence such crucial determinants of women's position in industry as hiring or job placement policies. These matters were left to management, while the unions concentrated on recruiting those workers already hired. The CIO did try to narrow sex differentials in wages in the 1930s, but achieved little in this area before the war. As we saw in chapter 3, the main impact of the unions on the sexual division of labor in the prewar period was to stabilize it by establishing seniority systems and by resisting female substitution.

With the mobilization for war, however, and the dramatic upheaval that it brought in the sexual division of labor, the unions could no longer avoid the issues of hiring and job placement. The basic achievements of the CIO in such areas as job security, wages, and working conditions were jeopardized by the employment of women on "men's jobs." Would women war workers share the gains the unions had won for men in the prewar era? Or would they be treated the way women workers traditionally had been? This dilemma thrust gender issues into the forefront of labor-management conflict during the war.

Management took the initiative in shaping both the sexual division of labor and the production process in which it was embedded. Union influence on the wartime sexual division of labor was twofold. First, union power was indirectly reflected in management's policies, which were developed with a view to the possibility of union resistance. Second, the unions could directly shape the sexual division of labor by challenging managerial initiatives after the fact. In both respects, union influence was shaped in the context of wartime industrial relations.

At first glance, one might presume that wartime conditions strengthened labor's hand. Union membership rose astronomically during the war years, especially in defense-related industries. By 1946, more than 80 percent of the work force in the auto and electrical industries (as well as in aircraft, meat-packing, rubber, steel, and shipbuilding) were covered by union agreements.[1] And full employment significantly undercut managerial control, especially relative to the 1930s. "Most employees are aware of the fact that if they are discharged for violation of plant rules that it merely means going from one plant to another to work, sometimes at an advanced rate of pay, and therefore see no particular reason why such things should be taken seriously," complained a manager at GM's A. C. Spark Plug division in April 1943. "Men who formerly did a splendid job of supervision are, during these trying times, having considerable difficulty in maintaining proper discipline."[2] Indeed, the level of shop floor militancy during the war years, especially the upsurge of wildcat strikes, is legendary.[3]

Yet the no-strike pledge, which the nation's unions took immediately after Pearl Harbor, significantly undercut labor's power. As Nelson Lichtenstein has skillfully demonstrated, the price of the organizational strength the unions gained during the war was the erosion of workers' shop-floor power. This was accompanied by large-scale bureaucratization within the CIO and, on the national level, a strengthening of business (in a conservative alliance with the military) at labor's expense.[4] Conflict between labor and management over the sexual division of labor necessarily reflected this larger context.

Wartime struggles over the sexual division of labor in industry were typically fought out between management and the prewar work force, which was made up primarily of male workers (especially in auto). Often the disputes arose even before significant numbers of women were employed. Moreover, most women war workers had no previous factory or union experience. They could hardly get their bearings, much less develop the skills needed to participate effectively in struggles with management, during the brief period when the wartime sexual division of labor was open to negotiation. And high-paying war jobs meant such an enormous improvement in the economic circumstances of many of these women that they were not overly concerned about their specific job placements.[5]

The same was true of many male workers who entered manufacturing industry for the first time during the war. Like women war workers, these men, many of whom migrated to war production centers from the South or the rural Midwest, had no relevant standards against which to measure the industrial situation they now entered. Thus, management could act with a much freer hand in plants newly built during the war, and in others where the labor force was entirely new, than in converted consumer goods plants with an experienced labor force and seasoned union leaders.[6] This is one reason why conflict with management over the sexual division of labor was more intense in the auto and electrical industries than in such new war industries as aircraft and ship-building, where the portion of the wartime labor force with prewar industrial experience was relatively small.

While wartime struggles over the position of women emerged in both auto and electrical manufacturing, their trajectories were quite different. In auto, where women had been a tiny minority of the prewar work force, conflict initially focused on hiring, with the UAW generally resisting the introduction of women into "men's jobs." Only after it became clear that large-scale female substitution was unavoidable did the UAW shift to the demand for "equal pay for equal work." By contrast, because of its long history of extensive female employment, in electrical manufacturing the issue of sex differentials in pay emerged immediately. It was apparent long before the war that an exclusionary strategy could not succeed in this industry. Accordingly, the demand for equal pay for equal work was raised at the very beginning of the war. The UE went even further by the war's end, questioning the overall basis of job segregation by sex and demanding "equal pay for comparable worth." Thus their contrast-ing histories of female employment produced distinct forms of struggle in the auto and electrical industries during the war.

From Exclusion to "Equal Pay": Conflict over "Women's Work" in Auto

The UAW's main goal when war production began was to prevent female substitution as long as there were unemployed men. Wage standards, as well as the newly won seniority rights of prewar auto workers (an overwhelmingly male group), had to be defended in the face of conversion unemployment. In October 1941, the major auto companies and the UAW agreed to a plan pro-posed by the federal government's Office of Production Management, which stipulated that prewar workers would be rehired in line with seniority in the course of the defense buildup. Under this "OPM Six-Point Transfer Agree-ment," laid-off auto workers who took defense jobs continued to accumulate seniority with their original employer, who could, in turn, recall them for defense work later on. The agreement also stipulated that transfers within a firm were to be made in line with seniority, and that local workers would be given preference in hiring for defense jobs.[7]

Almost from the beginning of the economic mobilization, planners consid-ered recruiting women into the auto work force to alleviate the expected labor shortage. But the UAW remained highly antagonistic to this idea as long as men remained out of work. In mid-1942, when conversion unemployment was still high, the War Production Board (WPB) provoked a hue and cry from the union when it undertook registration of Detroit women to ascertain how many might be available for war work. "A lot of these people walking the streets are saying, 'What in the devil are you registering women workers for when we are on the other side of the street and out of a job?'" Ernest Kanzler of the Detroit WPB reported. Walter Reuther had warned of this just a few months before at a meeting of the WPB's automotive branch. "If you carry out the policy of putting women to work before you put the idle men to work," he said, "you will have trouble."[8]

As it happened, the UAW's fears of early female substitution were unfounded, for the auto firms themselves strongly preferred men to women for war jobs. Most defense contracts were written on a cost-plus basis, so that the wage bill was passed on the government.[9] There was little effort to cut costs through female substitution in this situation. The union's fears were more justified when it came to guarding against other types of seniority violations, however, as employers often did hire inexperienced male workers before rehiring those with seniority. Continuing labor recruitment in the South also threatened seniority workers. "You have to get in line at the factory outside in the cold winter weather at 6 a.m. to get an interview card," George Abbott of UAW Local 602 complained. "They put out about 40 of them, at 8 o'clock [and] . . . you come back in after noon for an interview. And if you are a hill billy or a green horn with no seniority or knowledge of work you get hired or if you know some one."[10]

Similar problems arose within the small sector of the auto industry that had traditionally been a female preserve. Clara Shipski and Myrtle Hewitt wrote to Secretary of Labor Frances Perkins on behalf of several hundred women in Lansing, Michigan who were laid off when the Fisher Body plant there closed for conversion in February 1942. The women demanded the protection to which they were entitled under the O.P.M. Six-Point Agreement. "We feel that the Reo Motor Company showed discrimination by hiring four hundred women and only ninety-five were Fisher Body women," they wrote. "We understand that the people who were automatically laid off through no fault of their own should have preference to other wage earners who left their jobs to work for the Reo Motor Company."[11]

But in this period, with depression memories fresh and the seniority victory still fragile, the union gave priority to men in defending employment rights. In October 1941, forty to fifty women from various UAW locals met to discuss the effects of conversion unemployment on women and sent a delegation to George Addes, then the UAW's defense policy coordinator. Their request that a woman be appointed to the union's recently formed Unemployment Defense Committee was politely rebuffed. Addes advised them "not to make an issue at this time of women's rights, as their position was too precarious at present, as the Union men were jealous of their jobs, and employers were not any too favorable to them."[12]

Despite its commitment to the seniority principle, the UAW did little to protect women auto workers with seniority against employers' preference for men in conversion-era hiring. Seniority lists were generally segregated by sex at this time, so that management could define a new job as male or female and then hire from either the male or female list without violating seniority rules. And although the union feared that management would replace men with women during the conversion period, more often substitution was in the other direction. "I know of no plant at present that is employing women," Victor Reuther, then working in the UAW's War Policy Division, wrote Katherine Farkas on December 3, 1941. Farkas had written the union for help after the Detroit unemployment compensation office had advised her to "get something in my line of work now in defense plants for they have to train a lot just for that kind of work[,] but no one to place me (*sic*)."[13]

The UAW protested vigorously in the rare instances when management did hire women for "men's jobs" in the conversion period. An October 1941 strike at a newly built defense plant owned by the Kelsey-Hayes Wheel Company in Plymouth, Michigan illustrates this well. Although it took place before anyone realized the scale on which female labor would have to be incorporated into the auto industry, this strike clearly posed the questions that would have to be confronted in regard to women's wartime employment. "The issue, raised in its present form for the first time since defense production got under way," commented *Business Week*, "promises to become one of the most dangerous and troublesome ones Washington will have to meet."[14]

The October 28 walkout was the climax of a conflict that had been developing for some time between the company and the union over women's employment. On October 15, the UAW had filed a strike notice against Kelsey-Hayes, demanding a wage increase and "the removal of all girl employes from machine work which, it [the UAW] contends, is a man's job." Negotiations over these issues were underway when workers discovered that two new women had been hired on the night shift. They walked out at midnight in protest, because the company had agreed not to hire any more women pending the outcome of the negotiations. Significantly, "the strikers had no objection to women being hired, ordinarily on other jobs in the plant." But because women in the plant received a maximum of 85 cents per hour, while men earned $1 per hour, "workers feared the company would replace men with women workers in order to reduce labor expenses."[15]

The two-day strike was successful. In the final settlement, "It was agreed by the Company that girls would not be used on any Screw Machine Operations, nor would they be used on Profiling operations. The Company would use them, however, on Filing wherever possible, on Inspection (Bench) where they can be utilized, and on small assemblies wherever they can be utilized. Female employees at no time will exceed 25% of the total."[16]

Thus the main demand of the walkout was won: the exclusion of women from "men's jobs." The union did not object to women's lower pay, providing they were confined to "women's jobs" as the agreement stipulated. The maximum wage rates for the female job classifications established after the strike were 88 cents for women with two years seniority or more, and 85 cents for those with less than two years. Men's maximum rates under the agreement, in contrast, ranged from $1.01 to $1.13.[17]

The union's role in reinforcing job segregation is obvious here, but the dispute was more complex. Faced with a shortage of male labor, management sought to take advantage of the lower wages historically paid to women by making a marginal change in the existing sexual division of labor. This assault on the men's wage standards provoked the strike. In short, the underlying point of contention in the dispute was wage rates rather than the pros and cons of female employment, and yet, because it was so tightly intertwined with the wage issue, the sexual division of labor was directly shaped by the outcome.

The demand to exclude women from previously male job classifications was the auto workers' first line of defense in the mobilization period, as the Kelsey-Hayes strike illustrates. Although after the no-strike pledge there were no more officially sanctioned strikes against female employment, there were some wildcats.[18] And other means besides going out on strike were available to obstruct the incorporation of women into the industry, such as refusing to break in new workers properly or actively obstructing their work.

Such exclusionary tactics, however, became less and less viable as the demand for labor rose and the male labor supply was exhausted. As the war economy burgeoned, it became clear that resistance to women's employment in the auto industry's male preserves was doomed to failure. One response was to focus on the postwar period, accepting the presence of women during the war but demanding their exclusion subsequently. Many UAW locals succeeded in limiting women's employment to the period of the war emergency through such contractual provisions as separate seniority lists for war workers; special agreements providing for the integration of women "for the duration" only; or clauses giving the newly hired workers "trainee" status, with limited seniority rights.[19] However, such arrangements influenced the sexual division of labor in the postwar period without addressing the more immediate, and quite distinct, problem of the wartime sexual division of jobs.

Ambiguity and Conflict over Job Classification by Sex. "Will you please advise me on our particular job as to what is considered as major assembly and what is considered as minor assembly?" the President of UAW Local 249 asked

Mauro Garcia, an international representative of the union's Ford Department, in July 1943. "We cannot agree down here [Kansas City, Missouri] as to where we should draw the line. . . . Also, what is considered a light drill press and what is considered a heavy drill press?" Garcia in turn wrote to the Ford Motor Company's Rate Department with the same questions, saying, "I do not know what method you use in determining these classifications."[20]

Problems like this pervaded the auto industry in the conversion period. Before the war, there were clearcut boundaries between "women's" and "men's" jobs—boundaries that typically coincided with those between "heavy" and "light," or "major" and "minor" jobs. But classifying the jobs that came into existence for the duration was difficult not only for management, but also for workers (of both sexes) and their unions. There was some resemblance between many of the new war jobs and their predecessors in the peacetime auto industry. But with conversion, technological changes and dramatic shifts in the composition of the labor force created tremendous disarray in what had previously been a relatively stable set-up. The problem was not confined to the dilemma of where to assign sex labels, but this was especially troublesome given the tradition of sex differentials in wages.

Not only in classification systems, but also in actual job content, there was a difference between "heavy" and "light" work. Yet where the line should be drawn between the two was ambiguous. Its arbitrariness—along with that of the accompanying wage differentials—became increasingly transparent during the war. "Except that there is a division as to what's heavy and what's light, there's no difference in men and women's jobs," Irene Young remarked at a UAW Women's Conference in February 1942, "This is a carry-over from procedure they have had years ago. They just decide what our (*sic*) women's jobs and what are men's jobs. Men get all the way from ten to 20 cents more on the same job. We have many women doing similar types of work—I have seen a lot of men working alongside women and getting more pay for the same work. It is that sort of thing that has caused a certain amount of the split between women and men."[21]

Moreover, Young pointed out, there were many women in the plants whose jobs were physically taxing, protective legislation notwithstanding. "We have today any number of women who are doing heavy work, who lack safety devices," she said. "I've worked in any number of plants in Detroit where women worked on high production rates and lifted and were forced to carry packs of stock. They were forced to do this if they were to make a decent day's wage. This kind of hard work they were under for years. . . . The plant where I am from, all of our stock had to be gotten out of box trucks. It necessitated leaning over and pulling and hauling on box trucks."[22]

Eleanor Brenthal, another conference delegate, explained that women often accepted such working conditions because they feared that their jobs were at stake. "Women are to blame in some cases," she said. "We decided this work was very heavy. When the shop committee came to agree that this work was too hard for us, we denied it. We were afraid that if we couldn't do this particular heavy work . . . we'd be put out on the street. We said we agreed to do that work, but it was too heavy." Clearly women's placement in the industry's labor force was by no means consistently linked to their physique— and Brenthal for one would have been more satisfied if it had been. "Someone should point out to us just what work we are suited for," she concluded.[23]

Young's and Brenthal's comments were based on their prewar experience in the auto industry. But it was obvious to everyone at the conference that the war presented a situation where such problems would be compounded. Many delegates expressed uncertainty over which jobs were suited for women. "How would you determine whether a job was too difficult. . . ?" Bernice Cut wanted to know. "If they asked me to work on a lathe machine—would you label that as a man's job?" another delegate inquired. A third woman pointed out, "Some of our sisters are stronger than others—they could handle jobs that would about kill some of our other sisters in one or two days. How will we manage to distinguish this?"[24]

In response, UAW Secretary-Treasurer George Addes articulated the union's policy on the issue at the women's conference:

> First of all under this program you train the women for a particular job and machine. If said employer should assign women to jobs that are strenuous, too difficult because of the heaviness of the work; or materials that are detrimental, then it becomes a problem for the local union negotiating committee and the management to determine the type of work they should be placed on for the time being. Of course, when the male help is gone and these jobs must be filled it must be decided which jobs women are capable of performing—the jobs must be classified.[25]

The union's official policy, then, was to leave the initial decisions to management and to negotiate any necessary adjustments. None of the women at the conference objected to the idea of using some system of job classification arrived at this way; on the contrary, they thought that it might protect them from assignment to overly strenuous jobs. Evidence that such abuses had occurred in the prewar period only reinforced the women's support for a more systematic classification of jobs.

This view, however, was soon proven naive. Historically, the union had developed other principles of job assignment that conflicted with the notion that women war workers should be placed on the lighter jobs. Management was charged with manipulating the sexual division of labor in the mobilization period in order to undermine the seniority-based job preference rights of prewar workers. George Romney, then head of the Automotive Council for War Production, cited such a case in testifying before the U.S. Senate hearings on "Manpower Problems in Detroit" in 1945:

On September 13, 1943, company Y tried to discontinue the placement of men on jobs that women would be able to handle. Since that date, the company has tried on numerous occasions to effect this policy but each attempt has been met by positive union resistance. On May 26, 1944, a survey of the company's plants revealed that over 400 jobs then being held by men could be performed by women. Again the management requested, and the union refused, the re-placement of these men by women, even though the management offered to guarantee the rates of the men so transferred. . . . To date the union has not granted such approval.

The types of jobs to be vacated by men and filled by women were varied, but all were considered to be light enough for women to fill. The union's reasons for not granting approvals seemed to be that the men, for the most part, had worked long periods of time to acquire these lighter jobs, and did not feel that they should be removed from them just so the jobs could be filled by women.[26]

Many grievances of this type were filed by the UAW against GM in late 1943 and early 1944. "When female employees were brought into the plant and assigned to various jobs," according to the Umpire's summary of one set of grievances from the Chevrolet Gear and Axle Plant, "complaints arose from the male employes who were on the so-called "waiting lists" pending possible promotion to higher rated classifications. These male employes complained that the placing of women in the jobs above them in rate prevented the male employes from gaining the promotions to which they would ordinarily have been entitled."[27]

What provoked these grievances was not a belief that the idiom of sex-typing (on which both parties seemed to agree) had been incorrectly applied. Rather, the fear was that management was undercutting the seniority principle as a factor in hiring and job placement. As in the Kelsey-Hayes strike, where the real issue was wages, the outcome of these conflicts affected the sexual division of labor, but the underlying issue was quite different. Thus the shaping of the wartime sexual division of labor became intertwined with labor-management conflict over other issues.

The women workers who were most directly affected by these struggles over job classification did not play an active role in them. Instead, the key wartime conflicts over the sexual division of labor were fought out between management and the male UAW leadership. The union was primarily con-cerned with the implications of managerial actions for the wage and seniority standards it had won before the war. Initially, the union's exclusionary re-sponse to the feminization of auto employment defined the gender interests of male auto workers in opposition to women workers'. But there was another side to industrial unionism that stressed not gender but *class* interests. This took the form of a commitment to nondiscrimination and equality and came to dominate the UAW's stance on women's issues after the futility of exclusionism became evident. Nowhere was the ideology of equality more powerful than in the struggle for equal pay for equal work.

Tl.e UAW Campaign for Equal Pay for Equal Work. The equal pay issue, which became the central focus of struggles over women's position in industry during the war, was not new. Demanding equal pay for equal work had long been a standard union defense against the actual or potential replacement of men with women. But before World War II, actual incidents of such replacement had been relatively rare, especially in auto. In the mobilization period, though, the UAW's longstanding fears of large-scale female substitution finally materialized. Moreover, any wage cuts made while women occupied a given job might affect men after the war when the position reverted to them. And the wartime wage freeze meant that equal pay was one of the few avenues available for the pursuit of wage increases.

Some companies readily agreed to pay women equal rates on "men's jobs," without a protracted struggle (although perhaps in anticipation of one). Ford's recruitment handbills for the giant Willow Run bomber plant advertised the policy: "Women paid same rates as men," and Ford as well as Studebaker and Vultee signed national contracts with the UAW that had equal pay clauses.[28] Because war production was often done under cost-plus contracts, and because women's jobs were expected to revert to men after the war anyway, equal pay for equal work was a sensible policy for many employers. The federal War Labor Board (WLB), which was charged with resolving labor-management disputes for the duration of the no-strike pledge, also endorsed the equal pay principle early in the war period.

Although many voluntary equal pay adjustments were reported to the WLB, there were also numerous disputes over women's pay rates in the wartime auto industry.[29] The most important was a WLB case that the UAW and the UE jointly brought against GM in 1942. The decision in this case was widely regarded as a milestone, because it firmly established the equal pay principle as government policy. "Wages should be paid to female employees on the principle of equal pay for equal work," the September 26, 1942, decision stated. "There should be no discrimination between employees whose production is substantially the same on comparable jobs." The WLB also ordered GM to include an equal pay clause in its union contracts, which it did.[30]

Subsequently, however, disputes developed over the implementation of the equal pay contract clause, and when negotiations failed to resolve the matter, the UAW requested arbitration in June 1943. Hearings were held at three GM plants before arbitrator William Simkin, whose July 31 decision was later sustained by the National WLB. This case, typical of equal pay disputes in auto, turned on the question of whether or not jobs being done by women were "comparable in quantity and quality" to those done by men. The union contended that the jobs in question were new, first established in the conversion period, and were comparable to jobs previously performed by men. The company, however, insisted that the jobs were of the type that had always been "women's jobs," although because of the peculiar circumstances of conversion some had been performed by men during a brief "experimental" period. All three plants had had local wage agreements including job classifications explicitly designated as "female" before the September 1942 WLB ruling, and the issue now was whether or not the war jobs being performed by women fit into those classifications.

Simkin baldly acknowledged the ambiguity surrounding the assignment of sex labels to the jobs in a section of his decision aptly titled, "WOMAN'S JOB OR MAN'S JOB?" He noted that "exact and certain allocation of a specific operation to a given type is by no means easy."[31] But ultimately he accepted, at least in part, GM's detailed arguments about why the jobs in question were appropriate for women and not comparable to prewar "men's jobs," as the union insisted. GM's case was cast entirely in terms of the idiom of sex-typing, stressing that women did physically "light" work and had fewer responsibilities than men, and insisting that women's war jobs resembled their prewar jobs. A typical statement was that "it is not possible to assign to a woman all the duties that over a period of time can be assigned to a male janitor because of her physical capacity. Often the janitors are called on to do heavy work such as moving furniture. . . ."[32]

The arbitrator ruled that the existing wage differentials were too wide to be justified by the difference in the content of "men's" and "women's" jobs. But the ruling also perpetuated what had been *sex* differentials in wages in a new, if thinly disguised, form: as differentials between "light" and "heavy" work. "The only solution consistent with the 'equal pay' clause [in the union contract]," the decision stated, "is to wipe out the sex designation of the . . . jobs and establish . . . rates for various types of work which reflect only the type of work performed."[33] The detailed opinion issued by the Regional WLB drew out the implications of this ruling even more sharply:

Under the principle of equal pay for equal work, sex differentials are no longer proper. The principle . . . however, is consistent with differences in rates which are based upon differences in job content. It is upon this basis that the arbitrator *substituted* for the classifications "Inspection—Receiving—Male" and "Inspection—Receiving—Female" the classifications of "Inspection—Receiving—Heavy" and "Inspection—Receiving— Light" and fixed the rate for the former at $1.14 per hour and for the latter at $1.04 per hour. Roughly, the new classification "Inspection—Receiving—Heavy" corresponds to the former classification "Inspection—Receiving—Male" and the "Inspection—Receiving—Light" to the former classification "Inspection—Receiving—Female." *Rates of each classification imply whether the employees are men or women.*[34]

Thus the sexual division of labor was recodified for the duration.

Neither party to the dispute was happy with the arbitrator's ruling. The industry members of the Regional WLB issued a dissenting opinion, arguing that the work done by women was paid less because it was different, and rejecting out of hand the contention that the historical wage differentials were based on sex. "The fact that the Arbitrator has designated two different classifications for the work being done," they pointed out, "is certainly acknowledgment of the fact that there is different work being done by women than that being done by men."[35] The union, on the other hand, argued that no distinction should be made between heavy and light work, and that the women should receive $1.14 an hour just like the men. In the UAW's "Exception to Arbitrator's Decision," it frankly stated its concern about the implications of the decision for the postwar period:

> With such great numbers of women employed, displacing men for military service, it is essential that the wage-structure built up through years of laborious effort be maintained for the preservation of morale, on the part of the men so displaced.
>
> The future security and economic position of labor will deteriorate if the war effort is permitted to be used as an instrument in tearing down the hard-won gains of labor.
>
> To maintain such a sense of security is vital to the war effort, and the International UAW-CIO, therefore, insist that where new operations are introduced, having no previous classification, such operations should, wherever it (*sic*) is comparable to that performed by men, be classified and rated accordingly.[36]

Clearly, the primary motive for the UAW's opposition to the distinction between "heavy" and "light" or "men's" and "women's" work was its concern about the postwar implications for men's wages. Nevertheless, the union was now advocating the abolition of the sexual division of labor in the job categories at issue—in marked contrast to the stance it had taken in situations like the 1941 Kelsey-Hayes strike. There it was the company that purported to be interested in eliminating the sexual division of labor (although without altering wage differentials). The shift in the form of what was essentially a struggle (in both instances) over the wage bill thus reversed the "interests" of management and the union in relation to the sexual division of labor. In both cases, male auto workers had an interest in perpetuating women's subordination in industry to preserve their power as a gender. Yet there was a crucial difference.

In the Kelsey-Hayes case, fear of permanent displacement generated an exclusionary impulse to preserve the male monopoly of the bulk of the jobs. During the war, however, when women's presence in the industry was unavoidable, the same employment insecurity led men to define their interest as best served by equal pay for equal work for women.

But the equal pay demand challenged sex discrimination in a very limited way. The formulation "equal pay for equal work" itself precluded the equalization of *work* between women and men. The issue was instead confined to whether women within a relatively small spectrum of occupations were doing "men's work," or work similar enough to men's to merit similar compensation. The ensuing debate revealed the arbitrary aspect of the sex-labeling of jobs, yet it reinforced the legitimacy of the sexual division of labor as a whole. Indeed, the prewar pattern of job segregation became the reference point for evaluating wartime claims for equal pay in the grey area between "women's" and "men's" jobs. A more radical formulation of the issue would not merely challenge the pay rates of those jobs at the margin, but also confront the overall structure of job segregation and the systematic undervaluing of women's work. Although it certainly benefited many women war workers, the UAW's narrow definition of the issue could not fundamentally alter the sexual division of labor. In the electrical industry, however, the equal pay issue developed along very different lines during the war, anticipating by several decades the struggles being waged today for "equal pay for comparable worth."

Wartime Struggles over "Women's Work" in Electrical Manufacturing

For a number of reasons, the UE was better prepared than the UAW for the challenge wartime conditions presented in regard to the sexual division of labor. The electrical workers' union had always included large numbers of women, whereas even in the mobilization period the UAW's membership was overwhelmingly male, so that it had far less experience with women's issues. And although the UAW was initially preoccupied with the problems of conversion unemployment, particularly protecting seniority rights, it was not a major concern in electrical manufacturing, where the process of conversion was relatively smooth and the seniority principle was less firmly established. In addition, the auto workers' union was highly factionalized during the war, whereas the UE was relatively unified, with the Communist leadership and the Carey opposition in a de facto truce based on the union's productionist "win the war" program. The internal divisions within the UAW and the frequent wildcat strikes consumed energies that might otherwise have been directed to gender issues. In contrast, the UE's contingent of female activists and its strong ideological commitment to gender equality made it more likely to challenge management on women's issues.

The most important reason that the UE had more prescience than the UAW in these matters was simply that there were always large numbers of women in the electrical industry. The UE entered the war period with a history of struggles over female substitution. Thus the implications of the war mobilization for the wage structure were immediately obvious to its leaders. As early as May 1941, the Executive Council of UE District 6 took account of the danger in a special resolution on "Women's Wage Differentials." "The differential of women's rates below men's . . . supplies a constant opportunity for chiseling by employers," it stated. "If this situation continues, it would lead to a disastrous decline in wage standards in the case of war, where the withdrawal of men for the army would greatly increase the proportion of women employees."[37]

Exclusionary efforts of the sort that initially emerged in the UAW in response to this concern with wage standards were absent in the UE. Instead, the electrical workers put forward—from the very beginning—demands for equal pay for equal work and for narrowing sex differentials in wages. Women UE activists who had raised the issue of narrowing wage differentials before the war gained new support with the defense buildup and the accompanying increase in female employment. Women at the East Pittsburgh Westinghouse plant successfully organized around the issue locally in 1941 and then pressed the union to raise it in the national contract negotiations. As a result, the 1942 agreement between Westinghouse and the UE included a provision narrowing sex differentials by 2 cents an hour in all the company's plants.[38]

Immediately after Pearl Harbor, the UE began negotiating equal pay for equal work contract provisions with the industry's major firms. "Organized labor must be on its toes to prevent industry from switching from male to female on the basis of cheap labor only," declared the UE Local 201 newspaper in January 1942. The national GE contract, signed a few months later, provided that the company would notify the union "before a woman or a minor is placed on a job which has been done previously by a man . . . with the reason why it should be done." And already, in mid-1942, there were local negotiations over the wartime sexual division of labor. In Local 201, the general procedure was this: "As jobs are broken down, segregated into simpler operations due to expanding production, each job, as performed by one person, is viewed and discussed on its merits as to whether the job is a woman's job or a man's job . . . and a rate (job value), either male or female . . . is set comparable with other similar jobs."[39]

As the number of women workers in the electrical industry swelled, the UE continued to press the major companies for guarantees that female substitution would not lead to erosion of wage standards. In late 1942, Westinghouse agreed to pay women placed on "men's jobs" at men's rates "without question," and not to employ women on such jobs as long as qualified men were still available. Jobs that were "men's jobs" before Pearl Harbor, it was agreed, would remain so for the duration, and would only be subdivided into "a new lineup of operations" if this was absolutely necessary for women to be able to perform them. In such instances, some of the new jobs could be classified as women's jobs if they were "similar to jobs already in the plant classified as women's jobs." Any disputed classifications were to be handled through collective bargaining.[40] Similarly, the 1943 GE contract provided that "women placed on men's jobs shall receive men's rates of pay for the same quantity and quality of work," and that in cases of job breakdown, women would be paid the minimum men's rate at the plant involved.[41]

The UE's fears that employers would take advantage of the opportunity provided by the war to substitute women for men and to cut wages appear to have been well-founded. Both Westinghouse and GE went to great lengths to do so, shifting jobs from one plant to another and changing men's jobs into women's jobs—at substantially reduced pay.[42] At the GM Frigidaire plant in Dayton, Ohio, UE Local 801 complained that "supervision has gone wild in replacing males on their jobs with females. Management contends that because of both male and female on similar jobs in the same classification, they have the right to remove the male, place a female on the job with the other female and call them female jobs." Calling a job "female" determined its lower pay rate, and this aroused the greatest concern. "We are not opposed to the use of females if male help is unobtainable, providing such female help shall receive the proper rate," the Frigidaire grievance stated.[43]

Because the arbitrariness of the boundaries between men's and women's jobs in electrical manufacturing had always been so obvious, the UE could not claim, as the UAW had, that jobs being done by women during the war were intrinsically men's jobs. The only effective way to guard against wage cutting was to challenge the entire basis of wage discrimination by sex. The inadequacy of the equal pay for equal work demand was quickly recognized by the UE. As the 1943 *UE Guide to Wage Payment Plans* noted, "the guarantee of equal pay for equal work does nothing to raise the rates of women employed on jobs that were traditionally women's jobs. Neither does it prevent new jobs from being classified as women's jobs. The most it does is help maintain the existing men's rates. But even in this respect it is inadequate, unless guarantees are obtained that rates will not be cut when men's jobs are broken down and simplified for women operators." The UE argued that no new women's jobs should be created during the war; new jobs and new products should all be classified on the male keysheet, regardless of who performed them. The union also sought to narrow or wipe out existing sex differentials in wages.[44]

The UE often challenged managerial designations of new jobs as women's work where it had contracts and used this issue in its wartime organizational campaigns.[45] But the 1945 WLB case against GE and Westinghouse was the most comprehensive challenge on the issue. It made the demand feminists in the 1980s call "equal pay for comparable worth." "There is no complaint in these cases," the WLB decision pointed out, "that, in instances in which women have been assigned to work on jobs customarily performed by men, they have not received the men's rates on those jobs." Rather, the issue was "that the jobs customarily performed by women are paid less, on a comparative job content basis, than the jobs customarily performed by men" and "that this relative underpayment constitutes a sex discrimination."[46]

The electrical manufacturers' own job evaluation systems were used to attack wage discrimination by sex. Both companies admitted that they used separate evaluation and rating systems for men's and women's jobs. "We line men's jobs up with men's jobs. We do not line women's jobs up against men's jobs," George H. Pfeif, GE's employee relations manager, told the board. Westinghouse also used separate key sheets for men and women. "Although a single evaluation system is used and the labor grades . . . carry the same respective point values," the WLB's report noted, "the rates attached to the grades on the two key sheets differ."[47]

The UE attacked this practice, as well as the companies' wartime manipulation of the sexual division of labor in order to reduce wages. "When employers are allowed to make simple changes in men's jobs and classify them as women's jobs with rates of pay some 20 cents below the lowest male rates, and when women's jobs are paid at rates below the lowest man's job, then the working conditions of the entire population are threatened." The union's concern here paralleled that of the UAW in its equal pay for equal work cases. Although the scope of the UE's 1945 WLB case was much wider, again the key issue was the postwar wage structure and the protection of men's rates. "The rate structure of General Electric and Westinghouse, based as it is on substandard wages paid to women and historical differentials, represents a real threat to returning servicemen," the union asserted. "The 60,000 GE vets and 26,000 Westinghouse servicemen will find that many of the jobs they come back to have been changed to women's jobs at lower rates of pay."[48]

The electrical companies conceded that there were sex differentials in their plants, but argued that they were of long standing and had been implicitly recognized by the UE in collective bargaining. Women's rates, management claimed, were in line both with industry practices and with rates paid in the communities where the plants operated, so that any increase in women's wages would put the firms at a competitive disadvantage.[49] Management also argued, as General Motors had in the 1943 arbitration case discussed earlier, that women's work was different from men's and not worth as much. Women, they claimed, could not be deployed as flexibly over a range of jobs as men and could not do heavy lifting, so that special services had to be provided. "The women's jobs," Westinghouse told the WLB, "are chiefly of a light repetitive nature, involving very little physical strength, and they are performed under pleasant conditions."[50] As a WLB official wrote, "both companies maintain that although the point values [assigned to women's and men's jobs in the firms' own job evaluation systems] are the same, the job content is less for women."[51]

The companies also argued that great weight must be placed on "sociological factors." As a wage administration manual submitted in evidence by Westinghouse suggested, "The gradient of the women's wage curve is not the same for women as for men because of the more transient character of the service of the former, the relative shortness of their activity in industry, the differences in environment required, the extra services that must be provided, overtime limitations, extra help needed for the occasional heavy work, and the general sociological factors not requiring discussion herein [!]"[52] General Electric's representatives made clear "that they share the same general point of view, namely, that women are worth less for purposes of factory employment than men."[53]

The UE countered that women had special abilities that were undervalued, and which compensated for any extra costs associated with women's employment. "If men were to be substituted for women on the so-called women's jobs," the WLB concluded, "there would probably be a very real loss in efficiency and productivity since it is recognized that men are not as well adapted as women for light, repetitive work requiring finger dexterity."[54] In this way, the idiom of sex-typing was marshaled to the attack on wage discrimination. The UE noted, for example, that the rate for male unskilled "common labor" (the bottom or "anchor point" of the male rate structure) was higher than the rate for the vast majority of women's jobs, including some that the company's own records indicated required substantial training.[55]

The challenge posed by the UE was much more global than that involved in the UAW's campaigns for equal pay for equal work. Management testified to the depth of the issue by laying bare its presumption that the basis of sex discrimination in wages and in job assignments lay outside the factories, in "sociological factors," as well as in women's supposedly less valuable performance inside the plants. The union did not challenge the idiom of sex-typing but, on the contrary, used it to attack the electrical firms' wage policies.[56] As far-reaching as the UE's attack on wage discrimination was, it never suggested that men and women should be assigned to jobs throughout the industry on a sex-blind basis.

The WLB, convinced that the wage structure at GE and Westinghouse was inequitable, decided in the union's favor on November 29, 1945. The companies simply ignored the decision. Then, on December 17, the WLB ordered

GE and Westinghouse to raise women's pay by 4 cents an hour and to set aside a 2-cent-per-hour fund for each woman employed, the distribution of which was to be determined by collective bargaining. But the war had long since ended, and the WLB had no effective power. Within a few hours of the announcement of the December 17 ruling, the companies announced publicly that they would not comply.[57] The matter then became an issue in the massive 1946 strike against the giant electrical firms. As we will see in chapter 8, the strike settlement would set an important precedent in the industry for the principle of flat rather than percentage pay increases as a means of narrowing differentials.

The aftermath of this struggle had another outcome as well: GE now eliminated all references to jobs as "men's" or "women's," so that sex-typing became less explicit. Paralleling the GM equal pay case, in which the arbitrator changed the labels of jobs from "male" to "heavy" and from "female" to "light," GE began to call "men's jobs 'heavy and/or complicated' and women's jobs 'light and/or simple'" after the strike. Later, the company dropped even these "descriptive phrases," and introduced other subtle changes. "The company in a number of cases upped the rates of women's jobs with the most obvious discrimination, and made other changes in rates to eliminate the most flagrant discrimination. In a number of plants, a few men were placed by the company on the lower-rated jobs previously worked on only by women, to give the appearance that both men and women worked in all labor grades."[58]

Wage differentials were narrowed by the UE's efforts, then, but they were by no means eliminated, and the basic structure of the sexual division of labor in electrical manufacturing was preserved intact. Still, the UE's strategy on equal pay exposed the industry's sex-segregated job structure to unprecedented scrutiny. The UAW's equal pay campaign sought to demonstrate that women's war jobs were like prewar "men's jobs." But because the electrical industry had always had large numbers of women in its work force, the UE could only confront the equal pay issue effectively by challenging the discriminatory basis of the entire wage structure.

While the UE's breadth of vision must have been nurtured by Communist influence in the union, this does not explain its definition of the equal pay issue in terms of comparable worth. Communists and other leftists were active in all the important CIO unions, but only in the UE did the comparable-worth campaign emerge. And although the presence of the UE's female activists should not be discounted entirely, its significance can be easily exaggerated. The critical factor leading to the union's sophisticated approach to the equal pay issue was the structure of the electrical industry itself and its prewar sexual division of labor.

In both auto and electrical manufacturing, moreover, the unions' wartime struggles for equal pay were waged primarily on behalf of their prewar male memberships. While women workers benefited, the goal was to prevent management from taking advantage of the war either by substituting women permanently for men or by eroding the male wage standards established before the war. And these campaigns, necessarily pursued on the bureaucratic battleground of the WLB, were conducted by male union officials, primarily on behalf of men. This was true not only for the UAW, but also for the UE, even if the latter's approach to the equal pay issue more fully represented the interests of women workers.

In both industries, struggles over the sexual division of labor did not end at the conclusion of the war, but continued with even greater intensity in the period immediately following the military conflict. The postwar struggles differed in a number of ways from those of the war years, not the least of which was that women themselves participated more fully. While women played a marginal role in the wartime struggles over the sexual division of labor, they moved to center stage in the reconversion period, when the gains of the war years were directly threatened. While the interests of women workers lacked any politically effective vehicle for their expression during the mobilization period, by the war's end they emerged as crucial protagonists. The key change was the growth of women's influence within the unions over the war years. That transformation is the subject of the next chapter.

6 The Emergence of a Women's Movement in the Wartime CIO

World War II not only drew women into industry in massive numbers, but it also brought them into the organized labor movement. Female union membership nearly quadrupled during the war years, and unprecedented numbers of women became labor activists and leaders.[1] Moreover, the CIO unions, committed to fighting discrimination and to industrial democracy, served as the primary vehicle through which women pursued gender equality in the workplace during the 1940s. For although organized feminism was at its nadir during this critical decade in women's labor history, the industrial unions were at the peak of their strength, and had good reasons of their own to encourage women's participation. Opportunities for female activism were especially great in the UE and the UAW, which had more women members than any other unions in the nation during the war, and which, accordingly, paid special attention to women's concerns.

Women mobilized extensively within the unions in this period, fighting against sex discrimination in industry and in the labor movement and defining a range of specific "women's issues." However, all of this was justified as a way of strengthening the labor movement as a whole. Wartime union activity on behalf of women was undertaken not as a feminist project, but in the name of working-class unity. There was no political space for feminism or any other specifically woman-centered ideology within the labor movement, nor was there any autonomous source of power for women workers outside of the union structure. Thus although a women's movement did emerge within the CIO during the 1940s, the preexisting framework of unionism set limits on its ideological and organizational scope.

The Growth of Female Union Membership

The wartime economic mobilization generated enormous growth in union membership. The number of workers in American trade unions grew from 7.2 to 12.6 million between 1940 and 1944, and the proportion of the work force that was unionized grew from 12.7 to 22.2 percent over that period.[2] Growth in female unionization was even more dramatic, as the wartime shift in the sexual composition of the labor force led unions to recruit women on a vast scale. By the war's end, all AFL and CIO unions were free of restrictions barring female membership, and only one (the International Brotherhood of Bookbinders) still had separate women's locals, which had been widespread in the prewar years. Although hostility toward women persisted in some unions (particularly in the AFL), exclusionism was eliminated during the war at the institutional level.[3]

In an era of rapid union growth, female unionization grew disproportionately. The number of women union members rose from eight hundred thousand (9.4 percent of the total) in 1940 to three million (21.8 percent) in 1944.[4] Both female and total membership grew especially rapidly in auto and electrical manufacturing, reflecting the centrality of these industries to the burgeoning war economy. In 1939, there were forty thousand women in the UAW, or 10 percent of total membership; by 1945, women comprised 28 percent of what had become the nation's first million-member union.[5] Similarly, while at the beginning of 1942, 15 percent of the UE's members were female, by 1944, when it was the third-largest CIO union, women were 40 percent of its seven hundred thousand members.[6] In 1945, the UAW and the UE each had more than a quarter of a million female members—more than any other union in the nation.[7]

These dramatic strides in women's union membership were partly due to new organizing, but also to the "maintenance-of-membership" clauses in many wartime union contracts. The maintenance-of-membership formula, which emerged from a series of War Labor Board decisions in the mobilization period, provided that workers employed in a plant covered by a union contract automatically became dues-paying union members, and remained so either until they left their jobs or the contract came up for renewal. Because few workers made use of the "escape clause" that allowed new union members (or old members under a new contract) to withdraw from the union during the first fifteen days of their employment under the contract, maintenance of membership in practice was similar to a union shop. Unions gained not only members, but also new financial stability from the dues check-off, which typically accompanied the maintenance-of-membership arrangement.[8] By 1945 there were 3.7 million industrial workers covered by maintenance-of-membership clauses, 46 percent of all manufacturing workers under union agreements. The

number of workers in closed or union shops also grew during the war years
under agreements reached between employers and unions without WLB intervention. In 1945, 87 percent of all unionized manufacturing workers were
covered by closed-shop, union-shop, or maintenance-of-membership agreements.[9]

Many of the women who became union members during the war thus did
so automatically, as a byproduct of their employment in the unionized sector
of the economy, and not because of any special organizational efforts to attract
them. This was especially true in the auto industry, where the major firms had
granted union recognition before Pearl Harbor, and union-shop or maintenance-of-membership provisions were simply added to existing contracts.
(Most of the UAW's new organizing during the war was in aircraft plants.)
The UE, in contrast, did a great deal of new organizing during the war, winning 831 separate recognition elections in plants employing a total of 335,000
workers.[10]

Whether through new recruitment drives or through expansion of employment in organized firms covered by maintenance-of-membership clauses or
other forms of union security, the still precarious CIO unions not only grew,
but also gained new stability during the war. Nevertheless, the war years
presented the unions with a major challenge: to win the allegiance of their
newly acquired constituents, many of whom had no past experience of either
industrial work or unionism. Women made up by far the largest group among
these new workers. Even in the UE, which always had many women in its
ranks, more than one-half of the wartime female membership had not
been employed in the electrical industry before the war.[11] And at the
UAW-organized Willow Run bomber plant outside Detroit, 89 percent of
the women (and 40 percent of the men) had never been union members before the war.[12]

New war workers (of both sexes) often had an anti-union bias, particularly
if they were from the less industrialized regions of the country. Seasoned
unionists understandably harbored some resentment toward women (as well
as blacks, Okies, and other new workers), who effortlessly reaped the rewards
of the CIO's past struggles.[13] This was particularly true in auto, where women
had been a tiny minority of the prewar work force. "The women in our plant
have never belonged to a union before," one local UAW president pointed out
in 1944. "They have walked into the best wages in the area—the best conditions. They never had to struggle for this."[14] At the same time, in both the
UAW and the UE, the leadership cadres developed during the 1930s were
decimated by the war mobilization, as male unionists left industry in vast
numbers for the armed forces. So while maintenance-of-membership and other
such union security arrangements preserved the unions in a formal sense, the
radical change in the composition of the membership wrought by the war

nevertheless threatened the substance of unionism. Under these conditions, the CIO unions had a tremendous incentive to integrate women and other new war workers as fully as possible into their activities and organizational structures.

New Opportunities For Women in the CIO

As their numbers grew, women gained influence in the factories and showed growing confidence as rank-and-file activists. "The women have learned . . . to organize, learned to make their power and influence felt," the Army Air Corps Labor Relations office in Detroit reported to the War Department in 1943. "They have also learned how to improve their working conditions by fair means as well as what we who are responsible for war production consider unfair. . . . We have had in several vital facilities slow-downs that were traced to women."[15]

The evidence concerning female participation in wartime strikes is fragmentary, but it appears that women, like men, stopped work over a wide range of issues. In 1944, 19 percent of the workers participating in recorded work stoppages were female. Wartime strikes sometimes involved issues, such as clothing regulations, of particular concern to women, but more often the issues were not sex-specific, and most of the strikes in which women participated also involved men. In 1944, 39 percent of the recorded strikes involved workers of both sexes, while less than 2 percent were exclusively female.[16] Nevertheless, these strikes gave women valuable experience in shop-floor struggles, complementing the influence that they simultaneously accrued within the formal structure of the unions.

The industrial unions actively sought to educate women war workers and to win their allegiance. During the war, both the UE and the UAW hired female staffers in larger numbers than ever before, and also gave rank-and-file women special encouragement to seek leadership posts, particularly at the local level. Both unions developed educational programs around "women's issues," and offered women a greater voice within their central administrative structures. These creative activities directly reflected the fact that the war situation had made women's loyalty necessary to the unions. Indeed, male union leaders explicitly justified their new interest in incorporating women into the union structure in terms of the danger that the introduction of women into war industry presented. As UE President Albert Fitzgerald put it in the spring of 1942, "There are thousands and thousands of women being introduced into our industries. . . . If we do not encourage women to come into the organization, think what this will mean. After the war, you will have a group of unorganized women working in the factories taking your jobs and your living

10. "UE Local 1225 runs class for girls who want jobs in defense plants," Brooklyn, n.d. (United Electrical Workers)

11. UE Women's Conference committee meeting, District 2 (New England), December 1942. (United Electrical Workers)

away from you."[17] The electrical workers' union subsequently undertook a range of efforts to enhance women's participation and leadership.

Indeed, no union amassed a more impressive wartime record than the UE in increasing female representation in both appointed staff and elected union positions. In September 1943, the electrical union's top officials urged that "more women must be added to the staff, and the upgrading of women members of the staff must be given careful consideration and encouragement."[18] Even before this official statement was issued, the number of women in appointed staff positions had increased dramatically. In February 1943, 17 percent of the UE's national staff members were women, as opposed to 2 percent only a year earlier. By the end of 1944, Ruth Young had become the first woman on the UE Executive Board, and more than a third of the union's full-time organizers were female. There was also a large increase in female representation among elected UE officials. In 1944, eighteen women were local presidents, and thirty-three were vice-presidents, while in less powerful positions such as shop stewards, business agents, and local secretaries, women were even more numerous.[19] The number of women elected as delegates to the UE's national conventions also increased during the 1940s. In 1941, there were twenty-five women delegates, comprising 6.3 percent of the total; by 1944, one hundred and four women delegates made up 13.3 percent of the total.[20]

The UE's impressive record in increasing women's leadership was partly because of the fact that it had always had many women members, and expected to after the war as well. The considerable influence of the Communist Party within the UE also contributed to the rapid rise in women's representation in staff positions.[21] In any case, the results of the electrical workers' union's efforts to increase women's leadership were unmatched.[22] However, other unions, and especially the UAW, did take much more interest in recruiting women into leadership roles during the war than ever before.

"Sisters, I know we men have made some mistakes, dealing with you as you entered our industry and our union," implored UAW President R. J. Thomas in 1944. "[But] we want, we need more women leaders."[23] The growth of female representation in the auto union's leadership was less dramatic than in the UE, but still unprecedented. A 1944 UAW survey found that 60 percent of the union locals responding had women on their Executive Boards, and 73 percent had at least one female shop steward. Thirty-seven percent of the locals had women on their bargaining or negotiating committees.[24] While comparable data on local leadership in earlier years are not available, the parallel increase in women's representation among delegates to the annual UAW conventions suggests the magnitude of the wartime changes. In 1940, only eight of the elected delegates were women, about 1.5 percent of the total. Six years later, there were seventy-three female delegates, nearly a tenfold rise—although still only 4 percent of the total.[25]

The incorporation of women into union leadership posts was motivated largely by fear of the consequences of neglecting them. But it was also facilitated by the conscription of male unionists into the military. "Day by day we are losing more of our staff members, organizers, local union officers, to the armed services of this country," UE President Fitzgerald noted at the 1943 convention. "Unless we develop the proper leadership, unless we encourage women to take an active part in the affairs of our organization, the men of this union are going to find themselves in a position where the structure of the union will be weakened."[26] Indeed, the military draft created a leadership vacuum that, together with the phenomenal wartime growth in union membership, eased the entry of workers of both sexes into leadership posts in both the UE and the UAW. "During the war, a lot of the men had gone in service. . . . So places opened up. We got women on the staff," Ruth Young (Jandreau) recalled. "I don't think it was as much doing the right thing as it was having no choice. You couldn't get a draft deferment if you left the war plant. . . . They were better off keeping the guy in the shop and using him on lost time."[27] Florence Peterson, who would later become a UAW International Representative, also recalled the unusual opportunities available to women under these conditions:

> Many of the people who came to work at Irwin Pederson in war time, the women especially—and this was almost all women—had never been in a shop before. . . . It was more or less this kind of group with the exception of about three of us. . . . So I wasn't afraid to speak up. I was furious that they were asking us to work without lights. So I climbed all over the foreman when he came through. When he walked away after promising to do something, the group all turned to me and said, "You're our new shop steward." . . . So, I really kind of started at the top there. Only during war time could this have happened. Normally, you go to work in a plant and you work awhile before you get elected even to shop steward or to a committee.[28]

In addition to increasing the number of women leaders, the unions made special efforts to integrate the female rank and file into their organizations through a variety of educational activities. Both the UE and the UAW set up several women's conferences to explore specifically female concerns.[29] Both unions also published pamphlets and other educational materials especially for women. The UAW Education Department's magazine *Ammunition,* which began publication in early 1943, carried many feature articles about women workers as well as a regular column addressed to women, "Sister Sue Says." In August 1944, a special supplemental edition of the magazine appeared, "Women Work—Women Vote."[30] The UAW also issued pamphlets with special

12. (left to right): Mildred Jeffrey, Mabel Johnson, and Grace Blackett at a UAW Women's Conference, January 1945. (Wayne State University Labor Archives)

13. Front cover, special supplemental edition to UAW-CIO *Ammunition,* August 1944. (United Automobile Workers)

appeals to women such as "Sister, You Need the Union! . . . And the Union Needs You."[31] The UE, similarly, began issuing special women's pamphlets during the war.[32] The *UE News* carried a weekly column by Ruth Young, "Work and Play," and frequently dealt with women's concerns in regular news articles as well. In addition, the electrical workers' union ran special schools during the war to train women members in leadership skills.[33]

The top leadership of both the UAW and the UE systematically sought to incorporate women into their organizational structures, motivated by the need for the allegiance of the vast new female sector of their membership and by an ideological commitment to egalitarianism as well. In February 1944, the UAW established a Women's Department within its War Policy Division, which made policy proclamations on women's issues and served in an advisory capacity to the union's Executive Board. In the UE, the formal structure of a women's department was lacking, but women gained direct representation at the highest level in the person of Ruth Young, who in 1944 became the first woman member of the Executive Board. (In contrast, the UAW's Board remained an all-male preserve until the 1960s.) Significantly, however, Young joined the board not "as a woman," but as a unionist in her own right. She had worked closely with the union's top leaders for many years, and gained the Executive Board post by virtue of her elected position as the second ranking officer of the union's huge District 4 (New York and New Jersey). While during the war her work focused increasingly on issues affecting women, her power in the UE was based on a much broader contribution. As she put it, "I was never viewed as a woman. . . . I represented the union. . . . Really what started happening [during the war] was that the union would send me places, and once I got there I represented the whole union, even though they may have asked for a woman or the union felt it was a good idea."[34]

Although women gained power during the war in both the UE and the UAW, in neither was their influence commensurate with their huge representation in the membership. And female leadership was concentrated at the lower levels in both unions. A U.S. Women's Bureau study of union locals in the Midwest, which included both UE and UAW locals, found only four women local union presidents among the eighty-one locals surveyed. Although women held a variety of other union offices, most were of minor importance such as recording secretary, financial secretary, or trustee.[35] In some locals, the traditional social activities of the women's auxiliaries had become the focus of women war workers' participation in the union. Elizabeth Hawes's 1946 account of women in the wartime UAW cites an example of this in a Columbus, Ohio local, where "the men had allowed the women union members to cook and serve them a dinner after a big meeting."[36] Even in the UE, there was a sexual division of labor among the union staff: in the locals, women were overrepresented in

14. Ruth Young speaking at Women's Luncheon, 1944 UE Convention, with Pauline Newman (ILGWU), far left, and Josephine Timms (ACA), center, New York, September 1944. (United Electrical Workers)

15. UE National Executive Board. Ruth Young, center. Sitting, left to right: Merle Bennett, Harold Conroy, Ernest De Maio, Eldon Parr, Ruth Young, Albert Fitzgerald, James Matles, Julius Emspak, James McLeish. Standing, left to right: John Gojak, Leo Jandreau, Lem Markland, William Sentner, Joseph Vejlupek, Robert Wishart, Paul Seymour, Harry Phelps, George Harris, Tom Fitzpatrick, Joseph Price, and C. S. Jackson, New York, December 1946. (United Electrical Workers)

classically sex-stereotyped roles such as clerical functions and social committees, and women field organizers were hired exclusively to work in plants where
the majority of workers were female.[37] At the 1942 convention, Ruth Wellman
complained that women "have been rather discouraged and shoved into positions as recording secretaries or perhaps social activities or maybe house
committees to clean the windows."[38]

The limits on women's power in the unions were partly because of male
hostility. The UAW Women's Department's 1944 survey of local union policies
toward women found that men's attitudes were, at best, ambivalent. "We men
have not got used to women in [the] plant yet we try to give them equal rights
[but] we don't understand women's problems too well," acknowledged Howard
Pearson of Local 646. And Local 329's James Burswald frankly stated, "Our
first interest is in interesting male members in Union activity since women
very likely will not be employed in our shop after the war."[39] Similarly, in
1943, UE field organizer Marie Reed reported that "the girls [female activists]
felt that the attitude of the men toward them . . . was not good. . . .[They]
felt, therefore, that they had no place or a very small place in the war effort,
and in the union."[40]

At the upper levels, too, there was resistance to women among male UAW
leaders. "The policies of the UAW were always very good," recalled Mildred
Jeffrey, who headed the union's Women's Department from its founding in
1944 until 1948. "Getting them implemented was another story."[41] Grievances
from women in the locals that came to the Women's Department had to be
referred to the powerful UAW regional directors, who were then supposed to
resolve the issue with the local union involved. As Florence Peterson recalled,
"The only recourse for the Women's Department was to bring the case back
and attempt to get the people who had already made this decision [i.e., the
decision which had led women in the local to complain to the Women's Department in the first place] to reverse themselves. Considering that the only
power the Women's Department had was the power of moral persuasion, a
reversal did not often take place. It was an impossible situation."[42]

There were other obstacles to women's advancement in the wartime unions
as well. Culturally, organized labor represented an alien territory for many
women. Even more than the factory itself, the union was a traditionally male
world. "The trouble with the women," delegate Mary Catherine Eddy suggested at the UE's 1943 convention, is that "they have never participated in
the running of our country. And the sole problem . . . is giving the women
. . . the feeling of confidence to carry on, to do away with the feeling that,
'Oh, Tom Jones is a man, he can do it better than I can.' "[43] Compounding
this difficulty were the practical obstacles that women had to overcome if they
were to become active unionists. Most important, family responsibilities com-
peted with paid work and unionism for women's time and energy. This was

hardly a new problem, but it was greatly intensified under wartime conditions, when the number of married women in the labor force was at an unprecedented level, working hours were longer than ever, arranging transportation was often a problem, and rationing made for added difficulties in shopping. As the U.S. Women's Bureau reported, there was "literally no extra time for them [women] to even attend union meetings. They do not therefore get a very clear understanding of the union program."[44]

Both the UE and the UAW developed special programs to help women solve these problems. District 4 of the UE (New York) hired social workers to staff a "Union Personal Service Department" to assist women members with child care and other "personal and family problems." The UAW, similarly, set up a "union counseling" program inside the factories, which offered advice about various social services as well as personal counseling.[45] These services were certainly valuable to the women they reached, and they made it possible for some women to become active unionists who otherwise could not have. But these innovative union programs were never adequate to meet the enormous need they sought to address, and family responsibilities remained a critical obstacle to women's active involvement in union affairs during the 1940s.

For many women war workers, simply gaining access to "men's jobs" had brought such a huge increase in wages that the traditional economic appeals of unionism fell flat. As Irene Young pointed out at a 1944 UAW conference:

> When you went to these new women who were getting top wages of $1.00 or $1.50 an hour for running machines, you just couldn't tell them if they didn't join a union, if they didn't stay in the union, they weren't going to get a wage increase, because to these women they were getting more money than they ever heard of in all their life.
>
> As to working conditions, if these women had ever worked at all before, they had worked, most of them, in laundries, restaurants, and things like that, where the conditions had always been lousy, and when they come into a plant where the union has been in control for five or six years, it is like a paradise to them.[46]

This was less true in electrical manufacturing, because so many women had been employed in the industry before the war and had witnessed firsthand the economic improvements brought by unionization. But even in the UE, the majority of the women had come into industry only during the war.[47] And in both auto and electrical manufacturing, the upward mobility that women experienced in the 1940s was clearly due to the economic mobilization rather than to union efforts, so that women were often indifferent towards unionism.

Despite all these difficulties, a substantial women's movement did emerge within the CIO during the 1940s as a result of the unique war situation. But the composition of this movement was shaped by the impediments to women's union participation that were just discussed. Older women, especially those with prewar industrial and union experience, were particularly likely to be involved. Those whose children were already grown had more time for union work, and older women were also more likely to understand the gains that had accompanied unionization in the prewar years. Younger women from union families (especially the wives and sisters of union men in the military) were also disproportionately represented among female union activists for similar reasons.[48] Finally, leftist women made up a large proportion of the wartime CIO's female leaders and militants.

The women's movement in the CIO in the 1940s was constricted not only by the external problems that limited the numbers and types of women who could be active in it, but also by the internal organizational structure and world view of the unions. On the one hand, the labor movement was the only available vehicle in this period for the active pursuit of women workers' interests, in the absence of any autonomous women's organization or mass feminist conscious-ness. On the other hand, because the unions were ongoing organizations, with their own needs, internal structure, and ideology, there were definite con-straints on the ways in which women could contribute and on how issues could be defined.

The Limits of Unionism for Women Workers

The definition of women's issues in the wartime CIO was shaped by two contradictory notions. The efforts to recruit women into union leadership, as well as the educational and social service programs developed especially for women, implicitly acknowledged that women were in some respects different from men and had gender-specific needs. Yet at the same time, once women became active members and leaders, they could not recast the organization and ideology of unionism in any fundamental way to better respond to women's distinct needs. Women were welcomed into the labor movement, then, but only on the terms previously defined by men. There was a great deal of space for "exceptional women" like Ruth Young; there was little or none for a female perspective that might question the basic structure or ideology of unionism.

Unions were, after all, workers' organizations first and foremost. Their primary purpose was to unite their members in order to extract concessions from employers—always a difficult task. In this organizational setting, any effort to demarcate the special interests of a subgroup within the larger mem-bership was likely to be interpreted by union leaders as divisive and threat-ening. This severely restricted the political space in which female union activists interested in mobilizing women could operate.[49] They had to provide continual reassurance to male union leaders of their loyalty to the larger or-ganization, even as they sought to win broad support for women as a group with distinct interests.

The repeated insistence by female union activists that they were not seeking special treatment of any kind for women, either in the union or in industry, must be understood in this context. "We would make a mistake if we were to say we want special privileges because we are women," warned Ruth Young at a UE conference in 1942. "We don't have that right. We have to prove that we are equal to the tasks that face us." The vision articulated by women unionists of the struggle for women workers was thus circumscribed by a politics of class interest defined within the traditional framework of industrial unionism. "We are not fighting just for women," Ruth Wellman told the 1942 UE convention. "We are fighting to preserve all the standards that this Union has built up."[50]

The same position necessarily prevailed among UAW women activists. At the 1944 UAW Women's Conference, the alternatives were clearly posed when Florence Walton suggested that women should enjoy preferential seniority rights akin to those the union supported for veterans. "If we're going to get special provisions for others," she asked, "why not make special provisions for women and Negroes?" This position, written up as a "favoritism" amendment to a conference resolution on seniority, was rejected overwhelmingly by the female UAW delegates. The resolution they passed instead explicitly opposed any form of special treatment for women. "The more than 300,000 women in the automobile and allied industries represented at this conference do not want special consideration or privilege," it read. "We thoroughly endorse and stand back of the seniority system which has been built up in plants under the UAW's jurisdiction."[51]

In practice, women union activists found that they could not function effectively unless they accepted the overall world view of their male counterparts in the labor movement. That world view did offer certain avenues for mobilizing the union as a whole in support of gender equality. Indeed, the idea that unions should strive for unity among workers and equal treatment for all (which had led to women's inclusion in the CIO in the first place) became the basis for building opposition to sex discrimination in the 1940s. However, the scope of such struggles was restricted to efforts that clearly benefited the union as a whole—serving the interests of both male and female members. In effect, women could pursue their gender interest where—and only where—it coincided with the interest of the working class as a whole.

In most instances, the class and gender interests of women factory workers were not in conflict. Thus women were often able to mobilize effectively within the unions in order to secure equal treatment for all workers. On the local level, they enjoyed considerable success in campaigning for enforcement of the equal pay for equal work policies established in the mobilization period, as well as for nondiscriminatory seniority systems and other gender-blind employment practices. The extent to which discrimination was eliminated in these areas varied directly with the extent of women's activism and representation in local union leadership. Thus a 1945 U.S. Women's Bureau study found that, although separate seniority lists for women were written into only one-fifth of the local union contracts surveyed, in plants where no women were on the bargaining, grievance, or shop committees, three-fourths of the contracts provided for separate seniority lists.[52]

The wartime struggles against sex discrimination in pay and seniority systems clearly benefited women workers both as workers and as women. But if the gender and class interests of women workers generally coincided, this was by no means the case for men. Although discrimination was in their class interest, male workers might stand to lose from it as a gender. This presented a serious problem, for despite the growth of female union membership during the war, men were still in the majority and exercised power on a scale disproportionate even to their large numbers. Under such conditions, the political task of women trade union activists was to persuade male union members to put their class interests ahead of their gender interests if the two were in conflict. Women, therefore, not only had to suppress their own gender consciousness (as in the protestations cited earlier rejecting any notion of special treatment for women), but also had to effectively suppress gender consciousness among men.

This could frequently be accomplished during the war, for example with equal pay for equal work, which benefited both men and women in respect to both gender and class interests. However, after the war came to an end, uniting men and women along class lines would become far more difficult. Given the uncertainty over whether women would retain their wartime foothold in "men's jobs" during the postwar period, demobilization brought the gender and class interests of men into potentially explosive conflict. For if women workers' interests lay unambiguously in the active defense of their wartime gains, their male co-workers had two contradictory interests. As a gender with considerable privilege in relation to women (not only in the factory but also in the family and society), male workers' interests might be best served by a reconstruction of the prewar sexual division of labor. But if male workers defined their interests exclusively in class terms, they would instead support nondiscrimination and the equitable allocation of postwar jobs according to seniority. The outcome of the process through which this dilemma was resolved—a process in which the nascent women's movement in the CIO played a central role—would have a major impact on the postwar sexual division of labor. The working out of that process is the subject of the next two chapters.

7 Demobilization and the Reconstruction of "Woman's Place" in Industry

The war's end generated renewed upheaval in the sexual division of labor. As reconversion brought massive layoffs and then new hiring, the issue of women's position in industry came to the fore, just as it had in the mobilization period. Would there be a return to the "traditional," prewar sexual division of labor as the mobilization-era ideology of "woman's place" in the war effort had promised? Or would the successful wartime deployment of women in "men's jobs" lead to a permanent shift in the boundaries between women's and men's jobs? Or—a third alternative—would completely new, postwar exigencies reshape, or even eliminate, the sexual division of labor?

Reversion to prewar patterns, which ultimately did occur, might appear to have been the only real possibility. Had not the nation been repeatedly assured that women's entrance into industry was a temporary adaptation to the extraordinary needs of war? After all, the war's end would bring an end to full employment; the return of many male workers from military service; and the elimination of such direct forms of state intervention in the economy as wage and price controls, War Labor Board jurisdiction over labor disputes, and restrictions on consumer goods production. The no-strike pledge and popular front politics would also be abandoned. Was this not simply a long-awaited "return to normalcy," which for the female population heralded a return to home and hearth?

Such a view is consistent with the prevailing ideology of the demobilization period, but it obscures the significance of the war years themselves. Wartime conditions were indeed transitory, yet the extraordinary period between Pearl Harbor and V-J Day left American society permanently transformed. One legacy of the war years, from which no retreat would be possible, was the increase in female labor force participation. On an individual basis, to be sure, many women faced conflicting pressures after the war—to continue working for pay on the one hand, and to go back to the home on the other. Yet a permanent shift had occurred for women as a social group. Despite the postwar resurgence of the ideology of domesticity, by the early 1950s the number of gainfully employed women exceeded the highest wartime level. And as early as 1948, the labor force participation rate of married women was higher than in 1944, the peak of the war boom. The rise in female employment, especially for married women, would continue throughout the postwar period, and at a far more rapid rate than in the first half of the century. In this respect, far from being a temporary deviation, the war was a watershed period that left women's relationship to work permanently changed.[1]

The crucial issue, then, was not whether women would remain in the work force, but rather which women would do so and on what terms. What would the postwar sexual division of paid labor look like? Would women retain their wartime foothold in basic industries like auto and electrical manufacturing? To what extent would they be able to find work in fields that had been predominantly male before the war? For women who worked for pay, whether by choice or necessity, exclusion from "men's jobs" did not mean the housewifery first celebrated and later decried as the "feminine mystique." Instead, it meant employment in low-wage "female" jobs, especially clerical, sales, and service work—all of which expanded enormously in the postwar decades.

That the war brought a permanent increase in female employment made the demobilization transition particularly consequential. The opportunity was there for incorporating the dramatic wartime changes in women's position in industry into the fabric of a postwar order in which paid work would become increasingly central to women's lives. In the absence of any events affecting the labor market as fundamentally and cataclysmically as the war, there has been no comparable occasion for a wholesale restructuring of the sexual division of labor since the 1940s. The fact that the opportunity the wartime upheaval presented was lost had enormous implications for the entire postwar era.

Why, then, was the potential for an enduring transformation in the sexual division of labor not fulfilled in the 1940s? There are two standard explanations. One focuses on the postwar resurgence of domesticity, both as a practice and as an ideology, and suggests that women war workers themselves relinquished the "men's jobs" they held during the war—either because of the genuine appeal of traditional family commitments or because they were ideologically manipulated. The second explanation, in contrast, suggests that the key problem was the operation of union-instituted seniority systems, and their manipulation by male unionists, to exclude women and to favor returning male veterans in postwar employment.

This chapter argues that both these accounts of the postwar transition, while partially correct, are inadequate, and suggests an alternative explanation that focuses on management's role in reconstructing the prewar sexual division of labor. A large body of evidence demonstrates that management took the lead both in purging women from "men's jobs" after the war and in refusing to rehire them (except in traditionally "female" jobs) as postwar production resumed. Management chose this course despite the fact that most women war workers wanted to keep doing "men's work," and despite the fact that refusing to rehire women often violated seniority provisions in union contracts. The crucial question then becomes why management acted as it did—particularly in light of the success with which women had been incorporated into war industry and the economies to be gained from their relatively low wages.

I will offer a two-part explanation for management's postwar policy. First, in both auto and electrical manufacturing, the "traditional" sexual division of labor had a historical logic embodied in the structure of each industry, which remained compelling in the demobilization period. At one level, indeed, reconstructing the prewar sexual division of labor was a foregone conclusion from management's perspective. Wartime female substitution was an experiment that employers had undertaken unwillingly and only because there was no alternative. Despite the success with which women were integrated into "men's jobs," the war's end meant an end to the experiment, and management breathed a collective sigh of relief.

But that is only half of the story. The postwar purge of women from men's jobs also reflected management's assessment of labor's position on the issue. For one thing, the CIO's wartime struggles for equal pay for women workers, which narrowed sex differentials in wages considerably, made permanent female substitution less appealing than it might otherwise have been. Moreover, in the reconversion period, male workers displayed a great deal of ambivalence about the postwar employment rights of women war workers, even those with seniority standing. The CIO's official policy was to defend women's job rights in line with the seniority principle, but in practice there was substantial opposition to retaining women in "men's jobs." This, I will suggest, effectively reinforced management's determination to reconstruct the prewar sexual division of labor. Before developing this argument in detail, however, the other explanations that have been offered for the postwar transformation must be considered.

The Resurgence of Domesticity

For some commentators, the appeal of domesticity to women workers immediately after the war is sufficient to explain the postwar transition. "To understand American women in the 1940s, it is essential to concentrate, not on the formerly male roles that some women occupied, but on the family roles that the vast majority of women at the time defined as central to their lives," writes historian D'Ann Campbell, for example. "An insignificant proportion of American women seized upon the opportunities for new occupations that the war proffered as a permanent break with their past commitments, sense of themselves, and expectations."[2] However, a closer look at the preferences that women war workers themselves expressed at the time casts doubt upon this argument.

Surveys conducted during the war consistently found that the overwhelming majority of women war workers intended to continue working after the war and, moreover, to stay in the same line of work. A 1944-45 U.S. Women's Bureau survey of women in ten war production centers around the nation found that 75 percent of them planned to keep working in the postwar period. Moreover, 84 percent of the women employed in manufacturing who intended to keep working wanted to retain their factory jobs. "Postwar job openings as cafeteria bus girls," the Women's Bureau report noted acerbically, "are not apt to prove attractive to women who are seeking work as screw-machine operators."[3]

Surveys of women employed in auto and electrical manufacturing revealed similar preferences. A 1944 UAW survey of women in the union's war plants found that 85 percent of those responding intended to work after the war, and the majority preferred to continue doing factory work.[4] Similarly, a survey jointly conducted by the UE and the New York State Labor Department in the winter of 1944-45 found that 82 percent of the state's women war workers planned to keep working outside the home. In Schenectady, home of GE's giant headquarters plant, 84 percent of the women surveyed intended to remain in the labor market. Of those who expected to continue working, the survey found, five out of six wanted to keep their present jobs or to do similar work elsewhere.[5]

One might question the accuracy of surveys conducted *during* the war as predictors of women's postwar behavior. But there is strong evidence that the employment preferences recorded in the 1944-45 surveys persisted in the immediate aftermath of the war. In July 1946, almost a year after V-J Day, the Detroit office of the U.S. Employment Service had nearly twice as many applications on file for semi-skilled and unskilled manufacturing jobs from women as from returning (male) veterans, while the applicants for clerical and service work included a higher proportion of veterans than of women. Although officials alerted automakers and other manufacturers to the availability of women for the factory jobs being spurned by men, the demand for industrial workers remained overwhelmingly male.[6]

Ironically, the sex-typing of the factory jobs women did for the duration may have increased women's attachment to manufacturing employment. Still more important were the high wages women war workers earned—far higher than most had even dreamed of before. Indeed, the primary reason women gave for remaining in the labor force after the war was responsibility for the financial support of themselves or others. This was the case for 84 percent of the women who reported their intention to remain in the work force in the U.S. Women's Bureau survey discussed above. Similarly, 93 percent of the women surveyed by the UE and the New York State Labor Department who planned to continue working said that they would have to work to support themselves or others.[7]

While many women workers in key war industries like auto and electrical manufacturing had been drawn into the wartime labor force from homemaking or from school, fully half had been gainfully employed in the prewar period.[8] Most women in this second group faced economic circumstances that made leaving the labor market simply impossible. They knew that they would have to keep working. And they were not eager to return to the kinds of jobs they had before the war—dull and poorly paid service, clerical, or sales jobs, tra-ditional "women's" factory jobs, or (for black women especially) domestic work. Investigators repeatedly reported women's own comparisons between such prewar jobs and the well-paid, unionized, and generally more attractive positions that they held during the war. "Laundry work is much too hard," one woman said. "The [factory] work is much better than pressing shirts." Another woman who had been a domestic servant before the war expressed similar sentiments. "I love it here, better than housework. I love machines. In the factory you're finished at the same time every day."[9] Lola Weixel, too, who before the war had done the "light, repetitive" factory work to which employers believed women were best suited, very much wanted to keep work-ing as a welder after the war. "I liked welding better," she recalled. "It was a special thing. At the end of the day I always felt I'd accomplished something. It was good—there was a product, there was something to be seen."[10]

Even women who had not been in the labor force before wanted to keep their war jobs, according to the surveys. Of course, that women who did not *need* to work felt this way during the war does not mean that their preferences could not change once peace returned. Many commentators have emphasized the impact of the postwar "feminine mystique" in this regard, suggesting that it was not women's "true" preferences, but an externally imposed ideological emphasis on domesticity that led them to give up the "men's jobs" they had during the war. That, indeed, is probably the most widespread interpretation of the postwar transformation.[11]

It is indisputable that the ideology of domesticity was revived with a venge-ance after the war, and that it legitimated the reconstruction of the prewar sexual division of labor. Indeed, even during the war, women's stint in "men's jobs" in industry was ideologically defined as an extension of (rather than a challenge to) domesticity—its apocryphal retrospective construction as "feminist realism" notwithstanding.[12] And whether they were victims of manipulation or genuinely preferred to do so, it is undeniable that some women war workers *chose* to leave the labor force in the postwar period in order to devote themselves to domestic concerns—although there are unfortunately no data on precisely how many or who they were.

But this still leaves a great deal unexplained. How did the postwar shift toward domesticity operate *within* the sphere of paid labor to restore the prewar division of jobs between the sexes—even as the number of women workers continued to rise? And what about those women war workers who remained in the labor force? How were they removed from the "men's jobs" that they had during the war, which they apparently would have preferred to keep? The scholarship that addresses these questions focuses on the role of the industrial unions and of union-instituted seniority systems, to which we now turn.

Seniority, the Unions, and Women's Postwar Job Rights

The second major explanation for women's postwar exclusion from "men's jobs" takes women's desire to remain in those jobs as a starting point and argues that the critical obstacles that prevented them from doing so were the operation of the "last hired, first fired" seniority principle in favor of male veterans and against women and the reticence of the industrial unions to enforce the limited seniority rights women did have.[13] The scholarship in women's labor history that puts forward this view offers important insights into the role of the CIO in this crucial period. Indeed, as we shall see, unionists' failure to consistently defend women's seniority rights, which this literature documents, gave a key political signal to management that was very significant in shaping the postwar sexual division of labor.

The problem with this line of argument, however, is that it *presumes* that seniority systems played a critical role in shaping the gender composition of the postwar labor force in industries like auto and electrical manufacturing. In fact, as the following analysis demonstrates, seniority was ultimately of limited importance, for employment in these industries expanded very rapidly after the war, and turnover rates were extremely high. Even with the large influx of returning veterans, who enjoyed special seniority status, there were many vacancies in the industrial labor force that could easily have been filled by women, had management cared to hire them. Indeed, in the automotive industry, while women were excluded from most postwar jobs, black men were hired in large numbers despite the fact that, like women, they had very low seniority standing. In the end, management's *hiring policy*, not seniority, was the critical determinant of the composition of the postwar labor force.

In order to demonstrate this, the complexities of the postwar controversy over seniority rights and women workers need to be explored in some detail.

Let us begin by examining the dilemma that the CIO unions had to confront immediately after the war, when full employment, which had been the crucial precondition for female incorporation into "men's jobs" in industry in the first place, could no longer be sustained. Now women's desire to retain those jobs thrust them into direct competition with men—a problem intensified by the large influx of returning veterans into the labor force. Moreover, fear of a return to the high unemployment levels of the depression years was widespread after the war, especially among workers in durable goods industries, which had always been particularly sensitive to cyclical economic changes. "It scares you, it really does," one woman worker in New York City told an interviewer. "Girls want to work, boys want to work, and everyone is afraid the factory won't exist."[14]

In the late 1930s, the CIO had fought to establish seniority systems to distribute employment equitably in just such situations. During the war, it became obvious that demobilization would bring the first real test of the seniority principle. At the same time, the industrial unions' commitment to opposing discrimination provided an opening for women union activists to work to equalize seniority rights. They pursued this goal energetically during the war, and with some success. By the war's end, the official policy of the UE and the UAW was that women should enjoy the same seniority rights as men. Locals were urged to eliminate separate women's seniority lists and other discriminatory contract provisions, and many did so.[15]

In addition, the auto and electrical unions were active in the campaign for full employment legislation, which they saw as the optimal solution to the problem of postwar jobs. As Ruth Young put it at the UE's 1943 convention, "It is a political question and cannot be solved in a given plant. . . . We feel most strongly, in fighting for the principle of Freedom From Want, that it means that every working man and woman in this nation who desires to work shall have that right."[16] The result of the campaign, the Employment Act of 1946, was a highly diluted and generally ineffective version of the CIO's original program, however.[17] Having lost the battle to place legal responsibility for providing postwar jobs on the shoulders of management and government, the unions could influence the distribution of employment only through contractual seniority agreements.

However, in the absence of full employment, the seniority principle, even if properly enforced, had mixed implications for women war workers. Because their employment gains were so recent, concentrated in the three-year period of war production, the "last hired, first fired" principle embedded in the seniority system meant that women would be laid off in disproportionate numbers. Indeed, this is the basis for the argument *against* strict seniority systems advanced today by advocates of affirmative action for women and other industrial minorities. It was not a view that enjoyed much credibility in the 1940s, however. Even female union activists pressed not for preferential treatment, but simply for enforcement of the limited seniority rights that women war workers already had.[18]

There was one group of workers for whom preferential treatment *was* widely advocated: returning veterans. Popular appreciation of the hardships of military service thoroughly legitimized the position that veterans should not be penalized for their absence from the labor market during the war. Both UAW and UE contracts granted seniority equal to the time spent in military service both to veterans previously employed by a unionized company and to those newly hired after their discharge from the military.[19] This policy enjoyed widespread support among industrial workers of both sexes and was endorsed by the most vociferous advocates for women within the unions. "Women do not expect or want to hold jobs at the expense of returning soldiers," the Women's Trade Union League stated flatly. Ruth Young took a similar stance at the 1943 UE convention, where she introduced a report on the seniority issue from the union's Committee on Women by saying, "It is obvious that, in a given plant, any woman who has come into industry during the war will have to give way, because of seniority rights, to the boy who has gone off to the front and is now coming back to do that job."[20]

However, the unions were wary of potential divisions between veterans and other workers that might be fostered by employers, and strongly opposed so-called super-seniority rights for veterans that would have given them preferential status over virtually all other workers.[21] In regard to the potential effect of veterans' preference on women war workers, both the UAW and the UE came out strongly in favor of protecting women's seniority rights, limited as they were. The following formulation of the UAW's policy expresses the stance both unions ultimately adopted on this issue:

> Should veterans without seniority be given jobs over women who have seniority rights in UAW plants?
>
> Here is Jimmy Smith, he's just 22 and a veteran of two years in the Pacific. He's had miscellaneous jobs before he went into service—delivery jobs, drug and grocery store clerking, but no re-employment rights to a job he's interested in. He's hired at X auto plant, simply because he's a veteran. When he goes to work he cuts out Alice Jones who was next on the seniority list. With three and a half years in X plant Alice, who was laid off the day after V-J day, has exhausted her unemployment compensation and needs a job desperately . . . she's got two children to support.
>
> Should Alice Jones be responsible for providing Jimmy Smith with a job? *The UAW says no.*
>
> . . . No individual worker or group of workers should be expected to give up their jobs so that another group might work. It's not Alice's responsibility to go hungry and let her children suffer to provide Jimmy with a job. It's management's responsibility to provide jobs, and if free enterprise fails then it's government's job to see that every citizen able and willing to work has the opportunity for a useful job at decent wages.[22]

But official union policies were one thing; their enforcement was quite another. There was tremendous ambivalence about women's rights to postwar jobs on the part of both individual union leaders and the rank and file, despite the officially nondiscriminatory policies. In the face of widespread fears of a return to depression conditions, the issue was hardly one of abstract principles. "When it came to a question of fighting for a job, that came first," recalled Ruth Glassman of UE Local 427. "Everybody was fighting for his own job and the hell with everybody else. . . . It was a very divisive thing."[23]

The unions faced a serious dilemma in the women's seniority issue: a direct conflict between the imperative of protecting the seniority principle during its first crucial test and the longstanding working-class ideal of the "family wage," which led many union members to question women's rights to postwar jobs. Here the ideology of domesticity played a role in shaping the views of male unionists (and probably of some women workers as well). As Mildred Jeffrey, the UAW Women's Bureau director at the end of the war, recalled, "Women were needed for the war effort to support our men and produce the war material when they were fighting for our country. That was over. The time had come for women to go back to their homes and take care of their families and their children. That was the prevailing mood and attitude. . . . The UAW can be a great, progressive union, et cetera, but it reflects the society and the societal attitudes. It doesn't live in isolation from that which is going on in the rest of the community."[24] As we have seen, most women war workers would not go "back to their homes," but rather into traditionally female jobs. That the dominant ideology denied this did not prevent it from generating considerable hostility toward women who wanted to keep their wartime jobs in industry—both within the unions and in the larger society.

Within the UE, there was some explicit opposition to women's postwar employment. "Some men still maintain that the women ought to be in the home and not in the factory," Steve Rubicz noted at the union's 1944 convention. "We have men in the shops who don't believe in seniority rights for women. . . they say the women came into industry just for the war."[25] But given the long history of female employment in the electrical industry, no one really expected that women would be absent from its postwar labor force. However, there were two aspects to the women's seniority issue in this industry. "One is the matter of layoffs and whether or not women should be laid off before men," Ruth Young pointed out in March 1944. "The other is the question of taking women off the more skilled jobs which they had begun to work on when men were drafted and and sending these women back to their old jobs at less money and requiring less skill."[26]

On the first issue, the UE took a firm stand in defense of women's rights, although some locals did negotiate discriminatory contract clauses calling for denial of seniority to married women.[27] But the second issue—seniority protection for women in the "men's jobs" into which they had been upgraded during the war—was far more controversial. Some local contracts were explicitly designed to prevent permanent displacement of men by women war workers, specifying that women on "men's jobs" be displaced before *any* men, regardless of seniority. At the GE plant in Lynn, Massachusetts, for example, the contract provided that a woman with high seniority could bump other women, whether on "men's" or "women's jobs." But when layoffs affected a "male" department, women were to be downgraded to "women's jobs" in order of seniority, while *all* men, no matter how low their seniority, were to be retained until there were no women left in the department.[28]

Where such arrangements were not contractually established, local unions sometimes pressured women to relinquish "men's jobs" by other means. At the Philco plant in Philadelphia, for example. "About a month after the end of the war, the union held a meeting and women were asked to relinquish their rights and seniority on jobs classified as men's and allow not only Philco veterans but any veterans acceptable to the company to replace them, and the women agreed to this."[29]

At another UE shop, in Newark, New Jersey, one woman reportedly "volunteered" to be downgraded, suffering a substantial pay cut, "because of the hostile attitude of the veterans with whom she worked and whom she had trained."[30] And at the Leland Electric Company in Dayton, Ohio, UE Local 804's Executive Board unanimously passed a motion providing that "women put on men's jobs during the war emergency be returned to their former jobs." This contradicted the seniority clause in the local contract, but management and local union officials nevertheless came to a verbal agreement on this policy.[31] The women workers affected did not lose all rights to employment, but they did lose access to high-paying "men's jobs."

The UE's national office did little to discourage such local arrangements. In October 1944, Margaret Toy, a local union officer at the Camden, New Jersey, RCA plant, wrote to Julius Emspak at UE headquarters asking for guidance on the seniority issue in anticipation of cutbacks. She explained that many women with high seniority at RCA had been upgraded during the war, as the female proportion of the work force had increased from 35 to 55 percent. "We are looking for the Standard answer," she wrote, "and it better be good." Emspak replied that this was a local matter and was noncommittal: "The International Union . . . to my knowledge has taken no position, as you put it, with regard to 'Male versus Upgraded Female.' " The national office did encourage locals to try to narrow sex differentials in wages and to work toward eliminating the distinction between "women's" and "men's" jobs, but these were long-range endeavors and did nothing to protect women against downgrading during the crucial postwar transition.[32]

Even if there had been less ambivalence within the UE on the issue of women's postwar position, the seniority provisions of its contracts with the major electrical firms were so weak that management had a relatively free hand in shaping the postwar sexual division of labor. As late as 1945, the GE national contract allowed management to consider both "ability" and "family status" in allocating layoffs and transfers, and that year's contract was the first to specify length of service as the "major factor" governing reductions in force. Seniority did not become the principal factor governing rehiring and layoffs until 1950.[33] In this respect, the UE provided its members—of both sexes—with far less seniority protection than did the UAW. Yet women war workers were generally rehired in the electrical industry (although not in "men's jobs") in the postwar period; whereas in auto, where there were stronger seniority provisions, very few women were rehired.

Ambivalence about women's postwar employment was also manifest in the UAW despite the union's formal opposition to sex discrimination. Internal battles over women's seniority rights raged during and after the war in the UAW, and often the union's practice was inconsistent with its official policy. Separate women's seniority lists remained in effect at the war's end in some locals (although in many others women activists succeeded in eliminating them during the war). There were other blatantly discriminatory arrangements as well. The national GM contract, for example, provided that women employed on "men's jobs" during the war would accumulate temporary seniority applicable "for the duration only."[34] And in auto, in contrast to electrical manufacturing, excluding women from "men's jobs" usually meant excluding them from the industry as a whole.

Yet in both industries, the ambivalent posture of the unions was less consequential for the postwar sexual division of labor than it appeared. It is indisputable that seniority systems were stacked against women, even where they were nominally nondiscriminatory; and that women war workers' seniority rights, limited as they were, were honored as much in the breach as in the observance. However, this does not constitute an adequate explanation for the postwar reconstruction of the prewar sexual division of labor in basic industry. Ultimately, *hiring policy* proved far more crucial than seniority (properly enforced or not) in determining the composition of the postwar labor force—and here, managerial control was virtually complete. So many new workers were hired in these industries after the war that the seniority lists were of marginal significance. For, contrary to expectation, the postwar years saw enormous expansion in both auto and electrical manufacturing after a brief interlude of reconversion unemployment. The postwar boom was fueled by vast consumer demand for automobiles and electrical goods like appliances, radios, and televisions, as well as growth in demand for turbines, generators, and other capital goods produced by the electrical industry. By 1947, the number of production workers in the nation's auto factories was higher than at the peak of war employment, and by the early 1950s, employment in electrical manufacturing also exceeded the wartime high.[35]

The postwar expansion in these industries was so massive that despite the dramatic influx of veterans, with their preferential seniority treatment, there was plenty of room for the recall of women war workers with seniority and even the hiring of additional women workers. In electrical manufacturing, where employment expanded less rapidly than in auto, laid-off women war workers generally were recalled, although only to traditionally "female" jobs. Even in auto, the influx of veterans constituted less of a setback to women's reemployment prospects than is often presumed. The rapid expansion of employment in the industry after the war, the emigration of large numbers of war workers (mostly male) from war production areas, and normal attrition (always high in the auto industry), meant that the composition of the postwar labor force was shaped primarily by hiring policies.

That the auto firms hired many veterans in the reconversion period is indisputable: Between December 1945 and July 1946, veterans constituted (on the average) 47 percent of all new hires. By mid-1946 they made up fully 23 percent of the automotive work force.[36] But this high rate of veteran entry into the industry reflected not seniority, but employers' preference for young male workers. "Employers in the auto industry prefer white males, between 20 and 25, weighing over 150 pounds and in good physical condition," the U.S. Women's Bureau reported in July 1946.[37] These were precisely the characteristics that the military had sought in conscripting soldiers, and so it is hardly surprising that veterans were hired in large numbers. Andrew Court, a GM labor relations executive at the time, recalled that the 1945-46 strike against GM had the effect of increasing the representation of veterans in the firm's work force. "There was a lot of moaning and groaning about the strike," he said, "but really it was one of the best things that happened to our labor supply. We lost people we'd hired during the war who were not as desirable as the GI's. They went somewhere else and didn't come back after the strike, and it was settled when the GI's were coming back, so we had a fairly good supply of young, vigorous, fairly adequate men. A few years later they made a study, and General Motors got 'all A's' for having hired so many GI's, and this was the reason."[38]

Most veterans who found postwar employment in the auto plants were young men who had not worked in the industry before, so that even when granted credit for their time in the military, few had more seniority than the women whose wartime "service" had been in war jobs rather than in the armed forces. Only about 20 percent of the nation's returning World War II veterans were entitled to reemployment rights.[39] That those veterans without formal reemployment rights got a seniority bonus meant that employers' preference for them did affect the seniority system, but the impact of this was offset by a combination of other factors.

Turnover rates among veterans hired after the war were quite high, with quits alone averaging 5.4 percent monthly between December 1945 and July

1946.[40] Nonveterans, especially migrants, also left the industry in droves at this time. Between 100,000 and 150,000 people left Michigan between V-E Day and mid-September 1946 alone, many of them southerners returning home. Men predominated in this group.[41] Although the number of veterans with substantial seniority in the auto industry cannot be precisely determined, it can be estimated for the immediate postwar period at a maximum of 100,000.[42] In the twenty months between V-J Day and April 1947 alone, total employment in auto rose by more than twice that figure (230,000).[43] The high rate of veterans' employment in the auto industry clearly reflected employers' hiring preferences, but it cannot explain the exclusion of women from the postwar labor force.

The most convincing evidence that women's low seniority standing was not the cause of their poor representation in the postwar auto labor force is the contrast between the impact of reconversion on women and that on blacks. Like women, black workers as a group had relatively low seniority standing at the war's end, for they too had first entered the auto industry in large numbers during the war. The proportion of blacks in Detroit's automotive plants rose from 5.5 percent in May 1942 to 15 percent by the spring of 1945. Black workers gained access to semi-skilled auto jobs on a significant scale for the first time during the war, paralleling the expansion of jobs open to women.[44]

The experiences of these two groups, which were so similar during the war, diverged sharply with reconversion. Whereas women were ousted from the industry at the war's end, and in most cases not recalled, blacks were more fortunate. "Once the painful transition to peacetime was over," Meier and Rudwick conclude, "blacks found that they retained the foothold in semiskilled machine production and assembly-line work which they had won during the war."[45] Data on black employment in individual auto firms confirm this. The proportion of blacks in Chrysler's production work force actually rose just after the war, from 15 percent in 1945 to 17 percent in 1946, in stark contrast to the "exodus" of women from the industry. By 1960, blacks were 26 percent of the labor force in Chrysler's Detroit plants, and 23 percent of GM's production work force in that city. Ford, the one auto manufacturer that had employed blacks in significant numbers before the war, also increased black employment after the war, so that by 1960 blacks comprised over 40 percent of the production work force at the huge River Rouge plant.[46]

This divergence between the experience of women and blacks can only be understood in the context of management's hiring policies. The female proportion of the work force might have been marginally greater in the postwar years if the UAW had more effectively defended women's seniority rights. But given the high turnover rates for all auto workers and the vast postwar expansion of the industry, even if the union had secured the reinstatement of every woman war worker, there would still have been a sharp decline in female representation in the industry's labor force unless additional women were hired as well. Only an insistence on sex-blind hiring policy—which the UAW had no means to enforce—could have altered the situation.

Hiring policies, not seniority systems, then, were crucial in shaping the composition of the postwar labor force. To explain the retrogression of the sexual division of labor during demobilization, the central focus of analysis must be on management's employment policies. We can now examine the events that immediately followed the war's end—the massive layoffs and then the buildup of new employment for consumer goods production—with a view to developing an understanding of what management chose to do, and why, at this critical conjuncture in women's labor history.

The Postwar Layoffs and Reconversion Employment Policies

The massive demobilization layoffs disproportionately affected women from the outset. By September 1945, one-fourth of the women who had been employed in factories three months before had lost their war jobs, and by the year's end more than a million women had been claimed by layoffs. In manufacturing, the post-V-J Day layoffs affected women at a rate nearly double that for men. The disparity was even greater in heavy war industries such as auto, which had employed very few women before the war. Between October 1943 and October 1945, total employment in auto declined 40 percent, but women's employment fell 75 percent. In electrical manufacturing, with its long tradition of female employment, the sex disparity was less pronounced. The drop in total electrical employment between October 1943 and October 1945 was 40 percent (the same as in auto), but women's employment fell a relatively modest 50 percent.[47]

In both auto and electrical manufacturing, the proportion of women fell after the war, and in neither case would it ever again reach the wartime level. But women were hired much more frequently in the postwar electrical industry than in auto—although only in traditionally female jobs. The number of women electrical workers exceeded the wartime peak by 1951 and continued to rise subsequently. In auto, however, both the proportion and the absolute number of women workers declined drastically, and permanently, in the postwar period. Less than half as many women were auto workers in 1951 as in 1944, despite a substantial rise in total employment in the industry (Table 5).

Even before V-J Day, women auto workers were disproportionately laid off as war contracts were terminated. UAW president R. J. Thomas noted as early as March 1945 that "nearly 50,000 women have been laid off from Detroit war plants within the last year." A survey conducted around the same time of

Table 5.   Female and Total Employment in Auto and Electrical Manufacturing, 1939 to 1955—Selected Dates

Month and Year	Auto			Electrical		
	Women Workers	All Workers	Women as % of Total	Women Workers	All Workers	Women as % of Total
Oct. 1939[a]	29,500	446,000	6.6%	100,300	295,900	33.9%
April 1944[a]	185,000	746,000	24.8	380,400	778,000	48.9
April 1945[a]	158,100	706,000	22.4	347,200	730,900	47.5
Aug. 1945[a]	101,600	577,000	17.6	305,600	662,900	46.1
April 1946[a]	61,400	646,000	9.5	181,600	460,900	39.4
April 1947[a]	76,700	807,000	9.5	216,600	567,000	38.2
April 1950[b]	70,700	707,000	10.0	310,500	817,100	38.0
April 1951[b]	91,400	914,000	10.0	398,900	997,300	40.0
April 1953[b]	111,600	1,014,500	11.0	519,100	1,236,000	42.0
April 1955[b]	99,100	900,900	11.0	425,200	1,090,200	39.0

Sources:
a. U.S. Department of Labor, Bureau of Labor Statistics, *Women in Factories,* mimeographed (1947), 6-7. Production workers only.
b. U.S. Department of Labor, Bureau of Labor Statistics, *Women Employees in Manufacturing Industry* (1958), 16-17. Production and nonproduction workers.

twenty thousand women laid off from Detroit plants found that 72 percent of them could not find jobs after weeks of looking. Detroit employers, meanwhile, were complaining about having to pay for unemployment insurance to cover laid-off women war workers who refused to accept lower-paying jobs in other sectors of the economy. "Unquestionably many of these women could fill orders for priority jobs for which employers have demanded male labor," R. J. Thomas pointed out. "[But] such action would conflict with the plans of such corporations as General Motors to return to their prewar pattern of exclusively male employment in plants other than those engaged in small-parts manufacture."[48]

Indeed, management went to extraordinary lengths to purge women war workers from the auto plants, provoking frequent complaints of sex discrimination even before V-J Day. In July 1945, for example, women UAW members complained that plant rules were being selectively enforced in order to justify firing women. "Plant managements are awfully fussy about women workers now," they told the *Detroit Times*. "It's all right for men to wear wrist watches and rings, but just let a woman worker show up on the job wearing them. Bingo—she's fired."[49] Management was also accused of deliberately making work difficult for the women in hopes of inducing them to quit. "They'd hassle them by putting them on the broom—as it was called—janitorial [work]," recalled Mildred Jeffrey, then the head of the UAW Women's Bureau. "They'd hassle them by putting them on night shift or afternoon shift, midnight shift, or just putting them on one job after another. Say, 'do this,' and then in the same day, move them to two or three different jobs, giving them very hard jobs."[50]

One widely used management tactic that elicited numerous complaints even before the war's end was to assign women to new jobs and demand that they master the tasks involved in an abnormally short time, without the customary break-in period. At the Ford Highland Park plant, for example, a group of women bumped some men with low seniority in the same occupational group (but doing different work and on a separate floor of the plant) after a layoff in February 1945. Women had these bumping rights under the seniority system, but when they reported to their new posts in what had until that time been an all-male section of the plant, "management rebelled, which is evidenced in their refusal to accept a reasonable break-in period." The women were given only three hours to qualify for the new jobs.[51]

This was but one of the tactics that Ford management used to lay women off out of line with seniority at the Highland Park plant. The Women's Committee of UAW Local 400 complained that:

> When a lay-off was due men were loaned out to other jobs and subsequently transferred to them, while the women remained in the department to be laid off. . . . The red-apple system flourished while our good union women walked the streets. Women who fought for their rights were disqualified for the jobs they held on trumped up charges such as absenteeism, making scrap, not meeting production quotas, etc.
>
> They were threatened with the loss of their unemployment compensation, told to be good girls and go home and *bake pies*.
>
> Job leaders were forbidden to help women, but continued to assist the men.[52]

Such techniques induced some women to leave the auto plants "voluntarily" and justified others' being fired and losing their seniority rights. By July 1945, the proportion of women in the auto production work force had fallen to 19 percent from the wartime peak of 26 percent. And after V-J Day, the proportion of women fell from 18 to 10 percent in one month (from August to September 1945)![53]

Everyone expected women to be affected disproportionately by the postwar layoffs, because they tended to have less seniority than men. Furthermore, men were laid off in large numbers themselves, as the nation's factories reconverted to consumer goods manufacturing. Indeed, the layoffs were far less consequential than the rehiring that began as postwar auto production got underway. Union contracts theoretically required that women, like men, be rehired in line with seniority standing. As workers began to be called back, however, it became clear that management had no intention of rehiring women in auto production work except in those few jobs that had always been considered "women's work." In some cases, management simply ignored the women on the seniority lists and hired inexperienced men. As Ida Griggs of Local 306 complained at the UAW's 1946 convention, "In our plant, and I guess it is the same in most plants, we have women laid off with seniority . . . and every day they hire in new men off the street. They hire men there, they say, to do the heavy work. The women do light work. During the war they didn't care what kind of work we did, and still we have to work on hard jobs now, and some of the men with lesser seniority get on the small jobs."[54]

Explicit job classification by sex was still standard practice during this period, so management could simply reclassify jobs from female to male (or from light to heavy) to justify not recalling women. Protective legislation, which had been eased in many states due to the wartime labor shortage, was also used to reclassify jobs.[55] As Mildred Jeffrey recalled, "There were all sorts of excuses. That many of them [women] were on 'war work' and now it was a different job, different product, etc. Or, 'we can't hire women for second shift.' Oh, another dodge that was used over and over again was weight lifting. . . . Now that, I say, was absurd, because nobody, no plant or retail store ever had observed that [protective] legislation. But that would be used. . . . They grabbed at anything they could to deny the opportunity for recall."[56]

Management's determination to oust women from the plants became glaringly evident when the initial failure to recall women in line with seniority was corrected in response to union complaints. In such cases, the women were rehired, but once back in the plant they were subjected to intense managerial harassment involving techniques similar to those used in the earlier discriminatory layoffs. A letter from two women who worked at a Ford plant in Memphis, Tennessee is a representative complaint. "Every woman in the plant has been discriminated against," wrote Jennie Lee Murphy and Minnie Sowell:

When we are called back to work we are placed on the heaviest jobs available. Burnadette Dennis was called to work April 12, 2 men were . . . called at the same time. These men were placed on the trim line, Miss Dennis on the chassis line. Mr. McKinnon said, "That is the very job for you." He also said to her and to Mrs. Emma Howell that women were not wanted at Fords. . . . He personally conducts the girls through the plant and points out how hard the work is before they check in. . . .

April 10 I was called into Labor Relations because of my inability to hang car tops weighing 97 pounds. I picked up a side of the top and moved it about 5 feet and turned it over and pasted insulating in the top, but I was unable to then turn it straight up and walk about 10 feet and hang them in the ceiling. Lots of the men cannot do it. Mr. Perkins said I was to be given one more chance and if I couldn't do it I would have to quit or he would discharge me. I pointed out to him that men came to work on April 10, with less seniority than I and they were given window washing jobs. I asked him to move me to

one of those jobs for my benefit and the good of the company but he told me
flatly he would not move me. April 11 I was discharged along with another
girl on the same job.

   These women didn't stop eating when the war stopped, and the widows of
the soldiers need jobs worse than ever. We have offered to stay out of the plant
until the heavy jobs were filled, but this is no solution because even now girls
are placed on the heaviest jobs and the men lighter ones to run us out.[57]

Here the idiom of sex-typing, according to which women were suitable only
for "light" jobs, was turned on its head in the service of employers' determination to exclude women with seniority from postwar employment. Automotive management now assigned the jobs most remote from this criterion—the
heaviest and most difficult work—to women.

   Such incidents took place at many auto firms during the reconversion period.[58] Although it is difficult to document the process through which this
assault on women's job rights was developed and implemented, there does not
seem to have been much division on the matter within management's ranks.
From the shop-floor level on up, management marshaled a range of tactics to
reconstitute the prewar sexual division of labor. The results were unambiguous.
At General Motors, less than thirty-two thousand women were employed in
November 1945, about 16 percent of the firm's total work force; two years
earlier, the one-hundred-and-seventeen thousand GM women workers had constituted 32 percent of the total. The dropoff at Ford was even more dramatic.
At the peak of the war boom in November 1943, forty-two thousand women
had been employed there, comprising 22 percent of the work force. By January
1946, their numbers had shrunk to only forty-nine hundred, or 4 percent of
all Ford workers.[59]

   In contrast to auto, management in electrical manufacturing did not seek to
exclude women from postwar employment. Immediately after the war, to be
sure, women were laid off more often than men. In the industry's communication equipment branch, for example, two-thirds of all workers displaced in
the month after V-J Day were female, although in July 1945 women made up
less than 60 percent of the labor force in this industry segment. In electrical
machinery manufacturing, similarly, women were 60 percent of the workers
released after V-J Day, but only 40 percent of those employed in July.[60] There
was a permanent drop in the proportion of women among electrical production
workers overall, from 50 percent of the war peak to about 40 percent in the
postwar period (Table 5).

   Thus far the story seems to resemble that in auto. The difference was that
the electrical manufacturers were eager to rehire women once consumer goods
production commenced. In a study of women war workers' postwar work
experiences in Baltimore, the U.S. Women's Bureau found that nearly one-
half of those women who had been employed in electrical plants in 1944 were

working in the same plants in the fall of 1946. Although some had been laid off temporarily after V-J Day, they were later recalled to work. The study found that women workers were more likely to remain with their wartime employer after the war in electrical manufacturing than in any other war industry. Indeed, a representative of a major Baltimore electrical firm told the Bureau that he preferred to hire women with experience in the industry.[61] Similarly, in New York State, women's employment increased more in the electrical industry than in any other durable goods industry between April 1946 and April 1947. "Assembly work and other semi-skilled factory jobs . . . require the dexterity for which women are very well adapted," the New York State Department of Labor suggested. "Women received good training during the war and employers have commented favorably on the work efficiency of women on these jobs."[62] Still another study of women after V-J Day in Bridgeport, Connecticut, also found that women maintained their employment in the electrical industry at close to the wartime level.[63]

Women's access to employment in electrical manufacturing then, was not jeopardized after the war, in sharp contrast to what happened in auto. However, the position of women *within* the electrical industry did change between the war and postwar periods. While occasionally women permanently replaced men on jobs they had taken over during the war, far more frequently they were eliminated from "men's jobs" and transferred to lower-paid jobs that had always been performed by women. Employer representatives at one Baltimore electrical plant told a U.S. Women's Bureau investigator in 1946 that the jobs newly opened to women during the war—such as lathe, drill press, and other machine operations; tool room work; and testing—were now considered "men's work" again, and that no women had been kept on such jobs after the war. Similarly, in Bridgeport, the openings available to women in electrical factories were in "old-line women's jobs" like punch press operation and assembly. "We will keep women on assembly, and replace women with men on machines," stated an electrical machinery plant manager in 1944, in reply to a query about his firm's postwar plans for women.[64]

The removal of women from the high-paying "men's jobs" in the industry resembled what happened in auto in that women found themselves earning substantially less after the war, although most could remain in the electrical industry if they so desired. In New York City, 87 percent of all jobs available for women in the electrical industry in December 1945 were unskilled and paid between 50 and 60 cents an hour. In take-home pay, that was less than what many women UE members could collect in unemployment insurance from their war jobs. The majority of women who found postwar jobs in the industry, according to one survey, suffered pay cuts averaging 17 percent.[65] Women not only earned less, but they also preferred their war jobs to the traditional "women's jobs" in the industry. One complained that her postwar position as a bench assembler was inferior to her war job as a solderer in the same plant. The bench work involved stripping rubber from cords, which was hard on her hands, and she now was trained not to exercise skill but instead to "work up speed" to earn the piecework bonus.[66]

Another aspect of the reconstruction of prewar management policies toward women in electrical manufacturing was the revival of age and marital status as criteria for female employment. One Baltimore electrical manager explained to the U.S. Women's Bureau in 1946 that his firm did not hire any women more than thirty-five years old because after that age, "according to tests, their muscles stiffen" and they are less efficient than younger women. Similarly, the Newark, New Jersey, GE plant refused to employ women over age twenty-five. There was also discrimination against married women in plants where this had been prewar policy, sometimes by agreement with local unions. At GE in Newark, married women were barred by management policy, and at the Westinghouse plant in East Springfield, Massachusetts, a clause in the UE contract provided that married women hired during the war could not acquire seniority rights.[67] Such practices were less widespread than before the war and gradually declined over the postwar period. They are significant, however, as part of the broader revival of prewar managerial policy.

In both the auto and electrical industries, then, management reconstructed the prewar sexual division of labor. The key difference between the two industries was that in auto, few peacetime jobs had been defined as female, so that the hundreds of thousands of women employed in the industry during the war were permanently ejected from it afterward. Women were not denied access to employment in this way in electrical manufacturing, but they were eliminated from the "men's jobs" they did during the war and transferred into less desirable "women's jobs." Lola Weixel, a UE member who worked as a welder during the war, recalled her experience in trying to find a new welding job after the war. "I went to one place and, I remember, they laughed at me. They thought it was funny again. It was just as though it had been four years previous, and they had never heard of a woman welder."[68] Indeed, in both industries, only a short time after the conclusion of the military conflict, employers behaved as if the wartime incorporation of women into "men's jobs" had never taken place.

Managerial Policy Toward Women Workers during the War—and After

Why did this reversion to the prewar sexual division of labor occur? Why was management so determined to oust women from the positions that they had occupied during the war? Women war workers wanted to keep their jobs, and union seniority policies did not stand in the way of hiring women, yet they

16. Woman working on wires used in an electrical relay, Gilbert and Barker Mfg. Co., West Springfield, Massachusetts, c. 1950. (Wayne State University Labor Archives)

17. Women making automobile upholstery in a De Soto factory, Warren, Michigan, c. 1950. (Wayne State University labor Archives)

were purged. The problem is all the more puzzling in light of contemporary evidence that management was highly satisfied with women war workers' abilities and performance. While initially employers had strenuously resisted replacing men with women in war industries, once having reconciled themselves to the inevitable, they seemed very pleased with the results. Moreover, because sex differentials in wages, although smaller than before, persisted during the war, one might expect management to have seriously considered the possibility of permanent female substitution on economic grounds.

There is no doubt that women's wartime performance proved satisfactory to management. Under the impact of the "manpower" crunch in the seven months following Pearl Harbor, the proportion of jobs for which the nation's employers were willing to consider women rose from 29 to 55 percent. And management praised women's industrial performance extravagantly during the mobilization period. "Women keep piling up evidence that they *can do,* and *do well,* a multitude of jobs," proclaimed the American Management Association in a 1943 report. "The distribution of basic aptitudes between the two sexes does not differ to any appreciable extent. . . . What is needed is *training*— training to develop latent aptitudes, to increase mechanical knowledge and skill, and to overcome any fear of the machine."[69]

In the auto industry, management attitudes changed dramatically as the number of women workers increased. "The consciousness of the capability of women is growing all through the industry, reported George Romney, then the head of the Automotive Council for War Production, in June 1942. He cited as evidence a discussion of women's employment at a meeting of automotive employers held a short time before in which the idea of female substitution was pursued to its logical extreme. "One of the fellows said, 'Where will we have any use for men?' 'Why should there be any men?' One fellow said, 'At least one thing a man can still do better than a woman, and that is being a father.' That is where they wound up in their discussion."[70]

A 1943 article, "Why We Like Women in Our Shop," by W. G. Guthrie, the works manager of GM's Allison Division, claimed that women were better workers than men. Not only were women "more precise . . . more dexterous . . . better on repetitive work . . . and . . . more patient than men," Guthrie claimed, but they were also "more conscientious . . . less likely to loaf on the job . . . often more loyal to the company . . . and . . . less inclined toward radicalism or agitation."[71] And the New York *Daily News* reported that, according to "Henry Ford's efficiency experts," women workers hired to do the work of men in the four largest Ford plants had "job for job . . . outproduced the men in most cases."[72]

In electrical manufacturing, where women were a more familiar element, their proficient performance was less often remarked upon. But in the segments of the industry that had been predominantly male in the prewar era, managers were explicit in their enthusiasm for women war workers. "A woman can do everything a man can do," said one employer at a New York electrical machinery plant in 1944. In the Connecticut Valley, similarly, "employers often stated that, contrary to every expectation, women had filled some male jobs quite as efficiently as men and sometimes more so." At one electrical factory there, for example, women crane operators "proved more meticulously obedient to the signals of the riggers on the floor and therefore were more reliable; as wrappers in the packing room women were at least as proficient as men."[73]

During the war, there were numerous testimonials from management that women's production record exceeded men's on the same or similar jobs. In a 1943 National Industrial Conference Board survey of 146 executives, nearly 60 percent stated without qualification that women's production was equal to or greater than that of men on similar work. Similarly, a study by the Bureau of Employment Security of several California war plants found an increase in production per hour of workers of both sexes, and a lowering of costs per hour when women were employed, in every plant studied. The BES study also found that women were easier to supervise, and that labor turnover and accident rates decreased with the introduction of women.[74]

Many traditional management policies toward women workers were revised or eliminated with their successful incorporation into war industry. For example, physical segregation of the sexes was no longer deemed necessary; the belief "that men and women could work satisfactorily side by side" was held by the majority of executives questioned by the magazine *Modern Industry* as early as mid-1942. There were also many efforts to promote women to supervisory posts, especially at the lower levels, although women were almost never given authority over male workers, and there was a lingering conviction that women workers themselves preferred male bosses.[75]

Women workers' wartime performance, then, stood as evidence that they could be successfully incorporated into the industrial labor force. In addition, wage differentials between the sexes persisted during the war years—a consideration that one might expect to have enhanced management's interest in retaining women permanently in the postwar era. The unions, to be sure, had successfully contested sex discrimination in wages in many "equal pay for equal work" cases before the War Labor Board. But although sex differentials were narrowed as a result of these struggles, they were not eliminated. The Conference Board's composite earnings index for twenty-five manufacturing industries registered only a modest increase in the ratio of female to male average hourly earnings, from 61.5 percent in 1941 to 66.4 percent in 1945.[76]

In war industries, where female substitution was particularly extensive, the narrowing of wage differentials was correspondingly greater. In 1945, the average straight-time hourly wage for radio manufacturing workers was 76 cents for women and 99 cents for men, whereas in the electrical generating and distribution equipment industry, women averaged 80 cents and men $1.09—in both cases a female to male ratio of about 75 percent, considerably higher than the typical prewar ratio.[77] Still, women's labor remained cheaper than men's in the electrical industry as a whole. In auto, too, sex differentials were narrowed, but not eliminated, during the war. In August 1944, women's average straight-time hourly wage in Michigan's auto plants was 90 percent of men's.[78] Here the differential was narrowed much more than in electrical manufacturing, primarily because the latter had many more low-wage "women's jobs" that were untouched by the equal pay for equal work struggles.

Still, because men and women rarely did "equal work" even during the war, the outcome of successful WLB equal pay cases was to narrow sex differentials in wages, not to eliminate them. And the Board's equal pay policy was not fully enforced, so that even when jobs were identical, or nearly so, women were often paid less than men. The Conference Board found differentials in starting rates paid to men and to "women hired for men's jobs" in nearly half the one hundred and forty-eight plants that it surveyed in 1943, well after equal pay "for comparable quality and quantity of work" had become official WLB policy. Of the ninety-two plants in the survey that had systems of automatic progression in wage rates, twenty-five had sex differentials built into the progression systems despite the fact that the WLB had declared this practice improper.[79]

Similarly, a study of women's wages by the New York State Department of Labor found that 40 percent of the 143 plants surveyed had different starting rates for men and women on "men's jobs." When the state's investigators asked employers to account for such differences, most simply referred to "tradition," standard practice, prevailing wage rates, and custom. "It's also cheaper," said one manager.[80] When employers in basic industry overcame their initial reluctance to hire women to do "men's jobs," it was out of necessity, not a desire to save on wage costs—but they were well compensated for their acquiescence. Once having realized so substantial a savings, one might expect management to have wished to preserve it through permanent female substitution.

There were some extra costs associated with the employment of women, to be sure, particularly in previously all-male plants. Women's absenteeism was generally higher than men's, especially if they were married and had domestic responsibilities, although employers succeeded in narrowing or even eliminating the gap in some plants.[81] UAW President R. J. Thomas, summarizing the reasons auto industry employers were reluctant to hire women for postwar jobs, noted other costs associated with expanding or introducing female employment in a plant. "First is that as you know on most jobs equal rates are paid for equal jobs today," he pointed out. "Management doesn't want to pay women equal rates with men. Not only that but in many of these plants additional facilities have to be put in, such as toilet facilities to take care of women. More space has to be taken to give an opportunity of changing clothes and more safety measures have to be instituted. I think it is pretty well recognized that it is an additional expense to a management to have women."[82]

This is an accurate rendition of the reasons auto industry managers themselves adduced for their reluctance to employ women. Yet it is an inadequate explanation for managerial hostility toward female employment. The costs of maintaining special "facilities" for women were largely absorbed by the government during the war, and could hardly have been a major financial consideration in any event. Surely the savings associated with sex differentials in pay would outweigh any expense firms would incur in continuing to maintain such facilities. Indeed, if only the direct economic costs and benefits of female employment are taken into account, one would expect management to have consistently discriminated *in favor of* women and against men in postwar layoffs and rehiring. Particularly in view of the vigorous efforts of employers to increase labor productivity in the reconversion period, management should have preferred to retain women permanently in the "men's jobs" they had just demonstrated their ability to perform.[83]

Industrial employers chose the opposite course, however, defying not only the apparent imperatives of economic rationality, but also the stated preference of women war workers to keep their war jobs and the unions' official policy that layoffs and rehiring be done strictly by seniority. Rather than institutionalizing the wartime incorporation of women into male jobs, management returned to its prewar practices. There was a slightly greater degree of permanent female substitution in electrical manufacturing than in auto, but in both industries the net increase in women's representation in the labor force during the 1940s was modest and might well have occurred in the absence of the dramatic wartime events.

The Roots of Management's Postwar Policy

In retrospect, then, management's determination to restore the *status quo ante* seems altogether irrational. Yet from the perspective of employers themselves at the time, it was a foregone conclusion. Management viewed the successful performance of women war workers as, at best, the fortunate outcome of an experiment in which it had participated with great trepidation and only because there was no alternative. To be sure, women had proved better workers than anyone had expected during the war. But now men's jobs were men's jobs once more. The ideology of sex-typing emerged triumphant again, defining the postwar order along prewar lines in both auto and electrical manufacturing.

   In part, the explanation for management's postwar policy involves the logic of the sexual division of labor as it had first developed within the auto and electrical industries a half-century earlier. Not only did the traditions of sex-typing established then have a continuing influence in the post-World War II period, but the factors that had originally shaped those traditions remained salient. In auto, wage levels were still high relative to other industries and would continue to increase in the postwar decades. As in the prewar years, automotive management's efforts to boost productivity focused on tightening control over labor, not on reducing pay levels.[84] Under these conditions, female substitution had little to recommend it, and employers continued to indulge the conviction, rooted in the historic—and still compelling—logic of Fordism, that women simply were not suitable for employment in automotive production jobs.

   In electrical manufacturing too, prewar traditions of sex-typing persisted in the postwar. But in this industry, the prewar sexual division of labor was historically rooted in a logic of feminization linked to labor-intensity and piecework systems. So why should the further extension of feminization during the war have been rolled back? Even in the case of the automobile industry, why was there a permanent departure from prewar tradition in regard to black employment while the sexual division of jobs persisted virtually unaltered? The historical, industry-specific logic of sex-typing seems to constitute only a partial explanation for management's postwar determination to reconstruct the prewar order.

   It is tempting to look outside of the industrial setting to the arena of family and social reproduction in seeking a better solution to the conundrum of management's postwar policies. The interest of capital in reconstructing a family structure in which women are responsible for the generational and daily reproduction of the working class, one might argue, ruled out the permanent employment of women in the well-paid manufacturing jobs that they had during the war. In this view, if women—and more significantly, married women—were to be employed outside the home in ever-increasing numbers in the postwar era, it was crucial that they be confined to poorly paid, secondary jobs that would not jeopardize their primary allegiance to family.

   The difficulty with this line of argument is in specifying how the presumed interest of collective capital in reconstituting traditional family forms was translated into the actual employer policies with respect to women workers that emerged in this period. The historical record offers no evidence that such familial considerations played a role in shaping managerial policy in the postwar transition.[85] Although the idea that "woman's place is in the home" was pervasive in the postwar period, it was seldom invoked by employers as a justification for restoring the prewar sexual division of jobs. Instead, management tended to define the issue in economic terms and, above all, by reference to women's physical characteristics and supposed inability to perform "men's jobs."

Although it would be extremely difficult to demonstrate that management policy was rooted in conscious concern over social reproduction, there is evidence for a different kind of explanation: that the postwar purge of women from "men's jobs" involved employers' assessment of the implications of their policies toward women for labor relations. The wartime struggles over equal pay indicated that the unions were committed to resisting any effort to substitute women for men in order to take advantage of their historically lower wages. If wage savings could not be garnered from substitution, or if they could only be garnered at substantial political cost, then why attempt to preserve the wartime sexual division of jobs after the war? In addition, given the widespread fear of postwar unemployment, management might reasonably have anticipated that unemployed male workers would be a source of potential political instability, given the working-class cultural ideal of the "family wage" and the obvious ambivalence of male unionists about women's postwar employment rights.

In short, management had good reason to believe that a wholesale postwar reorganization of the sexual division of labor, in defiance of the wartime assurances that women were in "men's jobs" only for the duration, could precipitate widespread resistance from labor. The unions were at the peak of their strength at this time, and at the war's end they were no longer constrained by the no-strike pledge. As one contemporary analyst noted, consideration of labor's reaction figured prominently in employers' postwar policies:

> Employers in plants where women had long been assigned to some jobs were disposed favorably to widening the fields of work open to women, unless the job dilutions had proved complicated and costly. In fact, union men declared that some companies, unless prevented by organized labor, would try to continue to use women on men's work because they could be hired at lower initial base pay, be upgraded more slowly, and would be throughout more docile. With the installation of mechanical aids, which using women had necessitated, already paid for out of war profits, management had frequently no particular reason to oppose keeping women on. . . . Yet most companies frankly admitted that, given full freedom of choice after the war, if only out of deference to prevailing male opinion in the shops, management would revert to giving men's jobs, so called, only to men. *And employers generally assumed that labor would permit no choice.*[86]

Understanding management's postwar policy in these terms helps explain why, in the auto case, women and blacks were treated differently. Despite their common history of exclusion from most auto jobs in the prewar era, the two groups stood in very different positions at the war's end. Organized feminism was at its nadir in the 1940s, and the labor movement's commitment to sexual equality was limited, so that management had little reason to fear that purging women from the industry would meet with substantial political opposition. In contrast, at least in the North, there was a large and vital black civil rights movement, which enjoyed substantial UAW support and from which management could expect vigorous protests if it pursued racially discriminatory employment policies.[87]

Only a few years earlier, when blacks were first hired in large numbers in Detroit's auto factories during the war mobilization, white workers had been vocal in their opposition, most notably in the numerous hate strikes which erupted in the plants and in the race riot of the summer of 1943.[88] But during the war, Detroit became a stronghold of the civil rights movement. The Motor City had the largest branch of the National Association for the Advancement of Colored People (NAACP) of any city in the nation, with a membership of twenty thousand by 1943, and the UAW had become a strong ally of the NAACP and other civil rights groups. While racial discrimination persisted in the auto industry in regard to promotion to the elite skilled trades, no one contested blacks' claims to semi-skilled jobs in the aftermath of the war.[89]

The sharp regional variation in racial patterns of hiring within the auto industry suggests the critical importance of the political dimension in shaping management's employment policies. Although the proportion of blacks in Detroit's auto plants rose dramatically in the 1940s and 1950s, reaching well over 25 percent of the production work force by 1960, in the nation as a whole the percentage of nonwhite auto workers grew much more modestly, from 4 percent in 1940 to only 9 percent in 1960. The national figures reflect the continuing practice of excluding blacks from employment in southern plants. As a manager at a GM plant in Atlanta told the *Wall Street Journal* in 1957, "When we moved into the South, we agreed to abide by local custom and not hire Negroes for production work. This is no time for social reforming and we're not about to try it."[90]

The situation of women auto workers was entirely different from that of northern blacks. Although the incorporation of women into the industry during the war had not provoked riots or hate strikes, this was primarily because female employment was explicitly understood to be a temporary expedient, "for the duration" only. After the war, women were expected to go "back to the home." There was no parallel expectation regarding black men. And while women war workers wanted to remain in the auto industry, as we have seen, their preferences (unlike blacks') lacked legitimacy. While black workers had the civil rights movement behind them, there was no mass feminist movement or even popular consciousness of women's job rights at this critical juncture, when the sexual division of labor that would characterize the postwar period was crystallizing.

As it turned out, in both the auto and electrical industries, there were protests against the postwar purges of women from "men's jobs." These are the focus of the following chapter, which traces the trajectory of the political struggles that did emerge over women's postwar position in the labor force, analyzes the distinct form these struggles took in the auto and electrical industries, and suggests the reasons why in both cases they were generally unsuccessful. This helps to illuminate the political logic of management's reconstruction of the prewar sexual division of labor and shows how and why the unique opportunity of the demobilization era to radically alter women's position in industry was lost.

8 Resistance to Management's Postwar Policies

Conventional historical accounts of the postwar demobilization presume that women workers did not actively resist management's effort to reconstruct the prewar sexual division of labor.[1] Indeed, although the available records are fragmentary, it seems that there were few organized protests. Women workers often lacked the time, energy, and political skills necessary, and knew that it would be difficult to succeed in such a venture. Moreover, in the absence of a mass feminist movement, and in an era when few workers believed that women should have the same job rights as men, sex discrimination seemed perfectly legitimate.

Yet female unionists did, under certain conditions, challenge management's postwar policies. To be sure, because of the many forces arrayed against them, such efforts failed more often than they succeeded. And even where they achieved their goals, the results were modest. Protest typically focused on the job placements of individuals or relatively small groups of workers. Even in the rare cases where women challenged the overall structure of job segregation, the results were incremental improvements at best.

Virtually all of the protests against managerial sex discrimination in the postwar transition emanated from the labor movement. But the war's end also brought new attacks on union power, so that the political space for struggles over the sexual division of labor was limited. Moreover, male workers and unionists often colluded in the postwar expulsion of women from "men's jobs," directly undercutting women's efforts to defend themselves against such sex discrimination.[2] Yet, in some instances, women workers succeeded in mobilizing male union members in opposition to management's effort to restore the prewar sexual division of labor. Serious attention to the circumstances under which such unity between men and women workers was forged, and to the other conditions that facilitated effective resistance to managerial discrimination, is essential for understanding the postwar transition.

If few effective protests emerged, that there were any at all reveals the fluidity of the postwar situation. Reconstruction of the prewar sexual division of labor was not inevitable, but a product of complex political processes. To understand why it occurred, we must examine the ways in which women and men defined their interests with respect to the postwar sexual division of labor, how the definition of those interests varied under different conditions, and the political resources with which those interests were pursued. Exploring these issues will not only contextualize the exceptional cases where resistance was effective, but also, and more important, it will help to explain why more sustained opposition was lacking.

As in earlier periods, struggles over the sexual division of labor after the war took different forms in auto and electrical manufacturing. In auto, the main battlefront was the seniority system: Women protested layoffs out of line with seniority and management's failure to recall women with seniority as postwar production got underway. Women in the UAW mobilized their male co-workers to join their protests by arguing that the defense of women's seniority rights was merely sound trade unionism. As Tribly Riopelle of UAW Local 600 put it in 1945, "By throwing women out of the plant, management will set a precedent for breaking seniority rules that would soon spread and we would have no union. . . . Some of us [women] are a lot better trade unionists than some of the men."[3] This type of appeal, which sought to unite men and women on the basis of shared class interest, galvanized the postwar protests against discrimination in auto.

Postwar struggles over the position of women were more diverse in the electrical industry. In heavy electrical equipment plants that relied predominantly on male labor, the situation resembled that in auto, and protest focused on defending women's seniority rights. But this was relatively rare. Most postwar struggles over women's seniority in the electrical industry involved the question of *married* women's job rights. This was a conflict internal to the female labor market in the industry, rather than pitting male and female workers against one another, as in auto. As we saw in chapter 7, most electrical manufacturing employers were eager to rehire women war workers in the industry's traditional "female" jobs after the war. While wages and working conditions in such jobs were inferior to those women had enjoyed in wartime, in most cases there was no contractual basis for protesting such downgrading of women war workers, and it was seldom challenged.

In electrical manufacturing, not seniority, but equal pay for comparable worth was the central focus of struggle over the postwar sexual division of labor. We saw in chapter 5 how the equal pay conflicts in this industry developed in the course of the war, culminating in the 1945 War Labor Board comparable worth case against GE and Westinghouse. The issue was then carried over into the UE's massive 1946 strike against the electrical companies. There was a major postwar strike in auto, too, the famous "open the books" confrontation with General Motors. But the issue of women's job rights was not involved in the GM strike, and indeed it diverted energies from the concurrent struggles over women's seniority. In contrast, the issue of sex differentials in wages was an important aspect of the postwar electrical strike, and its resolution significantly affected women's position.

The UE had a more sweeping vision of change in the sexual division of labor than the UAW. But it was not much more successful in achieving practical results. The postwar split in the electrical workers' union was one major obstacle to change. Both the UAW and the UE had a history of internal factionalism, and in both it flared anew at the war's end. But whereas in auto the triumph of the Reuther caucus initiated an era of relatively peaceful industrial relations, the bitter factional rivalry in the electrical industry took the form of dual unionism. And as the UE and IUE battled, management's power flourished as never before. Just when the auto magnates were proclaiming their willingness to live peacefully with the UAW, the electrical employers were embracing the "take it or leave it" policy made famous by GE's Lemuel Boulware. The UE's comparable worth campaign stood little chance of success in this context.

In both industries, union activists faced an uphill battle in seeking to defend women's rights in the postwar transition. Not only did they have to find ways to mobilize women war workers, who were dispersed by reconversion layoffs, overburdened with family responsibilities, and often lacking in political experience. They also had to persuade male unionists to oppose rather than collude in the managerial reconstruction of the prewar sexual division of labor. Only where a unified work force could be mobilized in active resistance to management's policy did the campaign to preserve women workers' wartime gains have any hope of success.

The Seniority Issue and Women Auto Workers' Job Rights

Unifying the work force across gender lines was particularly difficult in the auto industry, where the desire for postwar jobs pitted women war workers directly against men. Knowing that women would be hardest hit by reconversion layoffs, female UAW activists focused on mobilizing support for enforcement of women's contractual seniority rights (limited as these were) in both layoffs and recalls. The "seniority resolution" passed by the December 1944 UAW Women's Conference simply urged the union to be vigilant with respect to management's treatment of women. "Far too few managements as they map their postwar production schedules are planning to employ large numbers of women workers," it read. "If such discrimination on the part of employers is to be overcome, the Union has a serious responsibility in eliminating any practices or policies over which they have control and which in any way may contribute to unfair or unjust treatment of women."[4]

It became apparent right away, however, that male unionists were not likely to pressure management to recall women with seniority unless there was considerable prodding from the women themselves. "Women are going to have to fight and fight hard to get their fair and equal seniority protection both in the layoff period and certainly when it comes to rehiring," noted Mildred Jeffrey, then head of the UAW Women's Bureau, in mid-1945. "Unless women demonstrate now that they are not going to take discrimination lying down, we are going to be in a much weaker position to combat it later on."[5]

A delegation of women from five Detroit locals showed up at the July 1945 UAW Executive Board meeting in Minneapolis to demand enforcement of the union's official policy of nondiscrimination in seniority. They also wanted "equal rights" for women in the UAW, specifically greater female representation in both the locals and the International. This "militant petticoat brigade," as it was dubbed by the *Detroit Times,* was made up of local officeholders who had already begun the fight to enforce women's seniority rights at the local level. In the face of management intransigence, they now sought the support of the UAW's top decision-making body.[6]

However, the Executive Board refused to even admit them to its meeting. "The inference we got from the board, and strongly, was: Just who do you women think you are?" the women complained. "The answer to that is: Dues paying members who wanted to talk to the top officers about how we are being discriminated against." Outraged, the delegates charged the union officials with "pushing us around more than management ever thought of doing," and vowed to "get even with the union brass hats by organizing all the women within the union." Local 600's Tribly Riopelle inveighed, "We are making the bullets now, and we will give the board members a blast that will blow them out of their shoes." This, the women promised, would be "a revolution the union will never forget."[7]

The UAW Executive Board's rebuff of the women's delegation made it clear that protecting women's seniority rights would require an extensive mobilization *within* the union. Within a week after their return from Minneapolis, the five delegates organized a meeting of women activists from nineteen Detroit-area locals and began their campaign, which became known as the UAW "Women's Revolt." Their central concern was the management assault on women's job rights. Riopelle told the *Detroit Times:* "Management is conducting a nationwide campaign to get women out of the factories, and we need our jobs. That is why we are organizing a women's division."[8] They also demanded that the UAW replace the Flint regional director, who was resigning that September, with a woman. Because regional directors automatically became Executive Board members, this would have led to female representation on the UAW's most powerful decision-making body for the first time.[9]

The strategy these women adopted was to appeal to the interest of their male co-workers in safeguarding the integrity of the seniority system as a whole. The task was to persuade the men that their *class* interest in protecting women's seniority rights was more compelling than their *gender* interest in colluding with management to oust women from the industry. The first step was to gain the support of the UAW's top leadership. At that level, the women's campaign enjoyed considerable success. In September 1945, the women were granted the hearing before the Executive Board that they had sought unsuccessfully three months earlier. There they extracted an official Board statement urging enforcement of nondiscriminatory seniority and calling for an end to union collusion with management. Shortly afterward, UAW president R. J. Thomas wrote to all the locals in support of the position the women had advocated. "If management is successful in disregarding seniority rights of women workers now, they will be in a stronger position to disregard seniority rights of other workers later on," he warned.[10]

Because of the UAW's tradition of local autonomy, however, this was a necessary but insufficient means of ensuring that women's seniority rights would be respected. Thomas's letter to the locals acknowledged this problem:

> It is unfortunately true that in some cases management has been successful because of the laxness of local unions. In one case, an entire department stopped working in protest when a woman was placed in the department on a job in line with her seniority and which she could perform. In another, until I intervened, the local was giving serious consideration to management's proposal that women's seniority should be terminated through payment of a bonus in the form of severance pay. In some locals, plant bargaining committees have failed to protect the seniority rights of stewardesses and committeewomen on the same basis as men. There have been several instances, too, in which separate seniority lists for men and women have been used to lay off all women before any men were laid off.
>
> The International union's policy is clear and unequivocal. *Every member must have the same and equal protection in line with the provisions of your contract.* I urge every local union to take immediate steps . . . to enforce our no discrimination policy.[11]

By itself, a letter from the union president would not stop local union collusion with management. But this was as much as the women activists could win from the Board. The next step was to see that the policy that Thomas's letter articulated was enforced at the local level.

Their prospects for success in that effort were often determined by the contractual seniority system that existed before demobilization began. Most

UAW locals had historically sought the largest possible seniority unit (plant-wide or, ideally, company-wide seniority), whereas management had pushed for the smallest unit in order to minimize transfers and "bumping" during layoffs and rehiring. In the 1940s, the prevailing arrangements were usually closer to the management ideal. Workers typically exercised seniority within "non-interchangeable occupational groups." These units could be located in a single department, a combination of departments (a building or division), a plant, or throughout the plants of a company (although this was rare). Each group consisted of a small number of occupations with similar skill and wage rates—for example, various kinds of welders or several types of assembly work. Workers' bumping rights were limited to positions within their occupational group. [12]

Insofar as jobs were sex-segregated, noninterchangeable occupational group seniority meant, *de facto,* a separate female seniority list. In addition, explicit provisions for separate women's lists still existed in some local contracts, although UAW women activists had succeeded in eliminating many of these during the war, and the union's national policy opposed the practice. Yet even when contracts did not formally provide for separate lists, women and men were often treated as noninterchangeable. "In our contract," explained W. G. Kult of UAW Local 72, "we have no separate seniority lists, although no female can replace a male, nor can a male replace a female, unless it is bargained between the Company and the Union." Similarly, in Local 172 the following arrangement prevailed:

> Seniority lists include both men and women listed by department and strictly according to date of hiring. In cases of lay-offs when such lay-offs involve men the youngest male employee in a department is laid off and the same is true when female help is to be laid off. In re-hiring the same procedure is followed. . . . If the job open is for male help and an older female is next on the list then her name is skipped and the oldest male employee called in. When the next female position is open she is the first one called. [13]

Given the rigidity of the boundaries between "women's" and "men's" jobs, some such arrangement was almost inevitable, even without separate seniority lists or occupational group seniority. But the war situation introduced special problems, for when women entered previously male occupations, their seniority status became extremely ambiguous. Some UAW locals expressed concern about this very early in the war. In July 1942, for example, an International Representative in Racine, Wisconsin wrote to UAW headquarters to inquire:

> Will the female hired if worked into the active seniority lists off [sic] all employees continue on her job after the War emergency is over and by so doing keep a male member off this job? Is it not at all possible if in some instances particularly in the smaller shops the female employees may exceed the male

employees in numbers and in turn pass union laws that would later in normal
times eliminate the men from those jobs previously done by men? For example
if a woman is hired prior to a man, and one seniority system prevails, she
would continue on after the male is laid off, even into peace time work?

We have many shops where two lists exist, this has helped us greatly in the
past to keep the women off the men's work. If they now become entrenched
within our seniority system how then will we be able to regulate this when
this War work is all over?[14]

There were several possible approaches to this dilemma. One is illustrated
by the wartime agreement between the Michigan Tool Company and the Mechanics' Educational Society of America (MESA), an independent union. It
provided that separate seniority lists be set up for women, that all women be
laid off before any man, and that all hiring advantages be given to men. In
1945, thirty-eight women who were adversely affected by this arrangement
were granted four weeks' severance pay in exchange for totally surrendering
their seniority rights. The Detroit War Labor Board ruled that the agreement
was legal, and the Regional WLB chairman praised it, saying, "We wish more
companies and unions would join in settling their grievances so sensibly." The
WLB maintained that the agreement was acceptable because the company
"expects" to produce items after the war involving parts weighing twenty
pounds, and the "male employees will have a productivity advantage."[15]

In response to pressure from women activists, the UAW formally protested
the MESA decision, arguing that it violated earlier WLB precedents banning
sex discrimination.[16] Yet there were also UAW contracts that permitted the
same kind of exclusionism, albeit less blatantly. For example, the national
agreement between the UAW and GM, the industry's largest employer, provided that women doing "men's jobs" would accumulate temporary seniority,
applicable only during the war. This meant that women laid off from GM
plants during reconversion could not apply their seniority to any peacetime
jobs unless they had worked for the firm before the war (in which case their
wartime seniority could be applied to their old positions).[17] Under this contractual arrangement, GM had little difficulty reconstructing the prewar sexual
division of labor as consumer automobile production resumed.

There was one struggle over women's job rights at GM. It involved women
hired *after* the war at the firm's Pontiac plant. Male labor was scarce at Pontiac
during the spring and summer of 1946, and so GM hired 150 women. Management, just as it had during the war, viewed hiring women as a temporary
expedient, and proposed an agreement with the local union giving the women
a different status from their male co-workers. But UAW Local 653 refused to
accept this—whereupon the company fired all the women just before their
probationary period was completed. The local then filed a grievance alleging
that the firings were discriminatory and won reinstatement for the 150 women.

Della Rymer, a member of the Local 653 Executive Board and a leader in the UAW Women's Revolt the previous year, played a key role in bringing this about.[18]

This effort significantly altered the position of women in the Pontiac plant. But the unusual circumstances under which the women were hired meant that the campaign for their reinstatement was not reproducible at other GM plants, where women were not hired in significant numbers after the war. Indeed, a crucial precondition for the emergence of a challenge to management's postwar policies was a seniority system that gave women job recall rights. If the union contract called for separate seniority lists, or, as at GM, temporary wartime seniority, there was no basis upon which women could mobilize support within the union, no matter how much they wanted to keep their jobs after the war. As a result, while things were quiet at GM, struggles for women's job rights took place frequently at Ford, Chrysler, and various smaller companies.

There was a dramatic protest over women's seniority rights at the Ford Highland Park plant. Thousands of women war workers there were laid off after V-J Day, and inexperienced men were hired in their places as production picked up again. Management failed to recall even those women with seniority rights dating back to the prewar years, claiming that women could not do the jobs that were available. Women activists in UAW Local 400 actively protested against this and persuaded the local union leaders to support them. In late 1945, 150 women picketed the plant's employment office, and the issue was taken up in negotiations between the company and the local union. Eventually, several hundred women were recalled to the plant on jobs that women were "permitted" to do (according to the protective legislation then in effect).[19]

Meanwhile, UAW Local 174 members at the Commerce Pattern Foundry and Machine Company on Detroit's West Side slowed down production and threatened a full-scale strike when the women who had worked there during the war were not recalled in line with seniority. Here too management claimed there was no work in the plant that women could do. Under the pressure exerted by the union, however, they recalled five women to work in the foundry. These women produced even more than the job standards required, leaving the company no alternative but to recall the other women as well.[20]

A third defense of women's seniority rights on the local level took place at Chrysler's Dodge Truck plant. After UAW Local 140 filed a grievance, thirty-one women who had been laid off at the war's end were recalled to work. Just like Ford and Commerce Pattern, Dodge had balked at hiring women, insisting that there were no jobs available that they could do. Once rehired, the women were harassed by management and then fired for "incompetence." The local then brought the case to the impartial appeals board and won reinstatement for the women, with back pay totaling $55,000.[21]

Successful resistance to managerial efforts to exclude women from postwar

18. Women picketing GM Ternstedt Plant #1 during national UAW strike against General Motors, Detroit, December 1945. (Wayne State University Labor Archives)

19. "A Complaint from the Women." Pickets at Employment Office Entrance, Ford Motor Co., Highland Park, Michigan, November 8, 1945. (National Archives)

jobs demanded constant vigilance by shop-floor activists and the support of local union officials. Even where contracts stipulated that women had seniority rights entitling them to postwar jobs, in the absence of active enforcement efforts, they could be excluded from the work force. Although some male unionists were committed to enforcing contract clauses protecting seniority women, most of the challenges to managerial sex discrimination came from women. Locals where women were especially active, indeed, were those most likely to protest violations of women's seniority rights.

In UAW Local 400, the women's committee led the fight for women's jobs that culminated in the picket line at the Highland Park employment office in November 1945. The women active in that struggle, which began well before V-J Day, were also prominent in the concurrent Women's Revolt, and worked closely with women unionists at other Ford plants in and near Detroit, where similar management policies toward women were in effect. Along with women activists from the River Rouge and Lincoln plants, the Local 400 women's committee appealed to the UAW's national Ford Department for assistance.[22]

Women were also active unionists at the Commerce Pattern Foundry and Machine Company, where the contractual seniority rights of female war workers were defended under threat of a strike. The account in *UAW-CIO Ammunition,* published by the union's Education Department, obliquely acknowledged this. "The West Side Local [174] has a woman's history," it reminded readers. "During the sitdown strikes the women . . . sat down to win equal pay for the men after they had won a boost for themselves. Since they sat down for us, we've got to stand up for them."[23]

There are no systematic data on the correspondence between women's union activism and the emergence of protests against management violations of women's seniority at the local level. In at least a few instances, male unionists initiated such struggles, as at Dodge Truck, for example.[24] Such men were motivated not so much by concern for women's job rights as by a commitment to the seniority principle. Many union officials objected to any seniority violations that came to their attention, regardless of the sex of the worker, and viewed management's assault on women's seniority as a dangerous precedent that threatened the seniority rights of all workers.

Women initiated most protests over women's job rights, but they could not succeed without the support of men. Because enforcing women's seniority rights under a union contract depended on local officers and stewards—an overwhelmingly male group—it was crucial to persuade these secondary union leaders that not only women's jobs but also the whole seniority principle was threatened by management's policies. The problems that this posed are well illustrated by what occurred at the Ford Highland Park plant. In April 1945, when 103 women were laid off out of line with seniority, women activists turned immediately to UAW Local 400 for help. However, the committeemen and building chairmen refused to write up their grievances. The women then appealed to the local president, John Carney. He wrote up the complaints, whereupon all 103 grievance forms, in triplicate, "mysteriously disappeared" from a committeeman's locker in the shop. Meanwhile, two members of the plant committee reportedly telephoned management and told them to go ahead with the layoffs, promising that no grievances would be filed.[25] And when the women's committee called a special plant-wide women's meeting, their male opposition stole the cards the committee had prepared for use in publicizing the meeting.[26]

In November, when women picketed the Highland Park Employment Office in protest against management's postwar policies, Ford managers told the press that local union officials had advised them to ignore the female pickets. "It has become apparent that some of our so-called union representatives voted us support with their tongues in their cheeks," complained Helen McLean, the chairman [*sic*] of the Local 400 women's committee, "for they have been systematically sabotaging our picket lines."[27] She brought the matter to the attention of the union's national convention in March 1946, commenting, "I am sorry to say that some of our Union representatives in my plant and the International Union have sided with the company."[28]

Others at that convention voiced similar complaints. Minnie Jones of Local 600, whose women members threatened later in 1946 to picket the *union* office if the local did not support their effort to defend women's seniority rights, told the convention delegates:

> We know we have been put out on the streets and people have been working on our jobs that have less seniority than we have. Some of our own Union men—I hate to say it, but it is so—say, "You should go back into your homes and cook on your stoves." Some don't have a stove to cook on, our husbands have died overseas. We have orphaned children to support and we are entitled to a decent wage and a decent living. . . . Certainly we are not going to work to organize the union and then go back to work for $15.00 a week.[29]

Joseph Biscay of Local 12 corroborated these accounts of collusion between management and male unionists and voiced support for the women's demands. "I think it is time that we considered this woman question the same as you consider the man question," he said. "We take their dollar; we take their dues. We take them in and give them the obligation just the same as the men, and then when it comes their turn to get laid off, or when management decides that, then we just kind of step aside and let the management get away with it. That is the attitude of a good many Local officers."[30]

Advocates within the UAW for the defense of women's seniority rights appealed to their fellow unionists not only on the basis of the longstanding CIO commitment to equality and nondiscrimination, but also by pointing to the self-interest of male workers in defending the seniority principle. In a leaflet publicizing the discrimination issue and calling a women's meeting to organize a protest, the Local 400 women's committee included a strong appeal to the men in the local. "LISTEN BROTHERS," it read. "We're Union Members Too—and We Intend to Stay that Way." The leaflet continued:

> The company is laying off women union members in violation of seniority. It isn't just a problem of the women, either. It's a union issue that concerns men, too. If the company is allowed to ignore the seniority provisions to do a job on one group—what's to prevent them from doing a job on you? Once the precedent is set what course will you follow if your group is singled out next? Will veterans be pitted against non-veterans? Foreign-born against American born? It's the old Ford Game! Don't be sucked in by company tricks![31]

Securing the support of men was clearly important, but the active involvement of women could not be taken for granted. Many of them perceived the union (sometimes all too accurately) as hostile to their postwar employment in the industry, and did not understand the potential protection that their seniority rights gave them under the union contract. "Many women feel as bitter toward the union as towards the Company," Helen McLean explained to the UAW's Executive Board. "Even tho [*sic*] a number of women are not fully acquainted with the details of seniority rights, they realize an injustice has been done them."[32] Women like McLean (and their male allies) faced an enormous organizational and educational task among workers of both sexes, as well as among union officials. It was not impossible to defend women's seniority rights on the local level, but it required shrewd and persistent organization to convince the rank and file that their true interest lay in the defense of the seniority system regardless of sex. In many cases, attempts to do this failed, so that an effective challenge to management could not be made.[33]

In Detroit, where the UAW had always been strongest, the women's seniority issue was most sharply defined and most vigorously pursued. Workers' understanding of such principles as nondiscrimination and the desirability of the broadest possible seniority unit was more advanced in the Motor City than elsewhere, both among rank-and-file activists and among union officials. Women UAW activists in Detroit had an edge on their counterparts in other cities in terms of both experience and mutual support in the postwar seniority battles, thanks to the 1945 city-wide Women's Revolt. Detroit men were also more easily won over to the women's cause because of their relatively strong commitment to the defense of seniority rights, regardless of sex.

Successfully combating management's assault on women auto workers on the local level, in short, required a contract that gave women equal seniority rights in layoffs and recalls, a core of union activists committed to the contract's enforcement, and an internal educational campaign to build support for women's seniority rights within the local union. It was rare that all these conditions were met, and even where they were, the best that could be hoped for was the protection of women who had accumulated seniority rights. Demanding that management also refrain from sex discrimination in hiring new workers—once the seniority lists were exhausted in the course of postwar expansion—was never on the agenda. While this would have been essential for the establishment of real equality in the occupational structure, it lacked the legitimacy that the protection of women war workers' seniority rights enjoyed in a period when women were not yet constituted as equal contenders in a competitive labor market.

Recognizing that conditions were seldom conducive to the success—or even the emergence—of struggles to enforce women's seniority rights, it remains important to assess the results of those that did materialize. How was the postwar sexual division of labor in auto affected by local union challenges to management's efforts to eliminate women from all production jobs other than those traditionally defined as female? To what degree did such challenges undercut the assumptions about "woman's place" in the work force upon which the edifice of job segregation by sex was constructed?

Numerically, the net results of even the most successful of these battles were trivial when viewed in the context of the auto industry as a whole, especially in light of the vast expansion of employment in the postwar years. At the Ford Highland Park plant, the protracted struggle to enforce women's seniority rights led to about four hundred women being recalled who otherwise would not have been between September 1946 and July 1947. The number of women who were not only reinstated, but who would also continue to work at the plant for a significant period of time was probably smaller. Even the number of women recalled was miniscule relative to the 5,300 women who had been laid off from the plant.[34] And this was one of the most *successful* challenges to management's postwar policy.

Certainly the gains to individual women recalled to jobs in the auto industry were substantial, and the sexual division of labor was different from that which management had sought to establish, in that these women occupied positions that would otherwise have gone to men. Yet the result was a marginal change in the sexual division of labor. Moreover, the postwar seniority struggles (like the mobilization-era conflicts over the sexual division of jobs) tended to take the idiomatic construction of "men's" and "women's" work as a reference point rather than challenging the ideology of sex-typing.

In launching their defense of women's job rights, women UAW activists developed a strong critique of management justifications for excluding women from postwar jobs, exposing the arbitrariness of the idiom of job assignment by sex. A leaflet produced by the Local 400 women's committee, for example, mercilessly ridiculed the managerial about-face from full acceptance of women workers during the war to its postwar hostility to women's employment. A cartoon in the leaflet depicted a Labor Relations man handing a quit slip to a distressed-looking women worker, with the caption, "Now that War is nearly over. . . . 'So Sorry.' Have suddenly remembered you are incapable of working in factory."[35]

As the protracted battles over women's seniority rights proceeded, however, and the focus of conflict narrowed to individual seniority cases, the women unionists abandoned this global critique of the idiom of sex-typing. As was discussed earlier, management approached the problem of purging women with seniority from the auto plants by reversing the usual application of the idiom, placing the women whom they were forced to recall on the jobs most remote from the criteria previously used to define "women's work."[36] Women's resistance to this put them in a difficult position. They could either demand "light work" assignments, in effect reinforcing management's view that the more difficult, "heavy" jobs were not suitable for *women as a group* (a view quite different from the actual situation, which was that many workers of *both* sexes—albeit more women than men—would find these physically demanding jobs difficult or impossible). Alternatively, the women affected could seek to demonstrate their abilities to do the most difficult jobs in the plant, implicitly accepting the idea that they should be tested by a standard most of their male counterparts were not required to meet. Wanita Allen, of the Ford Rouge plant, recalled the dilemma:

> [You'd say] "I think you're really a dog to give me a job like this." "Well, you wanted a job, didn't you? After all, if you'd stay at home. . . . This job, you know, is a man's job in the first place. They don't have no women's jobs out here now. The war is over. So you women just have to do . . . "
>
> "Yeah, but what about that man over there? That job, a child could do it."
>
> You'd be angry when they'd tell you [that], but there was nothing you could do.[37]

In Local 400, the issue seemed to be resolved shortly after the women picketed the plant employment office. A week and a half later, on November 19, 1945, the company agreed to "make a survey of all the potential jobs in the plant that women can do," and furthermore that "any suggestions from the union in regards to this matter would be accepted." Management also agreed to begin recalling women to jobs designated by the survey as appropriate for them.[38] Here the union was directly incorporated into the process of establishing the boundaries between "women's" and "men's" work in tacit recognition of the political dimension of the sexual division of labor. On the other hand, by accepting the idea of the job survey, the union directly bolstered the legitimacy of the idiom of sex-typing as rooted in physical job requirements.[39]

LISTEN, BROTHERS!
We're Union Members, Too—and We Intend to Stay That Way

Despite the efforts of the Ford Motor Company to turn women workers in the Highland Park plant against the union by carrying through a policy of discrimination, we intend to stick with our union and fight!

The company is laying off women union members in violation of seniority. It isn't just a problem of the women, either. It's a union issue that concerns men, too. If the company is allowed to ignore the seniority provisions to do a job on one group—what's to prevent them from doing a job on you? Once the precedent is set what course will you follow if your group is singled out next? Will veterans be pitted against non-veterans? Foreign-born against American-born? It's all the same! It's the old Ford Game! Don't be sucked in by company tricks!

LOOK, SISTER!
The Cartoon May Be Funny, But What's Happening to Us Isn't!

On April 20, the Ford Motor Company gave 103 women in the Bomber Wing Press Shop, slips reading: "Discharged, due to physical inability to perform job to which their seniority entitles them." The job in question is box car loading.

Under our new Interchangeable Occupational Seniority Agreement, known as Appendix A, workers can bump the employee with the least seniority, first in the occupational group, then in the labor pool.

In violation of the spirit and intent of the agreement the company interprets sections of the agreement to discriminate against groups of employees—in this instance, the women, in the future the men. The Company hypocritically implies that it is forced to interpret these sections in a discriminatory way. Our answer is:
WE WANT FAIR PLAY, NOT TECHNICALITIES!

When women with 2½ and 3 years seniority are laid off while probationary employees are still working in the plant there is foul play afoot no matter how many excuses are offered.

MAYBE YOU THINK YOU ARE GOING TO VACATION ON YOUR UNEMPLOYMENT COMPENSATION!

Well, the Company is fighting the claims of the women already laid off. Their legal staff is advising the Labor

Relations office how best to word the lay-off slips to avoid payment of benefits.

So there you are—not content with ignoring our seniority rights, the Company is out to chisel on our hard earned unemployment checks.

The first step in fighting these company tricks is to get together—to learn the facts, and to plan the fight! Let nothing stop you from attending the meeting Sunday! OUR JOBS ARE AT STAKE!

Issued by WOMEN'S COMMITTEE OF LOCAL 400, UAW-CIO

Pat McLean, chairman; Celia Paransky, vice-chairman; Caroline Garvey, secretary; Beatrice Madson, Lynne Moore, Janet Varrone, Gussie Oliver, Mary Vartanian, Sally Elias, Victoria Frederichs, Elvira Bivens, Beth Stuart, Dorothy Madson, Rose Shotenfelt, Hazel Hughes, Elizabeth Boehlin, Juanita Cunningham, and Tillie Martin.

PLANTWIDE MEETING
FOR WOME
—EXECUTIVE BOARD MEMBERS ARE INVITED

Sunday, May 6   2:30 PM
Northeastern High School   E. Warren at Grandy

20. Flyer for a meeting on sex-discriminatory layoffs called by the Women's Committee of UAW Local 400, Highland Park, Michigan, May 6, 1945. (Wayne State University Labor Archives)

The projected survey was abandoned a short time later, however, when a November 30 UAW-Ford Umpire decision proclaimed management's technique of laying women off by disqualifying them from arbitrarily chosen and especially difficult jobs to be contractually valid.[40] This decision gave the green light to management to proceed as before without violating its formal agreement with the UAW. Ford's policy was later embodied in a memorandum from the director of Labor Relations, issued to all the company's plants in August 1946:

> In conformance with our agreement with the UAW-CIO, females previously employed by the company who have been laid off have, in certain instances, recall rights. . . . This does not mean that they are to be called back for particular jobs but that they are to be called back and assigned to a job in line with their seniority, regardless of the nature of the job. The only exception is that they must not be assigned to a job which State Laws preclude them from doing.
>
> In the event they are unable to do the assigned job, they . . . will then be processed as quits and their call-back rights terminated. . . .
>
> This matter should be carefully and tactfully handled in order that the company may not be laid open to the charge of attempting in any manner to rid itself of female employees; however, you are again reminded that "soft jobs" are not to be picked out for these people.[41]

Local 400 continued to seek the recall of women with seniority to jobs it judged "suitable" for them. In February 1947, the union complained to Ford's Labor Relations department when three new men were hired to do jobs that women were permitted to do under state law. The union demanded "that the three individuals mentioned be replaced with Seniority Women." Management responded, "We have investigated this situation and have called in women to replace two of the above men; however TA 7583 [the third man involved] is working on a punch press which supervision feels women cannot do." The union persisted, stating, "the work performed by TA 7583 is definitely work that can be done satisfactorily by a woman."[42]

Such exchanges, which occurred frequently between Local 400 and Ford management in 1946 and 1947, suggest the limits within which struggle over the sexual division of labor was confined. As always, management retained the initiative in making job assignments. If management's decisions were challenged, the union might succeed in reversing the initial decision. But its power to affect the division of labor was confined, at best, to these marginal cases. Disputes focused on whether or not a particular job was sufficiently "light" for a woman to perform. Thus the point of contention became the boundary between women's and men's work, not the legitimacy of the system of job segregation. Just as in the mobilization period, struggle at the margin over "women's" work had the unintended consequence of helping to legitimate the idiom in which the overall division of labor by sex in industry was couched.

Despite their meager results, the women's seniority struggles during the demobilization period reveal the political dimension of the sexual division of labor. Had the labor movement actively and consistently opposed sex discrimination, the effect on women's position in the work force might have been far more significant. Conceivably, the wartime changes in the sexual division of labor could have been permanently incorporated into the postwar auto industry. This would have required the elimination of all sex-discriminatory seniority provisions (like the one in the national GM agreement) in UAW contracts, the consistent enforcement of women's seniority rights by both locals and the International union, and, crucially, securing equal rights for women in hiring as well as in seniority-based recalls. That this did not occur reflects the weakness of women within the UAW, who were seldom able to effectively challenge either the ideology of gender or the organized power of male workers loyal to that ideology. It also reflects the weakness of the UAW as a whole with respect to management. Indeed, even had its members been united on the desirability of instituting sex-blind hiring policies, the union lacked the power to do so. The return to prewar arrangements was not inevitable, then, but was predicated on historically specific political conditions that facilitated the managerial reconstruction of the prewar sexual division of labor.

Postwar Struggles in Electrical Manufacturing

There were some postwar seniority struggles in electrical manufacturing, too, primarily in the "heavier" branches of the industry that always employed relatively few women. The UE defended women laid off out of line with seniority in a number of situations where such discriminatory treatment jeopardized the seniority principle. At Westinghouse Airbrake in Pittsburgh, for example, UE Local 610 succeeded in having seniority women transferred to "men's jobs" rather than being laid off ahead of more junior men.[43] But such incidents were relatively rare in the electrical industry. As Ronald Schatz points out in his history of the UE, "Although protest might be voiced in cases in which layoffs did not proceed according to seniority, no protest arose in the large majority of cases in which [women's] seniority rights were respected."[44] In the absence of seniority violations, there was no legitimate basis for mobilizing the union in defense of women's wartime gains. And seniority rights *per se* did not offer women any protection from "downgrading" *within* the electrical industry from their wartime jobs to traditional "women's jobs." In fact, many locals had negotiated contract provisions specifically requiring such transfers.[45] Downgrading was the key mechanism by which management reconstructed the prewar sexual division of labor in electrical manufacturing, rather than denying recall rights to women war workers as in auto.

If seniority rights rarely divided men and women electrical workers, they did pit unmarried and married women workers against each other. The position of the industry's married women workers was ambiguous in the postwar period. Before the war, and especially in the 1930s, the "family wage" ideal along with employment insecurity had generated widespread hostility to married women's employment, and in electrical manufacturing, this reinforced the longstanding managerial preference for a youthful labor force. Some plants banned married women altogether, and elsewhere local union contracts denied them full seniority rights.[46] With the wartime labor shortage, such bans on married women's employment were lifted, but in anticipation of renewed unemployment after the war, seniority provisions in some UE contracts differentiated between married and single women, according preference to the latter. The national office of the UE recommended against this practice, but took little action to eliminate it in the locals. In the wake of the layoffs of the first postwar recession of 1948-49, however, married women themselves mobilized around the issue.

In 1948, following an employment cutback, Local 617, a large Westinghouse local in Sharon, Pennsylvania, negotiated a supplement to the national Westinghouse contract restricting the seniority and employment rights of married women. Because of job segregation by sex, the single women benefited most from this arrangement. "Let's keep the single girl on the job and put the married women back in the kitchen," read a leaflet issued by a Local 617 committee of single women. Apparently male workers, who made up 80 percent of the local's membership, also viewed the exclusion of married women as a brake on female substitution in the first postwar recession. In a special referendum, the local's members endorsed the discriminatory contract supplement by a vote of 2,700 to 700.[47]

The married women then protested that the supplement violated their seniority rights as specified in the national UE-Westinghouse contract. The Married Women's Steering Committee of Local 617 appealed to the union's District Council, emphasizing the implications for the seniority system as a whole. "Seniority rights are the very cornerstone of the Union movement," they wrote. "It is not in behalf of ourselves alone that we ask for a reversal of the actions of Local 617 and Westinghouse Electric Corporation, our appeal is planted firmly on the proposition that Union solidarity and the job of every worker who belongs to a minority group hang in the balance."[48] The women hired a lawyer and threatened to sue the union if their appeal was not favorably resolved. This tactic was effective; the discriminatory contract supplement was rescinded six months after it had been instituted.[49]

An otherwise similar case in Local 202 in Springfield, Massachusetts, another large Westinghouse local that in 1948 also negotiated a contract supplement restricting the seniority rights of married women, dragged on much longer. In Springfield, the married women ultimately sued the union, claiming that their seniority rights under the national Westinghouse contract had been violated. Before taking this step, they had appealed to UE President Fitzgerald and to the Executive Board. The UE national office had promised to try to settle the question, but in March 1949, more than a year after the controversy had begun, Marie Sutton wrote bitterly to Fitzgerald on behalf of Local 202's married women, "Don't you think we've had enough of this stalling? It's high time we get action to preserve the basic principles of Trade Unionism. 'The big cry' — No discrimination, job security, better standard of living, equal right's [*sic*] for everybody. Does anyone know what they mean? . . . It's heartbreaking Mr. Fitzgerald to see what we preach and fight so hard to gain through all these years be thrown out the window."[50]

In response to this, Fitzgerald did urge Local 202 officials to cancel the supplement, as Local 617 had done, warning that legal action might otherwise ensue. Subsequently the women sued the local, whose officers had meanwhile switched their allegiance from the UE to the IUE, and the issue became entangled in the rivalry between the two organizations.[51] Ironically, while in Springfield the national UE supported the married women's position, and the IUE defended the discriminatory supplement: the IUE took the opposite position in a 1950 election contest with the UE in Dayton, Ohio, at a GM plant employing large numbers of married women. They reproduced the old Local 617 agreement (which had long since been cancelled) as evidence that the "Red UE" wanted to fire all married women.[52]

These efforts to defend married women's seniority rights resembled the seniority struggles in the UAW in several respects, despite the fact that marital status, rather than gender, was the dividing point. In both industries, the challenges to discriminatory seniority practices were launched by women themselves, reflecting women's increased effectiveness as a political force within the unions. In the married women's seniority struggles in the electrical industry, women were active on both sides of the conflict, but the older, more experienced married women were far more involved. (In Local 617, indeed, the married women claimed that the single women had not previously participated in local membership meetings!)[53] Another parallel between the campaigns of the married women electrical workers and those of women UAW activists was that both won support from other workers by appealing to their interest in preserving the overall seniority principle. Although the idea of equal rights for women had limited legitimacy in the labor movement or in the larger society at this time, the seniority principle could be seized upon by women in pursuing what was actually an issue of gender equality.

Although the married women's seniority struggles resembled the protests over women's job rights by UAW women activists in many ways, the sexual division of labor was not directly affected in the electrical case. Rather, the outcome there shaped the distribution of jobs by marital status (and, indirectly, age) within the female labor market. In many ways these struggles were vestiges of an earlier era, for since the war the female labor force in general, and in the electrical industry in particular, had aged significantly and included a much higher percentage of married women than previously. Almost two-thirds of female electrical workers were married in 1950, compared to less than one-fourth twenty years earlier.[54] It was still possible to stir up feelings of antipathy toward married women in the conservative political and cultural climate of the immediate postwar period. But, at the same time, the increased demand for female labor and the growing supply of married women workers, stimulated by postwar inflation, was rapidly narrowing the gap between the labor force participation rates of married women and their single, widowed, and divorced counterparts. In any case, the shifting balance between married and single women in the electrical industry did not affect the sexual division of labor itself. At most, excluding married women was a potential stopgap against management's efforts to substitute women for men by limiting the female labor supply in a given community.

In electrical manufacturing, the struggles that significantly influenced the postwar sexual division of labor involved the "equal pay for comparable worth" issue that had crystallized during the war. While the UAW's wartime concern with equal pay for equal work was virtually dropped during demobilization, once it became clear that automotive management was not interested in female substitution (on the contrary), there was more continuity in electrical manufacturing. The UAW's successes in the equal pay fight had a major impact on women's wartime wages and indirectly contributed to management's postwar preference for male labor, but there was no impetus to pursue the issue further after the war's end. In electrical manufacturing, however, the pay equity issue became more salient than ever in the postwar transition.

As we saw in chapter 5, the UE's approach to equal pay during the war was much broader than the UAW's, going beyond the argument that women should be paid the same rates as men when they performed "men's jobs" to attack the historical differentials in wage rates for "women's" and "men's" jobs. While the UAW and the UE had both successfully fought to establish the former, more limited, principle early in the war in the landmark War Labor Board decision against GM, the more comprehensive approach adopted by the UE was elaborated gradually in the course of the war. It too ultimately won support from the WLB in its favorable decision in the union's case against GE and Westinghouse—but not until the end of 1945, after the war was over. Again, in contrast to the UAW, the UE did not drop the matter at this point, but incorporated it as one of the major issues in the massive 1946 strike against

GE, Westinghouse, and GM's electrical division. The same fear of permanent female displacement that led many UE locals to insist on contract provisions that automatically downgraded women from the "men's jobs" they had during the war also motivated the union to continue to pursue the pay equity issue in the postwar era.

The role of women activists in pressing the UE to pursue the equal pay struggle was less visible than that of women UAW activists, who were the protagonists in most of the seniority struggles in auto precisely because they were so isolated. That the male leadership of the UE took up the pay equity issue with such vigor may have made women's leadership less important. But after their brief taste of higher wages during the war, and knowing that they would be the immediate beneficiaries of any gains made on the equal pay front, women workers enthusiastically supported the union's equal pay strategy. They also succeeded in winning male support, both in the rank and file and among union leaders. In contrast to the seniority issue in auto, comparable worth did not polarize the men and women. As Sylvia Scribner, a UE organizer in New Jersey in the 1940s, recalled:

> The . . . men had a lot of questions about whether they *ever* wanted women to be equal. They had a lot of reservations about it. They had a deep commitment to preserving the family and social structure as they saw it. But they were ready to listen. I think that around the question of comparable worth there really is a basic commonality of interest, as long as it is not posed as a fight against men. We never said to any of the men, "We're going to fight *you*." We always said that we really had to fight the company on this. We told them to think about the future. We'd ask, "When the economy starts to decline and the company tries to save, do you think you are going to be better off or worse off with the dual wage structure?" . . . The men could see the issue. I think that this is one women's issue that is of general importance to all the employed; it is not a "them vs. us" matter.[55]

The UE's national leadership not only pursued pay equity in its case before the War Labor Board, but also made it an issue in the strike against the nation's three largest electrical employers in the first three months of 1946. When, on the eve of the walkout, GE made an offer of a percentage increase rather than the flat hourly raise the union sought, International Representative Joseph Dermody charged that this was a deliberate effort "to increase the exploitation of your women employees and to lower the wages of your male employees," in a typical statement of the issue.[56] The UE repeatedly demanded that Westinghouse and GE meet the terms of the recent (late 1945) WLB decision on women's rates. Strike negotiations over this issue were protracted. As James Matles, the UE's Secretary-Treasurer, later recounted, "[GE] said we'll improve our offer but we will not give the bobby-soxers the same as we give the men. 'Bobby-soxers' is what they called all the women. . . . So the fight then was for equality in the settlement in cents per hour. We stayed out another four weeks. Then [in the final settlement] it was eighteen and a half cents across the board for everyone in the plants including the bobby-soxers."

In addition to the 18.5 cent across-the-board increase at GE, the UE subsequently negotiated an additional 4.5 cent increase for two-thirds of the company's female employees.[57] After a much longer strike against Westinghouse, the union settled for an 18 cent across-the-board increase, plus a fund of 1 cent per hour per worker to be applied to equalizing women's rates. And in the first settlement of the long and dramatic General Motors strike, the UE signed a contract with an 18.5 cent increase and an 80 cent minimum hiring rate for both men and women in GM's electrical division.[58]

As a consequence, the wartime narrowing of wage differentials had lasting effects in electrical manufacturing, in contrast to auto. Downgrading women after the war inevitably led to some widening in average differentials. But in auto, the wage gap widened much more, both because the wartime narrowing had been almost entirely an artifact of the replacement of men by women on "men's jobs," and because the UAW did not negotiate narrowed differentials in the postwar transition.[59]

However, new developments in electrical unionism after the war, culminating in the 1949 expulsion of the UE from the CIO and the establishment of the rival IUE, diverted attention and energy from women's issues. Some women complained that the UE had not maintained its commitment to improving the conditions of women and developing women's leadership. "In the early period of the union and all during the war," a group of women in District 4 stated in 1949, "UE developed special campaigns in the shop and community to improve the conditions of its women members and to encourage their participation in the union. In the postwar period, however, UE has not been equally alert to the problems of UE women."[60] And the 1950 report of the UE's Fair Practices Committee noted "a serious weakness in the fight for women's rights. No districts reported any specific projects underway."[61] The wage gap also stabilized. At GE, the ratio of women production workers' straight-time hourly earnings to those of men rose from 70 percent in 1945 to 77 percent in 1951 and remained at or near that level for the next two decades.[62]

But the UE did remain committed to pay equity, at least in principle, even in the 1950s, when interest in women's issues in American society was at its nadir. In 1952, the union issued a pamphlet, "UE Fights for Women Workers," criticizing wage discrimination and job segregation in the electrical industry and stressing that this was "men's business too." "Low rates for women hold down the entire rate structure," it noted, citing several examples of management attempts to substitute women for men at lower pay.[63] The pamphlet

21. Women from UE Local 255 picketing their plant during national UE strike against General Electric. The woman in the fur coat is 70 years old. Pittsfield, Massachusetts, 1946. (United Electrical Workers)

22. "These Plutocrats in top hat and tails have been touring the UE Picket Lines in Pittsburgh, showing the strikers how the other half lives. . . . Underneath the stuffed shirts are Charles Copeland and Paul Carmichael of UE Local 601, and they claim to be none other than Robertson and Bucher, who make $149,000 a year but won't give women workers equal pay for equal work." Pittsburgh, February 9, 1946. (United Electrical Workers)

explicitly linked the equal pay issue to the structure of job segregation. "The majority of women in our industry," it pointed out, "are still segregated by the companies on jobs to which the companies do not assign men at all. They may not actually be labelled 'women's jobs.' But the companies deliberately maintain an artificial separation of the work done by women from the work done by men in order to prevent comparison on the basis of the actual content of the jobs."[64]

But the UE's sophisticated understanding of job segregation and wage discrimination by sex led to few practical achievements in the postwar period. If its breadth of vision in regard to sex discrimination was partially because of the strong influence of Communists in the UE, the structural features of the electrical industry also contributed significantly—and indeed, the anticommunist IUE has also taken up the comparable worth issue in recent years.[65]

Conclusion

When the postwar struggles in the electrical and auto industries are compared, the salience of industry structure in shaping them is striking. While women's efforts to enforce their seniority rights in auto were often undercut by collusion between male unionists and management, the pay equity issue unified men and women electrical workers. This was not because of any difference in the sympathies of male workers in the two industries for the cause of gender equality. Indeed, male electrical workers, like their counterparts in auto, had an interest in perpetuating women's subordination in industry in order to preserve their power as a gender. Yet they strongly supported the UE's campaign to equalize wage rates between women and men.

Because of the contrasting histories of female employment in each of these industries and their distinct structures, male auto and electrical workers defined their interests in crucially different ways. In auto, fear of unemployment made sex discrimination in seniority a means to preserve the male monopoly of the bulk of jobs, so that it was very difficult to mobilize male workers to defend women's job rights. In electrical manufacturing, however, the same employment insecurity led men to define their interest as the elimination of sex discrimination in wages, in order to reduce the likelihood of female substitution. The seniority struggles presumed a sex-stratified economy; the pay equity campaign challenged the very basis of job segregation by sex. Because automotive management had never seriously tried to replace men with women, the UAW had little incentive to pursue the broader issues involved in gender inequality, whereas the opposite was true in electrical manufacturing. The interests of male workers, then, rather than being located outside the wage labor market and ineluctably transcending the forces operating within it, could work either for or against women workers, depending upon the particular industrial setting.

In both industries, women sought to defend their wartime gains through strategies designed to bring together the interests of women and men. In both, they appealed to the men through an ideology of working-class unity. In auto, the appeal was unsuccessful because of the historical legacy of the industry's sexual division of labor and the limited political resources available to women activists. In electrical manufacturing, by contrast, the effort to attack job segregation in the critical postwar transition did gain male support but was rendered ineffectual by the union's overall weakness. Indeed, while the postwar period saw a general retrenchment of managerial power, it was especially extreme in electrical manufacturing. Although sex differentials in wages were significantly narrowed in the electrical industry in the late 1940s, the UE never even remotely approached its ultimate goal of closing the gap, and the overall structure of job segregation by sex persisted.

The isolation of the UE, with its radical vision of a transformation in gender relations in industry, reflected the general political impoverishment of the postwar period. The war years had offered a glimpse of the potential for gender equality in the workplace, and female union activists vigorously pursued this goal on the basis of an ideology of class unity. But in the conservative climate of the immediate postwar period, amid widespread fears of a renewed depression, class unity proved a very weak reed to lean on. Thus the unique opportunity that the wartime transformation offered to permanently alter the economic position of women was lost. Instead, management succeeded in reconstructing the postwar world along prewar lines, and the protests that did emerge were quickly obliterated from public memory.

9   Epilogue and Conclusion

The struggles of women workers during and after World War II were a crucial historical episode between the first wave of American feminism, which dissipated after the passage of the Nineteenth Amendment in 1920, and the second wave, which began in the 1960s. The absence of a feminist movement in the 1940s, indeed, helps explain the failure of women unionists' efforts to combat gender inequality in the workplace at that critical historical juncture. And yet today, after twenty years of feminist resurgence, job segregation by sex and pay inequality—the twin pillars of women's subordination in the workplace— have yet to be dismantled. Although women have made some inroads into male-dominated occupations in recent years, particularly in the elite professions, the vast majority of working women remains confined to poorly paid, low-status, pink-collar jobs with few opportunities for advancement. Despite enormous growth in the extent to which women work outside the home, the introduction of explicit legal prohibitions on sex discrimination in employment, and greatly increased popular support for economic equality between the sexes, surprisingly little progress toward gender equality has been recorded.

The gender gap in pay rates has remained remarkably stable during the postwar decades, with women's earnings consistently averaging about 60 percent of men's for full-time, year-round employment.[1] This is because occupational segregation by sex has consistently confined most women to jobs with relatively low pay. Although there have been shifts over time in the specific jobs men and women do, the extent of sex segregation in the labor market has changed very little during the course of the twentieth century. Statistical studies show that from 1900 to 1960, there was no change at all in the overall extent of segregation (except, of course, during World War II), and since 1960 the decline in segregation has been very modest.[2] The desegregation that did occur in the 1960s and 1970s was primarily because of increased female representation in traditionally male professions, and to a lesser extent in nontraditional blue-collar jobs.[3] But the sex composition of the jobs in which most women work has remained stable.

The most dramatic changes in women's employment have been in elite professions like medicine and law, where the proportion of women approached a record 15 percent by the early 1980s. However, despite their high visibility, these fields employ few persons of either gender. In 1981, the total number of women physicians, lawyers, and judges together comprised only 0.3 percent of all employed women. In contrast, more than one-third of all women workers are employed in clerical positions; another third are in sales, service, nursing, or (non-college) teaching jobs. And most occupations are still extremely sex-segregated. For example, in 1981, women were more than 99 percent of all secretaries, but less than 1 percent of all automobile mechanics; 97 percent of all registered nurses, but only 4 percent of all engineers.[4]

These facts may seem to contradict the widespread view, frequently expressed in the media, that women's position in the labor market has been radically altered in recent years. But it is crucial not to confuse the huge increase in female labor force participation with a change in the *types of work* available to most women. It is true that in the United States today more women are employed outside their homes than ever before, and that marriage and motherhood are far less frequently associated with withdrawal from the labor market than in the past. Women's attitudes toward employment have also shifted dramatically, with far less conflict between work and traditional family roles expressed today than in the past. The family wage ideology that was so prevalent in the first half of the century has almost disappeared; "woman's place" today includes *both* the home and the female labor market.[5] And a large majority of both men and women in the United States today support efforts to strengthen the status of women—which was not the case as recently as 1970.[6] These changes are real and, by all indications, ongoing. However, neither women's greater participation in the paid labor force nor the accompanying shifts in attitudes and ideology have generated much change in the overall structure of job segregation.

The modest structural changes that did take place are largely because of the passage and enforcement of antidiscrimination laws during the 1960s and 1970s. Title VII of the Civil Rights Act, which prohibits sex discrimination in employment, was passed in 1964. Its impact was limited until after 1972, when the law was amended to include effective enforcement mechanisms—the most important of which were affirmative action programs—and to extend its coverage. Similarly, Executive Order 11375, which was issued in 1967 and prohibits sex discrimination in employment under federal contracts, had little effect until after 1971, when specific enforcement mechanisms were added.[7] During the 1970s, when these laws were being enforced, they had significant results, as evidenced by the marginal decline in the extent of sex segregation that took place during the decade. In the 1980s, however, with economic contraction and an administration strongly committed to reduced enforcement of antidiscrimination legislation, progress has been slowed, if not halted altogether.[8]

The impact of the antidiscrimination laws was particularly great in the credentialed professions (such as law, medicine, and accounting), probably because educational institutions are the gatekeepers in these fields, rather than private employers, who have been more resistant to change. In addition, actual or threatened litigation and other efforts to enforce the legal prohibitions on sex discrimination led to significant increases during the 1970s in women's representation in many nonprofessional jobs. However, given the time and expense involved in such litigation and the relatively brief period of time during which the laws were enforced, the result was a modest increase in female employment in some traditionally male blue-collar jobs. In the female-dominated, pink-collar fields where most women are employed, the law has had virtually no impact, for because of the low pay and status associated with most of these jobs, their overwhelmingly female character has provoked few complaints of sex discrimination from men.

In auto and electrical manufacturing, as in the larger economy, the sexual division of labor underwent little change over the postwar period before the 1970s (Tables 6 and 7). The one exception is the small increase in the repre-

Table 6. Female and Total Employment in "Motor Vehicles and Equipment," 1950 to 1983—Selected Years

Year (average)	Women Employees (thousands)	All Employees (thousands)	Women as % of Total
1950[a]	76.8	775.5	9.9%
1955[a]	91.8	857.9	10.7
1960	68.4	724.1	9.4
1965	69.6	842.7	8.3
1970	71.1	799.0	8.9
1975	80.5	792.4	10.2
1980	110.8	788.8	14.0
1983[b]	95.9	682.9	14.0

Sources: Data for Standard Industrial Classification 371 from U.S. Bureau of Labor Statistics, Bulletin 1312-11 (1979) *Employment and Earnings, United States, 1909-78*, 351; U.S. Bureau of Labor Statistics, *Supplement to Employment and Earnings* (July 1983), 110.

[a]January (annual averages for women employees not available)
[b]January (preliminary data)

156 Gender at Work

Table 7.   Female and Total Employment in "Electric and Electronic Equipment," 1950 to 1984—Selected Years

Year (average)	Women Employees (thousands)	All Employees (thousands)	Women as % of Total
1950[a]	298.3	860	34.7%
1955[a]	432.5	1182.8	36.6
1960	518.5	1442.3	35.9
1965	620.6	1615.2	38.4
1970	728.0	1870.5	38.9
1975	659.2	1701.6	38.7
1980	890.5	2090.6	42.6
1984	960	2234.3	43.0

Sources: Data for Standard Industrial Classification 36 from U.S. Bureau of Labor Statistics, Bulletin 1312-11, *Employment and Earnings, United States, 1909-78* (1979), 286-87; U.S. Bureau of Labor Statistics, *Supplement to Employment and Earnings* (July 1983), 92; U.S. Bureau of Labor Statistics, *Employment and Earnings* 32 (March 1985): 52, 61.

[a]January (annual averages for women employees not available)

sentation of women in electrical manufacturing registered in the 1960s. However, this was not because of a decline in job segregation by sex, but rather the fact that electronic components production, a labor-intensive segment of the industry in which large numbers of women are employed, expanded its share of total domestic employment in the industry. That trend continued in the 1970s, and also explains most of the increase in the proportion of women in the industry (from 39 percent to 43 percent) between 1975 and 1980.[9] Although there were legal pressures on the electrical industry in the 1970s to eliminate sex-discriminatory employment practices, they seem to have had little effect on the overall proportion of women in the industry's work force, which had always been quite large.

In auto, there was a substantial increase in the proportion of women employed in auto over the 1970s, from 9 to 14 percent. The increase did not reflect any change in the industry's product mix, however, but was the direct result of the auto firms' equal employment opportunity programs, which were developed under pressure from the federal government.[10] In the 1980s, due to the drop in overall employment in the industry, and perhaps also to reduced enforcement of antidiscrimination laws, the female proportion of the auto work force has stabilized at just under 15 percent—a peacetime high, although well below the World War II level.

The postwar continuity in patterns of employment by sex, both in these two industries and in the labor market as a whole, while contradicting the popular view that women have made great strides in the world of work, is entirely consistent with the historical record. Just as the Great Depression of the 1930s and the economic transformation that accompanied World War II failed to dislodge the basic structure of job segregation or the ideology of sex-typing that accompanies it, so too the huge increases in female labor force participation and the resurgence of feminism in the 1960s and 1970s have left the sexual division of labor intact. Although overt discrimination has lost its former legitimacy, and some progress has been made toward integrating women into traditionally male jobs, in general occupational sex-typing still goes unquestioned.[11] That secretaries and nurses are and should be female and that truckdrivers and construction workers are and should be male continues to be the unexamined presumption of employers as well as most working people themselves.

This book has sought to demonstrate that such occupational sex-typing is deeply rooted in industrial structures and can only be understood historically. The sexual division of labor in a given industry or labor market develops as an integral part of the labor process and is shaped by the economic, political, and social forces operative at the historical moment when the labor process first crystallizes. Thus the relatively high labor intensity of electrical manufacturing and its reliance on piecework for managerial control over labor produced a very different sexual division of jobs than that which developed in the auto industry, which relied upon the moving assembly line and high wages to control labor. In other industries, the factors that were so important in auto and electrical manufacturing might be of little consequence; other economic, political, or social constraints might shape the sexual division of labor instead.

One direction for further research suggested by this argument is the analysis of additional historical cases. Perhaps by comparing a large number of case studies, a general theory of the relationship between industrial structure and the sexual division of labor—along the lines suggested by the theoretical literature on labor market segmentation but with greater explanatory power—could be constructed. But the historical analysis presented here also suggests that no set of static categories can be used to account for cross-industry variations in patterns of women's employment. Given the inertia that characterizes the sexual division of labor once it is established in an industry, any theoretical effort must accord a central place to the structural histories of particular industries and labor markets.

Ideology, especially the idioms differentiating women's and men's jobs, plays a central role in reproducing the sexual division of labor once it has crystallized in a particular labor market. There were repeated demonstrations of the supremacy of ideology in the analysis of the auto and electrical industries. Management strictly adhered to the established idioms of sexual division and showed little interest in female substitution, even in the face of the severe profitability crisis of the 1930s and the dramatic demonstration of the possibility of deploying women in men's jobs during World War II. Both during the war and in the 1970s, employers engaged in female substitution only when actively forced to do so by economic necessity or direct political intervention.

This is another issue that warrants much more investigation. What is the basis for the extraordinary staying power of the ideology of gender division in industry, even in the face of a direct conflict with economic rationality? Even if we assume, as early Marxist-feminist writings suggested, that the family is the ultimate "material basis" for this ideology, by what means is the collective interest of capital in preserving the family (and/or a labor force weakened by sexual divisions) transformed into the constraining idioms of sexual division?[12] And under what circumstances can such idioms, and the broader gender ideology in which they are rooted, be effectively challenged by workers themselves, female or male?

The historical analysis here suggests that struggles over women's position in the work force are themselves shaped by the sexual division of labor in an industry or labor market—particularly in regard to how male workers define their interests. This was illustrated in chapter 8 in the discussion of how the contrasting histories of female employment in the auto and electrical industries and their different structures led male workers to behave in crucially different ways during the postwar transition. In auto, the issue was *job* discrimination: Fear of unemployment made sex discrimination in seniority a means to preserve the male monopoly of the bulk of jobs, so that male workers colluded with management in opposition to women war workers' efforts to defend their job rights. In electrical manufacturing, however, the same employment insecurity led male workers to support the campaign to eliminate *wage* discrimination in order to reduce the likelihood of female substitution. The interests of male workers, then, rather than being determined outside the workplace by a hegemonic patriarchy, can work for or against women workers depending upon the characteristics of the industrial setting. Thus, the analysis of distinct industrial structures not only helps explain why women are concentrated in particular occupations and industries, but also illuminates the dynamics of political struggles over the sexual division of labor, past and present.

The efforts undertaken in the 1970s and 1980s to dismantle job segregation fall into two major categories: affirmative action and pay equity. There is an important parallel here to the contrast between the auto and electrical struggles in the 1940s. In industries and labor markets where women have historically been a small minority so that (as in the auto seniority struggles) job discrimination is the central issue, the main vehicle for change has been affirmative action in hiring and promotions. In industries where women have long been represented in substantial numbers, however, the key issue is wage discrimination, and pay equity or comparable worth campaigns have been the most viable strategy.

Affirmative action emerged as the key instrument used to enforce antidiscrimination legislation in the 1970s. Although it did produce marginal increases in women's representation in some traditionally male jobs, this success had its price. In a contracting economy, and particularly in basic manufacturing, where the most wrenching employment declines have occurred, affirmative action has engendered a strong popular backlash, not least among those who stand to lose job or promotion opportunities as a result of it. Part of the problem is that affirmative action is widely misunderstood to involve quotas or preferential hiring of women (and minorities) over more qualified white men. (In fact, affirmative action simply involves making special efforts to recruit members of underrepresented groups and giving them preference over *equally* qualified majority group members.)[13] But even when no such misunderstanding is involved, affirmative action has been an extremely divisive and difficult issue, very much like the seniority struggles in auto in the 1940s. To make this observation is by no means to suggest that affirmative action efforts should be abandoned—indeed, there may be no viable alternative strategy for change in predominantly male industries and labor markets. But strategies that can win broader support (from men as well as women) are far more likely to be successful, especially in the present period of economic contraction and restructuring.

In this regard, the current campaign for pay equity, or comparable worth, would seem to have better prospects. Unlike affirmative action, the demand for pay equity has engendered relatively little opposition from male workers. The definition of the issue is identical to that of the UE in its 1945 War Labor Board case: The basic argument is that "female" jobs are underpaid relative to "male" jobs requiring comparable levels of skill, effort, and responsibility, and that this constitutes sex discrimination. Significantly, the issue has been pursued exclusively in industries where large numbers of women are already entrenched—primarily in the public sector, but also in electrical manufacturing. Despite an inhospitable political climate and explicit condemnation from the Reagan administration, the pay equity campaign has won widespread popular support and has enjoyed considerable success both in the courts and at the bargaining table. The actual increases in women's pay rates that have been won have been relatively small. But the campaign has done much to undermine the legitimacy of job segregation by sex, and has focused public awareness on segregation as the underlying cause of women's low pay.[14]

The historical resilience of job segregation and of the ideology of sex-typing that accompanies it suggests that it will not be dismantled easily, and we must take a cautious, if not entirely pessimistic, outlook. Yet the prospects for change do seem better today than in the 1940s, despite the absence of anything comparable to the dramatic wartime demonstration of the malleability of the sexual division of labor as a contemporary reference point. There are more women working than ever, which means both more workplaces with substantial female representation and more two-income families, so that the prospects of unifying men and women in challenging gender inequality in the labor market are relatively favorable. The resurgence of feminism, which was totally absent in the 1940s, has given unprecedented legitimacy to the ideal of equality between women and men, especially in the economic arena. And the labor movement, which has a greater proportion of female members than ever before, has taken up women's issues to an unprecedented degree in the 1970s and 1980s—spearheading, for example, the drive for pay equity.[15] A major problem, however, is the fundamental weakness of organized labor in this period, as managerial power ascends to a new peak. For today, as in the past, the fate of women workers' struggles remains inextricably bound up with class issues. If the labor movement were revitalized in alliance with the movement for women's rights, the coming years could bring new struggles over the sexual division of paid labor—on a larger scale, and with better prospects for success, than at any time since the 1940s.

Notes

Chapter 1. Introduction

1. U.S. Department of Labor, Bureau of Labor Statistics, *Women in Factories*, mimeographed (1947), 6–7.

2. U.S. Department of Labor, Women's Bureau, *Women Union Leaders Speak*, mimeographed (1945), 32.

3. For a sophisticated statement of this position, see Alice Kessler-Harris, *Out to Work: A History of Wage-Earning Women in the United States* (New York: Oxford University Press, 1982), especially 300–19.

4. See Janet L. Norwood, *The Female-Male Earnings Gap: A Review of Employment and Earnings Issues*, U.S. Department of Labor, Bureau of Labor Statistics, Report 673, Sept. 1982, 2; "Earnings Gap is Narrowing Slightly for Women," *New York Times,* 3 Oct. 1983, B15.

5. The focus here is on the *reproduction* of job segregation and not the very different problem of its origins. To be sure, the existence of a clearly defined sexual division of labor is not a phenomenon unique to capitalist societies; quite the contrary. Yet, excepting perhaps certain biologically based theories (if they may be called theories), no matter how the *genesis* of the sexual division of labor, or its existence in noncapitalist societies, is understood, its persistence and continual reproduction within capitalist relations of production presents a distinct theoretical problem—and an especially paradoxical one. As noted in the text, the development of capitalism was widely expected to eliminate such "ascriptive" characteristics as sex from the process of allocating people to places within the social division of labor, and above all in the wage labor market; yet this has not taken place.

6. An extensive literature now documents this. The classic article on the persistence of segregation over time, covering the period from 1900 to 1960, is Edward Gross, "Plus Ca Change. . .The Sexual Structure of Occupations over Time," *Social Problems* 16 (Fall 1968): 198–208. See also Valerie Kincade Oppenheimer, *The Female Labor Force in the United States: Demographic and Economic Factors Gov-*

erning its Growth and Changing Composition (Berkeley: Institute of International Studies, Population Monograph Series, no. 5, 1970). For more recent data, see Donald J. Treiman and Heidi I. Hartmann, eds., *Women, Work, and Wages: Equal Pay for Jobs of Equal Value* (Washington, D.C.: National Academy Press, 1981), especially 24–29, and Andrea H. Beller, "Trends in Occupational Segregation by Sex and Race, 1960–1981," in *Sex Segregation in the Workplace: Trends, Explanations, Remedies,* ed. Barbara F. Reskin (Washington, D.C.: National Academy Press, 1984), 11–26.

7. Another comparative case study of women's work that addresses similar issues, although focusing on an earlier period, is Maurine W. Greenwald, *Women, War and Work: The Impact of World War I on Women Workers in the United States* (Westport, Conn.: Greenwood Press, 1980).

8. There are also "theories" of job segregation that purport to explain women's lower wages and their location in particular types of jobs in terms of "human capital" or in terms of workers' voluntary job "choices." These arguments will not be considered here, but excellent critiques of them have been made elsewhere. See Treiman and Hartmann, *Women, Work, and Wages,* 17–24, 53–54, for a useful overview of the literature.

9. The single most important statement of this position is Juliet Mitchell, *Woman's Estate* (New York: Pantheon Books, 1971). See also Peggy Morton, "A Woman's Work Is Never Done," in *From Feminism to Liberation,* ed. Edith H. Altbach (Cambridge, Mass.: Schenkman Publishing, 1971), 211–27; and Wally Secombe, "The Housewife and Her Labour under Capitalism," *New Left Review* 83 (Jan.-Feb. 1974): 3–24.

10. See Mitchell, *Woman's Estate,* 144; Paddy Quick, "Women's Work," *Review of Radical Political Economics* 4 (Summer 1972): 2–19; and Margaret Benston, "The Political Economy of Women's Liberation," *Monthly Review* 21 (Sept. 1969): 13–28.

11. See chapter 4 for specific examples and discussion.

12. The two most recent major works in this literature are Richard Edwards, *Contested Terrain: The Transformation of the Workplace in the Twentieth Century* (New York: Basic Books, 1979); and David M. Gordon, Richard Edwards, and Michael Reich, *Segmented Work, Divided Workers: The Historical Transformation of Labor in the United States* (New York: Cambridge University Press, 1982). A good example of the argument that the situation of women in the labor market is best explained by segmentation theory is R. D. Barron and G. M. Norris, "Sexual Divisions and the Dual Labor Market," in *Dependence and Exploitation in Work and Marriage,* eds. Diana Leonard Barker and Sheila Allen (New York: Longman, 1976), 47–69.

13. Edwards, *Contested Terrain,* explicitly refers to auto and electrical manufacturing as examples of the same mode of control over the labor process ("technical control"). For further discussion of this example, see chapter 2. A critique of labor market segmentation theory that in many respects parallels my own (although it does not focus specifically on gender) is Constance Lever-Tracy, "The Paradigm Crisis of Dualism: Decay or Regeneration?" *Politics and Society* 13 (1984): 59–89.

14. Richard C. Edwards, Michael Reich, and David M. Gordon use this phrase in the introduction to their jointly edited *Labor Market Segmentation* (Lexington, Mass.: D. C. Heath, 1975), xiii.

15. Heidi Hartmann, "Capitalism, Patriarchy and Job Segregation by Sex," in *Women and the Workplace: The Implications of Occupational Segregation*, eds. Martha Blaxall and Barbara Reagan (Chicago: University of Chicago Press, 1976), 137–69. Many of the criticisms of Hartmann that follow also apply to Edna Bonacich's "split labor market" theory. Although Bonacich is concerned primarily with racial divisions in the work force and does not enter into any detailed discussion of job segregation by sex, her characterization of the relationship between "higher paid labor" and "cheaper labor" is strikingly similar to Hartmann's view of the relationship between male and female workers. Patriarchy, nor for that matter "given" racial interests, is not the starting point for Bonacich as it is for Hartmann, but both make similar assumptions about the resources and interests of "higher paid"/male labor. See Edna Bonacich, "A Theory of Ethnic Antagonism: The Split Labor Market," *American Sociological Review* 37 (Oct. 1972), 547–59. It is telling that in this initial formulation of her theory, Bonacich does not even recognize the *possibility* of a cross-race alliance forming among workers, although she does incorporate this possible "outcome" into later expositions of her split labor market theory, starting with "Abolition, the Extension of Slavery, and the Position of Free Blacks: A Study of Split Labor Markets in the United States, 1830–1863," *American Journal of Sociology* 81 (Nov. 1975): 601–28.

16. Hartmann, "Capitalism, Patriarchy and Job Segregation"; and idem., "The Unhappy Marriage of Marxism and Feminism: Towards a More Progressive Union," *Capital and Class* 8 (Summer 1979): 1–33. An interesting empirical study that uses this theoretical framework is Cynthia Cockburn, *Brothers: Male Dominance and Technological Change* (London: Pluto Press, 1983). For a provocative critique of this perspective, see Iris Young, "Socialist Feminism and the Limits of Dual Systems Theory," *Socialist Review* 10 (March-June 1980): 169–88.

17. For an excellent critique of determinism with reference to theories of working-class collective action (but that makes no mention of the sexual division of labor), see Charles Sabel, *Work and Politics: The Division of Labor in Industry* (New York: Cambridge University Press, 1982).

18. This argument in some respects parallels that of Arthur L. Stinchcombe in his classic essay, "Social Structure and Organizations," in *Handbook of Organizations*, ed. James G. March (Chicago: Rand McNally, 1965), 142–93. It is questionable, however, whether the sexual division of labor in industry as discussed here would fit Stinchcombe's definition of an organization, which among other things entails "social relations *deliberately* created, with the *explicit* intention of continuously accomplishing some specific goals or purposes" (142, emphasis added). For a useful historical analysis of job segregation that illustrates this argument, see also David B. Tyack and Myra H. Strober, "Jobs and Gender: A History of the Structuring of Educational Employment by Sex," in *Educational Policy and Management: Sex Differentials*, eds. Patricia A. Schmuck, W. W. Charters, Jr., and Richard O. Carlson (New York: Academic Press, 1981), 131–52.

Chapter 2. Fordism and Feminization

1. Helen L. Sumner, *History of Women in Industry in the United States*, U.S. Congress, Senate Document no. 645, *Report on Condition of Woman and Child Wage Earners in the U.S.*, vol. 9, 61st Cong., 2d sess., 1910, 228.

2. Elizabeth Baker, *Technology and Women's Work* (New York: Columbia University Press, 1964), 195.

3. Transcript of Hearing no. 159, "Electrical Manufacturing," Hearings on the Codes of Fair Competition held under the National Industrial Recovery Act, 19 July 1933, 100, 109. Information on the Schenectady plant's product mix is from Milton Derber, "Electrical Products," in *How Collective Bargaining Works,* ed. Harry A. Millis (New York: Twentieth Century Fund, 1942), 747.

4. Sumner, *History of Women in Industry,* 228, notes that electrical manufacturing was "a new industry for both men and women, and consequently the women employed have not displaced men, unless it be considered that they have displaced potential men."

5. Hearing no. 159, "Electrical Manufacturing," 11.

6. However, the implication that the work was such as to exert little strain on the presumably fragile female constitution was highly misleading. A 1911 government report revealed the true meaning of "delicacy" in this context: "the operators are dealing with materials so delicate and minute that they can be clearly seen only in the best of light and by persons possessing at least normally good sight. This can be very easily appreciated by inspecting an ordinary carbon or tungsten lamp, the filament of which is not clearly visible unless the lamp is held close to the eyes and in strong light. To handle one such filament at leisure would be neither difficult nor trying; every day the housewife performs an equally delicate operation in threading a fine cambric needle. If, however, this needle-threading operation were repeated two or three thousand times a day, and particularly if it were done at a piece rate, which urges one to the highest speed in order to increase one's earning and to secure the higher rate paid for very rapid production, it would soon assume tremendous proportions to the person doing the work. There is perhaps no better illustration of the general nature of these occupations than of fine needle threading repeated at top speed day in and day out. Indeed there is in the tungsten department an occupation which is exactly like it. In this operation the gossamer-like tungsten filament, which can hardly be seen by the untrained eye, must be inserted in a tiny hole punched in the end of a copper wire no thicker than the finest needle, where it is kept in place by pinching the sides of the wire together. This operation is repeated a thousand times a day at the rate of about three every two minutes." See "Employment of Women and Girls Making Incandescent Lamps," *Glass Industry, Report on Condition of Woman and Child Wage-Earners,* vol. 3 (1911), 477–78.

7. Hearing no. 159, "Electrical Manufacturing," 109.

8. Elizabeth Butler, *Women and the Trades: Pittsburgh, 1907–1908* (New York: Russell Sage Foundation, 1909), 215–16.

9. Another piece of evidence indicating that the idiom was interpreted differently by different employers emerged in a 1929 U.S. Women's Bureau study of the radio industry, which found that "in some plants men predominated and in others

women." The report suggested that "in certain cases the manufacture of radios was a development from the making of motors or batteries that had been man-employing, and men were retained with the change in product. . . . The labor market was also a controlling factor. In one town there was a shortage of women while in another the radio factory was the only large woman-employing industry." U.S. Department of Labor, Women's Bureau, Bulletin no. 83, *Fluctuation of Employment in the Radio Industry* (1931), 27. See also U.S. Department of Labor, Women's Bureau, Bulletin no. 12, *The New Position of Women in American Industry* (1920), 113, for a discussion of variations in the extent of female substitution in electrical manufacturing during World War I.

10. Butler, *Women and the Trades,* 217.

11. Henry Ford, in collaboration with Samuel Crowther, *My Life and Work* (Garden City, N. J.: Doubleday, 1923), 79.

12. Charles Reitell, "Machinery and Its Effects upon the Workers in the Automotive Industry," *Annals of the American Academy of Political and Social Science* 116 (Nov. 1924): 43.

13. Examples of substitution are noted in Robert W. Dunn, *Labor and Automobiles* (New York: International Publishers, 1920), 73, 76; and in William H. McPherson, *Labor Relations in the Automobile Industry* (Washington, D.C.: Brookings Institute, 1940), 8–9.

14. See U.S. Bureau of Labor Statistics, Bulletin no. 438, *Wages and Hours of Labor in the Motor Vehicle Industry* (1927), 2–3. The other three job categories with large numbers of women were "final assemblers," "inspectors," and "trim bench hands." Only 11 percent of the men surveyed were in the four job groups employing 68 percent of the women.

15. William H. McPherson, "Automobiles," in *How Collective Bargaining Works,* 576.

16. Dunn, *Labor and Automobiles,* 74.

17. U.S. Bureau of Labor Statistics, *Wages and Hours of Labor in the Motor Vehicle Industry,* 4, 26–36 (percentages computed by the author). No parts plants were included in this survey, so the geographical variation cannot be explained by a preponderance of parts plants in some regions. Nor is there any significant variation in the number of employees per plant among seven of the eight states surveyed (the exception is Michigan, which had virtually all of the largest plants in the industry in this period), and in any case, plant size does not correlate with the proportion of women workers employed. This survey offers evidence of many specific state-by-state variations in the sexual division of labor in addition to the two examples cited in the text, and a less aggregated data set would probably reveal even more.

18. Horace L. Arnold and Fay L. Faroute, *Ford Methods and the Ford Shops* (New York: Engineering Magazine, 1915), 1, 58; interview with Edith Van Horn, Detroit, 14 Feb. 1980; interview with Morley Walker, Detroit, 7 Oct. 1980; Judy Rosen, "Women in the Plant, the Community, and the Union at Willow Run" (M. A. thesis, University of Pittsburgh, 1978), 47–48.

Comprehensive statistics on employment by sex for individual firms are unfortunately not available for this period. See however, R. J. Thomas's testimony in the U.S. Senate Hearings on *Manpower Problems in Detroit,* 79th Cong., 1st sess.,

9–13 March 1945, 13107f; and also the survey conducted in May 1945 by the U.S. War Production Board, a copy of which is in the UAW Research Department Collection, Wayne State University Archives of Labor History and Urban Affairs [hereafter WSU Archives], box 22, folder: "Reconversion 1944–1945, 1 of 2."

19. *Wall Street Journal,* 22 Nov. 1936, cited in Dunn, *Labor and Automobiles,* 72; U.S. Bureau of Labor Statistics, *Wages and Hours of Labor in the Motor Vehicle Industry.*

20. My interviews with former auto industry managers show this repeatedly. See also *Exploitation from 9 to 5: Report of the Twentieth-Century Task Force on Women and Employment* (New York: Lexington Books, 1975), 65–67.

21. Richard Edwards, *Contested Terrain: The Transformation of the Workplace in the Twentieth Century* (New York: Basic Books, 1979), 20. Edwards uses the example of a General Electric plant in discussing technical control. See also the discussion of labor market segmentation theory in chapter 1.

22. Ronald Schatz, *The Electrical Workers: A History of Labor at General Electric and Westinghouse, 1923–60* (Urbana: University of Illinois Press, 1983), 23.

23. "Women and Girls Making Incandescent Lamps," 479–80.

24. See Frederick Taylor, *The Principles of Scientific Management* (New York: W. W. Norton, 1967 [1911]); F. L. Roethisberger and William J. Dickson, *Management and the Worker* (Cambridge: Harvard University Press, 1939); David Loth, *Swope of GE* (New York: Simon and Schuster, 1958); Schatz, *The Electrical Workers,* 17–24, 53–60; W. D. Stearns, "Placing the Right Man in the Right Job: Outline of Methods Used by the Westinghouse Electric Mfg. Co., East Pittsburgh, for Selecting the Right Man for Each Job in the Shop and for Standardizing Rates of Compensation," *Machinery* 26 (Sept.-Oct. 1919): 30–33, 136–39; John C. Bower, "Westinghouse Employment Department Methods Used by the Westinghouse Electric and Manufacturing Company, East Pittsburgh, Pennsylvania, in Hiring Men and in Retaining an Efficient Working Force," *Machinery* 26 (Nov., 1919): 243–46; and United Electrical Workers, *Exhibits* in the case of the EEOC against General Electric (1976), 1355. (A copy of the *Exhibits* is in the UE Archives, University of Pittsburgh.)

25. Schatz, *The Electrical Workers,* 29–30 notes that in the smaller northeastern cities where most electrical plants were located, black populations tended to be low, and the industry's prewar labor force was "nearly lily-white."

26. "Sixteenth Keysheet—Effective April 1, 1937," in Margaret Darin Stasik Papers, University of Pittsburgh Archives of Industrial Society, folder 14; National War Labor Board, *War Labor Reports* 28, 679f.

27. David Montgomery, *Workers' Control in America* (New York: Cambridge University Press, 1979), 37.

28. Keith Sward, *The Legend of Henry Ford* (New York: Rinehart, 1948), 48.

29. Ford, *Life and Work,* 91–102, 126; Sward, *Legend of Henry Ford,* 1.

30. Reitell, "Machinery and Its Effects," 42.

31. U.S. Bureau of Labor Statistics, *Wages and Hours of Labor in the Motor Vehicle Industry,* 2–3; U.S. National Recovery Administration, *Statistical Materials,* no. 4, "The Electrical Manufacturing Industry" (1935).

32. Andrew T. Court, *Men, Methods and Machines in Automobile Manufacturing* (New York: Automobile Manufacturers' Association, 1939), 9.

33. In 1925, women auto workers averaged 47 cents per hour, compared to 73 cents for men in the industry. Similarly, in April 1934, women averaged 52 cents an hour in auto factory jobs, against 73 cents for men. A third survey in September 1934 found average earnings of 54 cents for women and 75 cents for men. (All three sets of figures exclude auto-parts plants, where wages were substantially lower for workers of both sexes). See U.S. Bureau of Labor Statistics, *Wages and Hours of Labor in the Motor Vehicle Industry*, 2–3; and N. A. Tolles and M. W. La Fever, "Wages, Hours, Employment and Annual Earnings in the Motor-Vehicle Industry, 1934," *Monthly Labor Review* 42 (March 1936): 527.

In spite of these differentials, a 1925 survey of Flint, Michigan found that the $20.10 per week that women averaged in the auto industry (this survey *did* include parts-plants workers) was more than they were paid in any other type of work. See U.S. Department of Labor, Women's Bureau, Bulletin no. 67, *Women Workers in Flint, Michigan* (1929), 19.

34. McPherson, "Automobiles," 611–12; Robert Blauner, *Alienation and Freedom* (Chicago: University of Chicago Press, 1964), 89–92; "Automotive Parts: Wage Structure, March-April 1950," *Monthly Labor Review* 72 (Jan. 1951): 37.

35. Philip S. Foner, *Women and the American Labor Movement: From World War I to the Present* (New York: Free Press, 1980), 260, 270.

36. Sward, *Legend of Henry Ford*, 56.

37. Ford, *Life and Work*, 128. For an insightful discussion of this aspect of Fordism, see Martha May, "The Historical Problem of the Family Wage: The Ford Motor Company and the Five Dollar Day," *Feminist Studies* 8 (Summer 1982): 399–404.

38. U.S. Commission on Industrial Relations, *Industrial Relations*, vol. 8: *Final Report and Testimony* (1916), 7637.

39. Sward, *Legend of Henry Ford*, 57, 60. See also Stephen Meyer, *The Five Dollar Day: Labor Management and Social Control in the Ford Motor Company, 1908–1921* (Albany: State University of New York Press, 1981). As both Sward and Meyer recount, Ford's high-wage system of control was supplemented by not only the velvet glove of the Sociology Department, but also the iron fist in the shape of the organized terrorism of the infamous Ford Service Department, especially after World War I.

40. Blanche Bernstein, "Hiring Policies in the Automobile Industry," WPA National Research Project on Reemployment Opportunities and Recent Changes in Industrial Techniques, mimeographed (1937), in W. Ellison Chalmers Collection, WSU Archives, box 1.

41. See U.S. Women's Bureau, *Women Workers in Flint, Michigan*, esp. 2–5; and Alan Clive, *State of War: Michigan in World War II* (Ann Arbor: University of Michigan Press, 1979), 185.

42. U.S. Women's Bureau, *Fluctuation of Employment in the Radio Industry*, 27; Derber, "Electrical Products," 747; *War Labor Reports* 27, 687; Finn Theodore Malm, "Local 201, UE-CIO: A Case Study of a Local Industrial Union" (Ph.D.

diss., Massachusetts Institute of Technology, 1946), 252; Hearing no. 159, "Electrical Manufacturing," 91f.

43. "Women and Girls Making Incandescent Lamps," 480.

44. U.S. Women's Bureau, *Fluctuation of Employment in the Radio Industry,* 26–27

45. See Schatz, *The Electrical Workers,* 21–22, 125. In the prewar period, the female labor force as a whole was generally youthful, but the women employed in durable goods industries like electrical manufacturing and auto were considerably younger than average. In 1930, 62 percent of all women workers were aged 34 or younger (as opposed to 45 percent of all men workers), but in electrical manufacturing, 87 percent of the women workers (and 59 percent of the men) were in this age group, and in auto, 82 (and 53) percent. Percentages computed from *15th Census of the United States: 1930, Population,* vol. 5, 115, 469, 533.

46. See note 14 regarding sex segregation in auto. The data available for the electrical industry are not sufficiently disaggregated to permit comparison with those, but it is clear that jobs were highly sex-segregated there as well. See "Wages and Hours of Labor," *Monthly Labor Review* 10 (June 1920): 82–94, for evidence from the 1919 Industrial Survey, which included thirty-eight electrical apparatus plants. Women made up 27 percent of the workers surveyed, but more than 90 percent of them were in six job classifications (as were about half of the men workers).

Chapter 3. The Depression and Unionization

1. For discussion of the poll as it compares with surveys in other periods, see Valerie Kincade Oppenheimer, *The Female Labor Force in the United States: Demographic and Economic Factors Governing its Growth and Changing Composition* (Berkeley: Institute of International Studies, Population Monograph Series, no. 5, 1970), 44. The best account of the experience of married women in the 1930s economy is Lois Scharf, *To Work and to Wed: Female Employment, Feminism, and the Great Depression* (Westport, Conn.: Greenwood Press, 1980). See also Winifred D. Wandersee, *Women's Work and Family Values, 1920–1940* (Cambridge: Harvard University Press, 1981), and Susan Ware, *Holding Their Own: American Women in the 1930s* (Boston: G. K. Hall, 1982).

2. For elaboration of this argument, see Ruth Milkman, "Women's Work and Economic Crisis: Some Lessons from the Great Depression," *Review of Radical Political Economics* 8 (Spring 1976): 73–97.

3. Jules Backman, *The Economics of The Electrical Machinery Industry* (New York: New York University Press, 1962), 328; U.S. Federal Trade Commission, *Report on Motor Vehicle Industry,* U.S. Congress, House Document no. 468, 76th Cong., 1st sess. (1939), 7.

4. N. A. Tolles and M. W. La Fever, "Wages, Hours, Employment and Annual Earnings in the Motor-Vehicle Industry, 1934," *Monthly Labor Review* 42 (March 1936): 529, 532; U.S. Federal Trade Commission, *Report,* 668; U.S. National Recovery Administration, *Statistical Materials,* no. 4, "The Electrical Manufacturing Industry" (1935); Ronald W. Schatz, *The Electrical Workers: A History of Labor at*

General Electric and Westinghouse, 1923–60 (Urbana: University of Illinois Press, 1983), 59–62.

5. In 1930, the U.S. Bureau of the Census enumerated 12.6 percent of male auto workers, 12.5 percent of male electrical workers, 6.1 percent of female auto workers, and 13 percent of female electrical workers in "Unemployment Class A," defined as "Persons out of a job, able to work, and looking for a job." An additional 4.1 percent of male auto workers, 3 percent of male electrical workers, 3.9 percent of female auto workers, and 4.7 percent of female electrical workers were in "Unemployment Class B," which included "Persons having jobs but on layoff without pay, excluding those sick or voluntarily idle." (All figures include both "operatives" and "laborers.") Percentages computed from *15th Census of the United States: 1930, Unemployment,* vol. 2, 14–15.The 1937 count found 8.8 percent of male and 9.6 percent of female auto workers to be unemployed, while in electrical manufacturing the rates were 8.7 percent for males and 16.7 percent for females. Computed from U.S. Bureau of the Census, *Census of Partial Employment, Unemployment and Occupations, 1937,* vol. 1, 17. The problems with the enumeration methods used and the reasons for the official rejection of the 1937 count are discussed in Stanley Lebergott, "Labor Force, Employment and Unemployment, 1929–1939: Estimating Methods," *Monthly Labor Review* 67 (July 1948): 50–53.

6. See Schatz, *The Electrical Workers,* 54; Robert S. Lynd and Alice C. Hanson, "The People as Consumers," in *Recent Social Trends in the United States,* Report of the President's Research Committee on Social Trends (McGraw-Hall, 1933), vol. 2, 906–9.

7. Schatz, *The Electrical Workers,* 20–21.

8. Ibid., 13–24; Gerard Swope, "Management Cooperation with Workers for Economic Welfare," *Annals of the American Academy of Political and Social Science* 154 (March 1931): 131–37; David Loth, *Swope of GE: The Story of Gerard Swope and General Electric in American Business* (New York: Simon and Schuster, 1958); Ruth Meyerowitz, "The Development of General Electric's Labor Policies, 1922–1950" (M.A. thesis, Columbia University, 1969).

9. "Personnel Activities of Motor Vehicle Manufacturers" (Jan. 1940) in records of the Automotive Council for War Production, Automotive History Division, Detroit Public Library, folder: "Manpower: Committees: Manpower Utilization Committee: Personnel Policies and Practices Sub-Committee."

10. U.S. Commission on Industrial Relations, *Industrial Relations,* vol. 8: *Final Report and Testimony* (1916), 7628.

11. Loth, *Swope of GE,* 132–33; Joyce Peterson, "A Social History of Automobile Workers Before Unionization, 1900–1930" (Ph.D. diss., University of Wisconsin—Madison, 1976), 196, 225.

12. Computed by the author from plant records in the papers of the Automobile Labor Board, Records of the National Recovery Administration, National Archives, Record Group 9, tray 1403: "Records Relating to Rehiring."

13. See Schatz, *The Electrical Workers,* 31–33; oral history of Dorothy Haener, *The Twentieth Century Trade Union Woman: Vehicle for Social Change,* Oral History Project of the Program on Women and Work, Institute of Labor and Industrial Relations, University of Michigan and Wayne State University (1978), 13 (copy in

Wayne State University Archives of Labor History and Urban Affairs [hereafter WSU Archives]).

14. Nathan D. Sleames to Dear Sir, 5 Jan. 1935, Records of the National Recovery Administration, National Archives, Record Group 9, box 7682, folder: "Automobile Industry: Letters Received in Washington."

15. "Preliminary Report on the Individual Conferences with Workers," NRA Research and Planning Division, *Preliminary Report on Study of Regularization of Employment and Improvement of Labor Conditions in the Automobile Industry* (23 Jan. 1935), appendix B, exhibit 19, copy in the Records of the National Recovery Administration, National Archives, Record Group 9, box 8281.

16. Finn Theodore Malm, "Local 201, UE-CIO: A Case Study of a Local Industrial Union" (Ph.D. diss., Massachusetts Institute of Technology, 1946), 278–79.

17. Ethel Erickson to Mrs. Hilton, 2 April 1951 (with attached field reports), Records of the U.S. Women's Bureau, National Archives, Record Group 86, box 1600, folder: "Equal Pay Study." The Philco case is discussed in more detail later in this chapter (see pp. 43–44).

18. Irving Bernstein, *The Lean Years: A History of the American Worker, 1920–1933* (Boston: Houghton Mifflin, 1960), 319–20; Sidney Fine, *The Automobile under the Blue Eagle* (Ann Arbor: University of Michigan Press, 1963), 123.

19. Transcript of Hearing no. 159, "Electrical Manufacturing," Hearings on the Codes of Fair Competition held under the National Industrial Recovery Act; 19 July 1933, 200.

20. U.S. Department of Labor, Women's Bureau, Bulletin no. 218, *Women's Occupations through Seven Decades* (1947), 221–22, 237.

21. Schatz, *The Electrical Workers,* 54; Lynd and Hanson, "The People as Consumers," 906–9.

22. U.S. Department of Labor, Women's Bureau, Bulletin no. 103, *Women Workers in the Third Year of the Depression* (1933), 10; *Proceedings of the UAW Convention,* 1940, 264–65.

23. Claire Howe, "Return of the Lady," *New Outlook* 164 (Oct. 1934): 34.

24. Records of UE District 9, UE Archives, University of Pittsburgh, Archives of Industrial Society, folder 594; *Proceedings of the UAW Convention,* 1940, 264–65.

25. See Milkman, "Women's Work and Economic Crisis," 83.

26. See Alice Kessler-Harris, " 'Where Are the Organized Women Workers?'," *Feminist Studies* 3 (Fall 1975): 92–110; Sharon Hartman Strom, "Challenging 'Woman's Place': Feminism, the Left, and Industrial Unionism in the 1930s," *Feminist Studies* 9 (Summer 1983): 359–86; Ruth Milkman, "Organizing the Sexual Division of Labor: Historical Perspectives on 'Women's Work' and the American Labor Movement," *Socialist Review* 10 (Jan.-Feb. 1980): 95–150.

27. Gladys Dickason, "Women in Labor Unions," *Annals of the American Academy of Political and Social Science* 251 (May 1947): 71.

28. See Strom, "Challenging 'Woman's Place'"; Ware, *Holding Their Own,* 87–115.

29. Strom, "Challenging 'Woman's Place'"; Milkman, "Organizing the Sexual Division of Labor."

30. Julius Emspak to Bertha Owens Scott, 26 May 1936, Records of UE District 9, UE Archives, folder 185.

31. "Local 601 Constitution," Margaret Darin Stasik Papers, University of Pittsburgh Archives of Industrial Society, folder 1; "Local 301 Organization," Records of UE District 3, UE Archives, folder 210.

32. Nancy Felice Gabin, "Women Auto Workers and the United Automobile Workers' Union (UAW-CIO), 1935–1955" (Ph.D. diss., University of Michigan, 1984), 15–55.

33. Interview with Mary Voltz, The Life and Times of Rosie the Riveter Film Project, series 4, Oral History of the American Left Collection, Tamiment Library, New York University.

34. Margaret Darin Stasik Papers, folder 7; Linda Nyden, "Women Electrical Workers at Westinghouse Electric Corporation's East Pittsburgh Plant, 1907–1945" (M.A. thesis, University of Pittsburgh, 1975), 50–60.

35. *Proceedings of UE Convention,* 1939, 141.

36. Ronald Schatz, "Union Pioneers: The Founders of Local Unions at General Electric and Westinghouse, 1933–1937," *Journal of American History* 66 (Dec. 1979): 586–602; Ruth Meyerowitz, "Women Unionists and World War II: New Opportunities for Leadership" (paper delivered at meeting of the Organization of American Historians, San Francisco, April 1980); and see Theresa Wolfson, *The Woman Worker and the Trade Unions* (New York: International Publishers, 1926), 20, 167–68, and passim.

37. Gabin, *Women Auto Workers,* 24–26; Ruth Meyerowitz, "Organizing the UAW: Women Workers at the Ternstedt General Motors Parts Plant," in *Women, Work and Protest: A Century of U.S. Women's Labor History,* ed. Ruth Milkman (Boston: Routledge and Kegan Paul, 1985), 235–58.

38. Nyden, "Women Electrical Workers," 52.

39. This was true of the industry's largest firms; smaller ones (such as RCA and Maytag) were much more resistant to unionism, and in such situations there were long strikes, as in auto. See Schatz, *The Electrical Workers,* 66f; Loth, *Swope of GE,* 168, 258; Walter Galenson, *The CIO Challenge to the AFL: A History of the American Labor Movement, 1935–1941* (Cambridge: Harvard University Press, 1960), 239–65; James J. Matles and James Higgins, *Them and Us: Struggles of a Rank-and-File Union* (Boston: Beacon Press, 1974), 76; Irving Bernstein, *Turbulent Years: A History of the American Worker, 1933–1941* (Boston: Houghton Mifflin, 1970), 603–15.

40. See Fine, *The Automobile under the Blue Eagle;* Bernstein, *Turbulent Years,* 499–571; *Violations of Free Speech and Rights of Labor,* Hearings before a Subcommittee of the Committee on Education and Labor, U.S. Senate, 75th Cong., 1st sess., pt. 6: 2111–26.

41. Dollinger Oral History, cited in Ruth Meyerowitz, "Women in the UAW, 1935–45," unpublished manuscript (n.d., copy in author's possession), 46; Gabin, *Women Auto Workers,* 21–22 and passim.

42. Steve Babson et al., *Working Detroit: The History of a Union Town* (New York: Adama Books, 1984), 76–79

43. On Flint, see Meyerowitz, "Women in the UAW"; Patricia Yeghissian,

"Emergence of the Red Berets," *Michigan Occasional Papers in Women's Studies* 1 (June 1975); and the documentary film, *With Babies and Banners: The Story of the Women's Emergency Brigade* by the Women's Labor History Film Project (Franklin Lakes, N. J.: New Day Films, 1978). Lyrics to "Union Maid" are from the brochure for the record *Talking Union* by Pete Seeger and the Almanac Singers (Folkways Records), 3, 6. The song was written by Woody Guthrie, but the verse quoted here was added by Millard Lampell of the Almanac Singers, according to Philip Foner, *Women and the American Labor Movement: From World War I to the Present* (New York: Free Press, 1980), 334.

44. This is a good example of what Temma Kaplan calls "female consciousness." See her insightful article, "Female Consciousness and Collective Action: The Case of Barcelona, 1910–1918," *Signs: Journal of Women in Culture and Society* 7 (Spring 1982): 545–66. For a study of a 1930s' auxiliary that explores these issues, see Marjorie Penn Lasky, "'Where I Was a Person': The Ladies' Auxiliary in the 1934 Minneapolis Teamsters' Strikes," in *Women, Work and Protest*, ed. Milkman, 181–205.

45. Yeghissian, "Emergence of the Red Berets," 24.

46. See *Proceedings of UE Convention*, 1938, 165–66; Report of District #3 to the 1937 UE Convention, 4 (included in the mimeographed minutes of the convention).

47. Matles and Higgins, *Them and Us*, 53–55; Julius Emspak to Stanley Newton, 22 Sept. 1939, Records of UE District 4, UE Archives, folder 336.

48. Strom, "Challenging 'Woman's Place,'" 371–72.

49. "Annual Averages of Hourly and Weekly Earnings and Average Hours per Week for Male and Female Wage Earners in the Automobile Industry," 28 June 1944, Research Department, UAW-CIO, in UAW Research Department Collection, WSU Archives, box 10, folder 10–19: "Employment, Detroit, 1941–1947"; Milton Derber, "Electrical Products," in *How Collective Bargaining Works*, ed. Harry A. Millis (New York: Twentieth-Century Fund, 1942), 760, 769, 804; Leo Jandreau to Dear Sir and Brother, 24 July 1941, in Records of UE District 3, UE Archives, folder 166 [GE 1941 wages]; Margaret Darin Stasik Papers, folders 6 and 14 [Westinghouse 1937 and 1940 keysheets].

50. W. H. McPherson, "Automobiles," in *How Collective Bargaining Works*, ed. Millis, 617f; Schatz, *The Electrical Workers*, 105–11; "GE Contract Clauses on Seniority in Layoffs," in United Electrical Workers *Exhibits* in the case of the EEOC against General Electric (1976), 1411 (copy in UE Archives).

51. Interview with Sadie Rosenberg, Oral History of the American Left Collection, Tamiment Library, New York University; UE Local 924, "Note," 19 March 1939, in Records of UE District 9, UE Archives, folder 594; Meyerowitz, "Women in the UAW," 33f.

52. Bernstein, *Turbulent Years*, 551; Jonas Silver and Everett Kassalow, "Seniority in the Automobile Industry," U.S. Bureau of Labor Statistics (mimeo, April 1944); Schatz, *The Electrical Workers*, 113–14; "GE Contract Clauses on Seniority in Layoffs."

53. *CIO News* 2 (11 Sept. 1939): 7, cited in Strom, "Challenging 'Woman's Place,'" 370. See also Gabin, "Women Auto Workers," 33.

54. Local #2 Edition of the *United Automobile Worker*, 15 Nov. 1939. At the 1942 UAW Woman's Conference, a delegate recalled, "back in 1937 . . . in Dodge local the men had just been emancipated from industrial slavery and were looking around for more worlds to conquer. They brought a motion on the floor to put all married women out of the plant [but] they didn't even put it to a vote. When we obtained wages necessary to make men able to support a family, then we could take married women out of the factory; and the time hasn't come yet," p. 30, transcript of conference in UAW War Policy Division—Victor Reuther Collection, WSU Archives, box 2, folder: "Conferences."

55. Nyden, "Women Electrical Workers," 58.

56. "Fifteen Years with 201: August 1933-August 1948," pamphlet in Records of UE District 2, UE Archives, folder 166.

57. "Mansfield, Ohio, October 1, 1941," notes on meeting with UE officials, in Records of the U.S. Women's Bureau, National Archives, Record Group 86, box 1416, folder: "Region V, Magee, Lowrie, Settle and Manning—Early 1941 thru 6/1943." Information about a similar case at the Schenectady GE plant may be found in Records of UE District 3, UE Archives, folder 214.

58. George Myers to UE/GE Conference Delegates, 28 Aug.1940, in Records of UE District 9, UE Archives, folder 594.

59. James B. Carey to Herbert R. Bates, 20 Jan. 1938, in Records of UE District 9, UE Archives, folder 219. See also letter from Alice Roth, "Should Married Women Work?" *UE News* 1 (20 May 1939).

60. *Proceedings of the UE Convention*, 1939, 140.

61. See Strom, "Challenging 'Woman's Place.'"

62. Milton Derber, "Electrical Products," 789–90; Ethel Erickson to Mrs. Hilton, April 2, 1951 (with attached field reports), Records of the U.S. Women's Bureau, National Archives, Record Group 86, box 1600, folder: "Equal Pay Study."

63. Ibid.

64. "Women off Late Shift in Westinghouse; Union Victory Brings Many New Members," *UE News* 1 (21 Oct. 1939).

65. Charles Newell, "Equal Pay for Equal Work Advanced as Solution for Problem in Westinghouse," *UE News* 1 (23 Dec. 1939).

66. Nyden, "Women Electrical Workers," 63.

67. "UE Wins Poll in Lima Westinghouse," *UE News* 1 (24 Aug. 1939).

68. "Mostly for Women," *Wayne-UE Victory News*, 14 Aug. 1942, 3, in Margaret Darin Stasik Papers, folder 27. See also folder 6 for a copy of the Westinghouse agreement, and Nyden, "Women Electrical Workers," 58–63.

69. The original grievance, management's answer, and transcripts of two sets of negotiations between the local union and management on this issue are in UAW Local 212 Collection, WSU Archives, Series 2, box 11, folder: "Grievances Briggs Local 212 Mack Ave. Plant 1941."

70. Ibid.

71. Ibid.

72. Laura Hayward Oral History, cited in Meyerowitz, "Women in the UAW," 35.

73. Four of the women worked in the paint shop on a job called "touch up and

stripe." Before 1934, this was a "woman's job" exclusively, but that year GM employed some men on it who were taught their jobs by the women. Three other women involved in the case worked as inspectors and performed their work in teams that included men, with tasks rotated among all team members. The other twenty-two women worked in the plant's small-press room, a division of the sheet metal department, where both men and women operated punch presses and other machines. In the small-press room, workers were shifted around from machine to machine depending on production requirements. Each machine had a tag fastened to it that specified the production quota that management expected of the work done on it, regardless of the sex of the worker. See "Opinion of the Court," in *Florence St. John* vs. *General Motors Corporation,* Circuit Court, County of Ingham, Michigan, 29 May 1942, in Records of the U.S. Women's Bureau, National Archives, Record Group 86, box 1469, folder: "AA Work Eq Pay: WLB and Other War."

74. Ibid.
75. Ibid.
76. Ibid.

Chapter 4. Redefining "Women's Work"

1. Karen Skold has documented the persistence of job segregation by sex in the wartime shipbuilding industry in "The Job He Left Behind: Women Shipyard Workers in Portland, Oregon during World War II," in *Women, War and Revolution: A Comparative Perspective,* eds. Carol Berkin and Carol Lovett (New York: Holmes and Meier, 1980), 55–75. Documentation is offered below for the electrical and automotive industries. See also Karen Anderson, *Wartime Women: Sex Roles, Family Relations and the Status of Women in World War II* (Westport, Conn.: Greenwood Press, 1981), 35f.

2. *16th Census of the United States: 1940, Population,* vol. 3, 75–80; U.S. Department of Labor, Women's Bureau, Special Bulletin no. 20, *Changes in Women's Employment during the War* (1944), 15.

3. Computed from U.S. Department of Labor, Bureau of Labor Statistics, *Women in Factories,* mimeographed (1947), 6–7.

4. For example, a study of the electrical appliance industry found that "despite drastic changes in products, the plants surveyed found, for the most part, that their usual machinery was adaptable to the manufacture of war materials." See "Earnings in Manufacture of Electrical Appliances, 1942," *Monthly Labor Review* 56 (March 1943): 527.

5. In a survey of its locals, the UAW found that of 105 Michigan plants studied, in July 1942, 41 employed no women at all, whereas the balance (64 plants) had 11,806 women workers at that time. A year earlier, 14,675 women had worked in those 64 plants. See "Women's Questionnaire" (typescript), 2, UAW Research Department Collection, Wayne State University Archives of Labor History and Urban Affairs [hereafter WSU Archives], box 32, folder: "Women—Employment Survey A to D, 1 of 2, June, 1942." A summary of this survey may be found in "Women in War Industries," *UAW Research Report* 2 (Sept. 1942): 1.

Another survey, conducted by the Michigan office of the U.S. Employment Service, showed a decline in the percentage of women in 185 Detroit-area war plants from 9.4 percent in June 1941 to 8.6 percent a year later, whereas total employment rose by thirty thousand in the plants surveyed over that period. See U.S. Employment Service for Michigan, Reports and Analysis Section, 7 Dec. 1942, Table E, "Trend of Female Employment in Major War Plants—Wayne County Area," UAW Research Department Collection, WSU Archives, box 10, folder 10–19: "Employment, Detroit, 1941–7."

6. Alan Clive, *State of War: Michigan in World War II* (Ann Arbor: University of Michigan Press, 1979), 24–25, 28; see also U.S. Department of Labor, Bureau of Labor Statistics, Employment and Occupational Outlook Branch, Post-War Division, Industrial Area Study no. 10, *Impact of the War on the Detroit Area* (mimeo, July 1943).

7. U.S. Department of Labor, Women's Bureau, Bulletin no. 197, *Women Workers in Some Expanding Wartime Industries: New Jersey, 1942* (1943), 7; William A. Dopierala, "A Study of the Worker at the Erie General Electric," *Journal of Erie Studies* 2 (Spring 1973): 56.

8. Clive, *State of War*, 34–35; U.S. Bureau of Labor Statistics, *Impact of the War*, 49.

9. Blanche Bernstein, "Hiring Policies in the Automobile Industry," Works Progress Administration National Research Project (1937), marked "not for publication," copy in the W. Ellison Chalmers Collection, WSU Archives, box 1.

10. Clive, *State of War*, 94–95, 172; Anne Gould, "Problems of Women War Workers in Detroit," 20 Aug. 1943, Records of the War Production Board, National Archives, Record Group 179, box 203, folder: "035.606 Service Trades Division, WPB Functions"; Memorandum from Laura Vitray to George Romney et al., 7 Sept. 1943, Records of the Automotive Council for War Production, Detroit Public Library, folder: "Manpower: Comm: Manpower Supply Comm: New Workers Sub-Committee: Women (Women's Advisory Comm—WPB)"; Keith Sward, *The Legend of Henry Ford* (New York: Rinehart, 1948), 436–37.

11. Ernest Kanzler to John L. Lovett, 3 July 1942, with attached "Outline of Proposed Drive to Recruit Women for War Work in Wayne County Area," Records of the War Production Board, National Archives, Record Group 179, box 1016, folder: "241.11 Labor—Women—Recruiting Drive" (quote is from p. 3 of the "Outline"). See also Memorandum from Ernest Kanzler to J. S. Knowlson, 16 April 1942, Records of the War Production Board, National Archives, Record Group 179, box 1014, folder: "241 Labor Supply and Demand (April-June 1942)."

12. "Meeting for Discussion on Labor Supply and Future Labor Requirements," 26 June 1942, Detroit, Records of the War Production Board, National Archives, Record Group 179, box 1016, folder: "241.11 Labor—Women—Recruiting Drive," 29–31 of transcript.

13. "Women in War Industries," *UAW Research Report* 2 (Sept. 1942): 1.

14. Interview with Edward Cushman, 25 June 1981, Detroit.

15. August Meier and Elliott Rudwick, *Black Detroit and the Rise of the UAW* (New York: Oxford University Press, 1979), 213; "Summary of Activities, Racial Relations Unit—Michigan State Employment Service," 13 Feb.—31 March 1941,

Records of the U.S. Employment Service, National Archives, Record Group 183, box 185 (Blue Series), folder: "Michigan 533.01–533.06 1941"; memorandum from Anthony Luchek to Joseph D. Keenan, 14 July 1943, "Degree of Utilization of Negro Workers," in Records of the War Production Board, National Archives, Record Group 179, box 1017, folder: "241.3 Labor Negroes."

16. Robert C. Weaver, *Negro Labor: A National Problem* (New York: Harcourt, Brace and World, 1946), 15, 80, 82; Theodore Purcell and Gerald Cavanaugh, *Blacks in the Industrial World* (New York: Free Press, 1972), 14, 19; "Labor Market Problems of Selected Firms Manufacturing Radio and Radar Equipment," 11 Jan. 1943, Records of the War Manpower Commission, National Archives, Record Group 211, Series 109, box 649, 1,3.

17. Weaver, *Negro Labor,* 81.

18. Memorandum from Luchek to Keenan, 14 July 1943 (see note 15); "Women Seek Factory Jobs," *Detroit News,* 26 Oct. 1942, UAW Public Relations Department Collection, WSU Archives, box 14, folder: "Women"; Weaver, *Negro Labor,* 81, 285–86; Karen Tucker Anderson, "Last Hired, First Fired: Black Women Workers during World War II," *Journal of American History* 69 (June 1982): 82–97.

19. Purcell and Cavanaugh, *Blacks in the Industrial World,* 14.

20. U.S. Senate Hearings, *Manpower Problems in Detroit,* 79th Cong. 1st sess., 9–13 March 1945, 13534, 13638; interview with Edward Cushman.

21. Reference to such a survey made "to determine those operations which were suitable for female operators" is made on pages 2–3 of the Summary Brief Submitted by Buick Motor Division, Melrose Park, General Motors Corporation, "In the Matter of GMC—Buick, Melrose Park, Ill., and UAW-CIO," 14 June 1943, Walter Reuther Collection, WSU Archives, box 20, folder: "WLB, GM Women's Rates." A survey of this type was also conducted at the Ford Willow Run plant; see the section on "Training of Women" in *Willow Run Bomber Plant, Record of War Effort* (notebook), vol. 2, pt. 2, Jan.-Dec. 1942, 30, La Croix Collection, Accession 435, Ford Archives, Dearborn, Michigan, box 15.

22. Computed from data in U.S. Department of Labor, Bureau of Labor Statistics, Division of Wage Analysis, Regional Office no. 8-A, Detroit, Michigan, 3 Dec. 1943, serial no. 8-A–16 (mimeo), "Metalworking Establishments, Detroit, Michigan, Labor Market Area, Straight-Time Average Hourly Earnings, Selected Occupations, July, 1943," UAW Research Department Collection, WSU Archives, box 28, folder: "Wage Rates (Detroit) Bureau of Labor Statistics, 1943–5." These figures include only workers in machining departments, which employed 99 percent of the women and 92 percent of the men covered in this survey of 180 Detroit-area plants, including "substantially all of the establishments which made up the peacetime motor-vehicle industry [and] a large representation of those plants heretofore producing automotive parts." Women made up 22 percent of the workers surveyed. If these data are compared to that collected by the Bureau of Labor Statistics in a 1940 survey, the degree of segregation by sex in the auto industry during the war is put into better perspective. In 1940, women were 2.5 percent of the labor force, and two occupational categories accounted for one-half of the women in the industry. In 1943, five occupational groups accounted for one-half of the women, which, given the much greater representation of women in the industry's work force (22

percent), does not indicate a significant decline in the degree of segregation. For the 1940 data, see U.S. Department of Labor, Bureau of Labor Statistics, Bulletin no. 706, *Wage Structure of the Motor-Vehicle Industry* (1942), 23–24.

23. Computed from data in "Earnings in Manufacture of Electrical Appliances, 1942," 532.

24. Computed from data in U.S. Department of Labor, Bureau of Labor Statistics, Bulletin no. 952, *Wage Structure—Metalworking Industries, 1945* (1949), 78, 83.

25. Regarding GE and Westinghouse, see U.S. National War Labor Board, *War Labor Reports,* vol. 28, 677–78. The questionnaires from the UAW survey are in the UAW War Policy Division—Women's Bureau Collection, WSU Archives, Series 1, box 5, folders 5–10, 5–11 and 5–12. (responses tabulated by the author). Of the 160 locals and subdivisions of locals that returned the questionnaires, 61 responded "yes," 83 "no," and 16 did not answer the question: "Are jobs set up on a male and female basis in your plant?" Of those responding "no," 7 indicated that there were no women in their plant at all; this was also the case for 9 of those not answering this question. Another 9 all-male locals did not return the questionnaire, but sent notes indicated that they had no women members. Given the low response rate (614 locals attended the UAW's 1944 convention), caution should be used in interpreting these data.

26. Computed by the author from "Ford Motor Company—Rouge Plant, Factory Count, December 14, 1943," one of several years' worth of weekly "factory counts" in Accession 732, Ford Archives, Dearborn, Michigan, box 1.

27. See "Summary Employment Status Report for Michigan," 30 April 1943, Records of the U.S. Employment Service, National Archives, Record Group 183, box 181, folder: "Michigan Statewide."

28. Exhibit 1, accompanying G. H. Pfeif to Aileen Lenk, 1 Oct. 1945, Records of the War Labor Board, National Archives, Record Group 202, case file 111–17208.

29. Press release of Office of Production Management, Labor Division, 5 Dec. 1941, UAW Research Department Collection, WSU Archives, box 32, folder: "Women Employment 1941."

30. "Engineers of Womanpower," *Automotive War Production* 2 (Oct. 1943): 4–5 (emphasis added). This was the organ of the Automotive Council for War Production, an industry association that included all the major auto firms except Ford.

31. "What Women Are Doing in Industry," *Factory Management and Maintenance* 100 (March 1942): 63.

32. "Provisions in Plants for Physical Differences Enable Women to Handle Variety of War Jobs," *Automotive War Production* 2 (Sept. 1943): 7.

33. "Report of Two Special Meetings on Employing and Training Women for War Jobs," attended by executives from 85 N. A. M. companies from the East and Midwest, 27 and 30 March 1942, in Records of the Automotive Council for War Production, Detroit Public Library, folder: "Manpower: Source Material: New Workers," 1.

34. "Provisions in Plants"; Constance Green, "The Role of Women as Production Workers in War Plants in the Connecticut Valley," *Smith College Studies in History* 28 (1946): 32. See also "New Workers," *Manpower Reports,* no. 10 (published by

the Manpower Division of the Automotive Council for War Production); "Technological Advances in Automotive Plants Help to Combat Growing Manpower Crisis," *Automotive War Production* 2 (Sept. 1943): 3; and "Automotive Industry Reducing War Costs through Improved Production Techniques," *Automotive War Production* 2 (March 1943): 3. Although the application of new technology was important in auto and electrical manufacturing, it was far more dramatic in some other war industries that had not previously adopted mass-production techniques. For an interesting and extremely detailed discussion of this process in the shipbuilding industry, see Frederic C. Lane, *Ships for Victory: A History of Shipbuilding under the U.S. Maritime Commission in World War II* (Baltimore: Johns Hopkins University Press, 1951), chaps. 7, 8.

35. W. Gerald Tuttle, "Women War Workers at Vultee Aircraft," *Personnel Journal* 21 (Sept. 1942): 8–9.

36. National Industrial Conference Board, *Wartime Pay of Women in Industry*, NICB Studies in Personnel Policy, no. 58 (Oct. 1943), 8. See also American Management Association, *Supervision of Women on Production Jobs: A Study of Management's Problems and Practices in Handling Female Personnel*, Special Research Report no. 2 (1943), which comments that, "Some of the equipment that has been added and the simplification of processes involved lead one to wonder why many of these changes were not made while men were still operating these machines, since the gains in production that have resulted would have been no less a fact for men than for women" (10–11).

37. "Women Work for Victory," *Automotive War Production* 1 (Nov. 1942): 4; "Engineers of Womanpower," 4.

38. "There's a Job for You at Sperry . . . Today" (pamphlet), Records of UE District 4, UE Archives, folder 877; "Hiring and Training Women for War Work," *Factory Management and Maintenance* 100 (Aug. 1942): 73; "Engineers of Womanpower," 4.

39. The transcript of this newsreel was made available to me by the Rosie the Riveter Film Project, Emeryville, California.

40. "Engineers of Womanpower," 4.

41. "New Workers," 4; "Problems of Woman War Workers in Detroit," 2.

42. U.S. Women's Bureau, *Changes in Women's Employment*, 18.

43. Dopierala, "Erie General Electric," 55; Ronald W. Schatz, *The Electrical Workers: A History of Labor at General Electric and Westinghouse* (Urbana: University of Illinois Press, 1983), 126.

44. Helen Baker, *Women in War Industries* (Princeton: Princeton University Press, 1942), 15.

45. "Report of Mrs. Betty Sturges Finan on Cleveland Detroit Trip, February 9–17 [1943] inclusive," 3–4, Records of the War Manpower Commission, National Archives, Record Group 211, Series 137, box 977, folder: "Consultants—Betty Sturges Finan." See also "Report of Two Special Meetings," 6.

Chapter 5. Wartime Labor Struggles

1. U.S. Bureau of Labor Statistics, Bulletin no. 909, *Extent of Collective Bargaining and Union Recognition, 1946*, 2.

2. W. E. Milner to R. J. Emmert, 20 April 1943, in Records of the Automotive Council for War Production, Detroit Public Library, folder: "Manpower: Committees: Manpower Utilization Committee: Work Control Sub-Committee."

3. There were record numbers of work stoppages in the United States in 1944 and 1945, exceeding in frequency even the organizational strikes of the 1930s. The number of strikes in auto exceeded those in any other industry, with a majority of the industry's wartime labor force participating in the wildcats. The interdependence of production processes in auto had always made the industry particularly strike-prone, and this remained true during the war years (although the proportion of assembly-line jobs decreased somewhat with conversion to war production). As Abraham Raskin reported to the War Production Board in a 1944 memorandum on "Industrial Conflict in Detroit," "the integration of Detroit production lines makes it easy for a handful of employees to shut down an entire plant over a minor grievance that applies solely to their department." In contrast, the electrical manufacturing industry had relatively few strikes. Raskin was struck by the difference between the GM plants under contact to the UAW and those in the UE's jurisdiction (parts and appliance plants): "Basic management policies and grievance machinery is the same, but there have been virtually no strikes in the plants under UE contracts whereas there have been frequent walkouts in the UAW plants." Nationally, only 4.4 percent of the workers employed in electrical manufacturing were involved in strikes in 1944, compared to 50.5 percent in auto. The electrical industry's production processes were less integrated, and indeed it had been less strike-bound in the prewar years as well. See "Memorandum to the Chief, Industrial Services Division, Subject: Industrial Conflict in Detroit," 9 June 1944, in Records of the War Production Board, National Archives, Record Group 179, box 1029, folder: "2.45 Labor Relations." See also Nelson Lichtenstein, "Auto Worker Militancy and the Structure of Factory Life, 1937–1955," *Journal of American History* 67 (Sept. 1980): 342, on the decline in the percentage of assemblers. The national strike statistics are from "Strikes and Lockouts in 1944," *Monthly Labor Review* 60 (May 1945): 961. See also Ed Jennings, "Wildcat! The Wartime Strike Wave in Auto," *Radical America* 9 (July-Aug. 1975): 77–112; Martin Glaberman, *Wartime Strikes: The Struggle Against the No-Strike Pledge in the UAW during World War II* (Detroit: Bewick Editions, 1980); Jerome F. Scott and George C. Homans, "Reflections on the Wildcat Strikes," *American Sociological Review* 12 (June 1947): 278–87.

4. See Nelson Lichtenstein, *Labor's War at Home: The CIO in World War II* (New York: Cambridge University Press, 1982), and also Howell John Harris, *The Right to Manage: Industrial Relations Policies of American Business in the 1940s* (Madison: University of Wisconsin Press, 1982).

5. For example, 68 percent of the women employed at the Ford Willow Run bomber plant earned at least three times as much in their war jobs than in their prewar jobs, while this was true for less than 15 percent of the men. See "Work and Wage Experience of Willow Run Workers," *Monthly Labor Review* 61 (Dec. 1945): 1086.

6. Lichtenstein argues that shop-floor militancy was generally led by secondary union leaders. See *Labor's War,* 126ff. My interviews with contemporaries confirmed that conflict over gender issues was greatest in established plants. Interview

with Morley Walker, Berkeley, California, 7 Oct. 1980; interview with Ronald Haughton, Washington, D.C., 4 June 1981.

7. The full text of the "Six-Point Agreement" may be found in the *Minutes of Proceedings of War Emergency Conference, UAW-CIO*, 7–8 April 1942, Detroit, 83–89.

8. "Telephone Conversation Between Mr. Ernest Kanzler and Mr. Bob Nathan, July 20, 1942," p. 3 of transcript; and "Transcript of Conference, February 4, 1942, Detroit—Automotive Branch, WPB," 7, both in Records of the War Production Board, National Archives, Record Group 179, box 2101, folder: "631 Automotive Industry."

9. Under cost-plus contracts, the government reimbursed firms producing military goods for all their costs, including labor, raw materials, plant and equipment, plus a fixed fee over the top, ensuring a profit regardless of cost overruns.

10. Enclosed with letter from James Wishart to Victor Reuther, 25 Feb. 1942, UAW War Policy Division—Victor Reuther Collection, Wayne State University Archives of Labor History and Urban Affairs [hereafter WSU Archives], box 9, folder: "Research Dept. Material 1941–42." See also Alan Clive, *State of War: Michigan in World War II* (Ann Arbor: University of Michigan Press, 1979), 38.

11. Clara M. Shipski and Myrtle H. Hewitt to Miss Frances Perkins, 18 Sept. 1942, in UAW War Policy Division—Victor Reuther Collection, WSU Archives, box 16, folder: "Women's Auxiliaries—UAW-CIO." The same folder contains a copy of another letter Shipski wrote three days later to J. W. Gibson of the Michigan Department of Labor and Industry, which includes a more detailed account of their situation:

> There were 500 women laid off, and they registered at our unemployment office to be placed as soon as possible on defense work. . . . After Reo opened its own employment office there were three Fisher women and myself, Clara Shipski, who went there for employment and Mr. Lamond asked if we had experience [and] if we were married. We told him we knew he was hiring inexperienced and married women and we stated how we knew. His reply was, "I will hire to suit myself, and I would like to see anybody stop me." He refused us application blanks.

12. Caroline Manning to Bertha Nienberg, 15 Oct. 1941, "Interviews with Union Members," in Records of the U.S. Women's Bureau, National Archives, Record Group 86, box 1416, folder: "Region V, Magee, Lowrie, Settle and Manning—Early 1941 thru 6/1943." See also "Interview Ternstedt Local UAW, CIO," 29 Sept. 1943, in same folder.

13. Katherine Farkas to Victor Reuther, n.d.; Victor G. Reuther to Miss Katherine Farkas, 3 Dec. 1941, in UAW War Policy Division—Victor Reuther Collection, WSU Archives, box 3, folder: "Miscellaneous 'F' Sept. 1941-Nov. 20, 1942."

14. "Labor 'Dilution,' " *Business Week* 636 (8 Nov. 1941): 59.

15. "Strike Is Threatened at Kelsey Hayes Plant," *Detroit News*, 28 Oct. 1941; "Workers Reject Plea for Truce," *Detroit News*, 29 Oct. 1941, in Joe Brown Collection, WSU Archives, scrapbook no. 21, 85.

16. "Clarification of Female Work," 5 Nov. 1941, enclosed in letter from Caroline

Manning to J. H. Wishart, 17 Nov. 1941, in UAW War Policy Division—Victor Reuther Collection, WSU Archives, box 11, folder: "U.S. Dept. of Labor."

17. "Kelsey Hayes—Plymouth Plant, Productive Rates," 5 Nov. 1941, UAW Research Department Collection, WSU Archives, box 9, folder: "Dept. of Labor, U.S., 1940–2."

18. Nelson Lichtenstein, "Industrial Unionism under the No-Strike Pledge: A Study of the CIO During the Second World War," (Ph.D. diss., University of California at Berkeley, 1974), 366–67, suggests that such strikes occurred, but cites no specific examples. There were certainly many fewer exclusionary strikes directed against women than "hate strikes" (which were particularly widespread in auto) in protest of the introduction of blacks into the factories. See August Meier and Elliott Rudwick, *Black Detroit and the Rise of the UAW* (New York: Oxford University Press, 1979), 125–34, 162–72. A hate strike that occurred at Western Electric in Baltimore is discussed in Robert C. Weaver, *Negro Labor: A National Problem* (New York: Harcourt, Brace and World, 1946), 201. There are several possible reasons why the hiring of blacks provoked strikes more often than the hiring of women. Certainly workers were quite accustomed to women's presence in the electrical plants, if not on "men's jobs." And even in auto, the introduction of women did not have the explosive character of the race issue, framed as it was by the ideology that proclaimed women to be temporary war workers who would simply disappear from industry after the war. Moreover, as discussed in chapter 4, most women war workers were drawn from the local community.

19. This is discussed more fully in chapter 8.

20. Gene Minshall to Mauro Garcia, 29 July 1943; Mauro Garcia to DeWitt Patterson, 9 Aug. 1943, in UAW Ford Department Collection, WSU Archives, box 13, folder: "Patterson, DeWitt, Ford Motor (Rouge)."

21. Transcript of 7 Feb. 1942, Women's Conference, Detroit, Michigan, 27, in UAW War Policy Division—Victor Reuther Collection, WSU Archives, box 2, folder: "Conferences."

22. Ibid., 24.

23. Ibid., 26.

24. Ibid., 23.

25. Ibid., 23.

26. U.S. Senate Hearings, *Manpower Problems in Detroit,* 79th Cong., 1st sess., 9–13 March 1945, 13595. See also Example no. 29, Ibid., 13594–95, for a similar instance.

27. Umpire Decision No. C–139, 29 Nov. 1943, "Hiring of Women," *Decisions of the Impartial Umpire Under the October 19, 1942 Agreement between General Motors Corporation and the International Union, United Automobile, Aircraft and Agricultural Implement Workers of America—Congress of Industrial Organizations,* vol. 1 (privately published, Detroit: GMC and UAW), 465–67.

28. "Sample handbill announcing arrival of company employment representatives to interview recruits for Willow Run," in *Willow Run Bomber Plant: Record of War Effort,* 2, notebook 2, 8, La Croix Collection, Accession 435, Ford Archives, Dearborn, Michigan, box 15; "History of the Support of the Equal Pay Principle by Official Federal, State, and International Action, and by Unions and Management,"

Exhibit A submitted by Frieda Miller of the Women's Bureau, in U.S. Senate Hearings on S. 1178, *Equal Pay for Equal Work for Women,* 79th Cong., 1st sess., 29–31 Oct. 1945, 34.

29. Between November 1942 and October 1943 alone, more than two thousand voluntary equal pay adjustments were reported to the National WLB. The number of dispute cases was relatively small. (These figures are for all industries). National War Labor Board, *The Termination Report: Industrial Disputes and Wage Stabilization in Wartime, Jan. 12, 1942—Dec. 31, 1945,* vol. 1, 297. See also Ella J. Pollinsky, *National War Labor Board Policy on Equal Pay for Equal Work for Women,* National War Labor Board, Program Appraisal and Research Division, Research and Statistics Report no. 32 (1945).

30. Bureau of National Affairs, *War Labor Reports,* vol. 3, 355–56. For discussion, see NWLB, *Termination Report,* vol. 1, 290–97. The UE, which represented GM appliance division workers as well as some parts plants workers, was also a plaintiff in this case.

31. "Arbitrator's Decision—Women's Rates at Buick Division—Melrose Park, Ill.; Buick Division—Flint, Mich.; Chevrolet Division—Bay City, Mich.," In the Matter of General Motors Corporation and United Automobile, Aircraft and Agricultural Implement Workers of America, C.I.O., case no. 125, 31 July 1943, 5–6, in UAW Research Department Collection, WSU Archives, box 32, folder: "Women—Statistics and NWLB Cases 1943–5."

32. "Summary Brief Submitted by Buick Motor Division, Melrose Park, General Motors Corporation," In the Matter of General Motors Corporation, Buick Motor Division, Melrose Park, Ill., and International Union, United Automobile, Aircraft and Agricultural Implement Workers of America, C.I.O., 14 June 1943, 8, in Walter Reuther Collection, WSU Archives, box 20, folder: "WLB, GM Women's Rates."

33. "Arbitrator's Decision—Women's Rates," 6.

34. "Opinion Explaining Directive Order," NWLB Region 11, case 125, 9 Oct. 1943, in Walter Reuther Collection, WSU Archives, box 47, folder: "WLB, GM Women's Rates" (emphasis added).

35. "Dissenting Opinion of Industry Members," NWLB Region 11, case 125, n.d., in Walter Reuther Collection, WSU Archives, box 47, folder: "WLB, GM Women's Rates."

36. "Opinion Explaining Directive Order," 2; "Exception to Arbitrator's Decision," case no. 125, 18 Aug. 1943, in Walter Reuther Collection, WSU Archives, box 47, folder: "WLB, GM Women's Rates."

37. "Resolution: Women's Wage Differential," passed at District 6 Executive Council meeting, 25 May 1941, in Papers of the International Union of Electrical Workers, Rutgers University Library, New Brunswick, N.J., box A2.03, folder (bound): "District Council #6 Minutes Years 1938–1945."

38. Ibid.; "History of UE Local 601 . . . 1935–1945," in Records of UE District 6, UE Archives, folder 320B; *War Labor Reports,* vol. 28, 690; "Program of Local 601 for Women Workers of Westinghouse, to be submitted to Westinghouse Conference," Oct. 1941, in Records of UE District 6, UE Archives, folder 310; Margaret Darin, "Westinghouse Conference Acts on Women's Demand," *Union Generator* 4

(Nov. 1941): 1, in Records of UE District 6, UE Archives, folder 314; *Proceedings of UE Convention,* 1941, 184.

39. Finn Theodore Malm, "Local 201, UE-CIO: A Case Study of a Local Industrial Union" (Ph.D. diss., Massachusetts Institute of Technology, 1946), 280–81.

40. "Women Employes during the War Emergency," 23 Dec. 1942, enclosed with James Matles to Dear Brother, 29 Dec. 1942, in United Electrical Workers, *Exhibits* in the case of the EEOC against General Electric (1976), 1044. (A copy of the *Exhibits* is in the UE Archives.) The Westinghouse contract with this provision was printed in the *UE News* 5 (10 July 1943).

41. Malm, "Local 201," 281.

42. *UE News* 5 (25 Dec. 1943): 12; *UE News* 6 (10 Feb. 1945): 12. See also Philomena Di Siena, "Weekly Organizer's Report," week ending 4 Sept. 1943, Syracuse, N.Y., in Records of UE District 3, UE Archives, folder 80.

43. "Plant Two—Step #3 Grievance Meeting Held on June 22, 1944: Grievance No. 10775," in Records of Local 801, IUE, Wright State University Archives, Fairborn, Ohio, box 14, file 1: "Grievances Plant No. 2 3rd Step Minutes April-Aug 1944." See also the previous agreement between the UE and Dayton Frigidaire, "Understanding Regarding Method of Application of Directive Order of the National War Labor Board with Reference to Equal Pay for Equal Work for Female Employes," 25 Feb. 1943, in Records of UE District 7, UE Archives, folder 1010. It is interesting that GM's Frigidaire division behaved so differently in regard to female substitution than the same corporation's automotive division, manifesting within a single firm the contrast between the electrical and auto industries discussed in the text.

44. United Electrical, Radio and Machine Workers of America, *UE Guide to Wage Payment Plans, Time Study, and Job Evaluation* (1943), 90–91, copy in Records of the U.S. Women's Bureau, National Archives, Record Group 86, box 1600.

45. See, for example, "Women Doing Men's Work at Lower Pay in Transmitter," Local 301 *Electrical Union News* 4 (30 May 1942): 3, in Records of UE District 3, UE Archives, folder 237, and subsequent stories on this case in the same folder; Charles Newell to James J. Matles, 18 May 1942, in Records of UE District 6, UE Archives, folder 666; correspondence regarding case at Cleveland GE Lamp Works, Records of UE District 7, UE Archives, folder 289, 290; "Back Pay Won on UE Equal Pay Clause," *Local 724 UE News* 1 (April 1943): 1, in Margaret Darin Stasik Papers, University of Pittsburgh Archives of Industrial Society, folder 21; "Frigidaire Women Collect Half Million in Back Pay," *UE News* 6 (15 July 1944): 12; "Women Collect $162,000 in Back Pay at GE Plants," and "Raise Female Rate at Two GE Plants," both in *UE News* 6 (2 Sept. 1944): 12.

46. *War Labor Reports,* vol. 28, 668.

47. Ibid., 358–59.

48. "Extracts from UE's brief to the War Labor Board (in connection with the Westinghouse Electric Corp. and General Electric Company)," 19 Sept. 1945, in Records of the U.S. Women's Bureau, National Archives, Record Group 86, box 1599.

49. *War Labor Reports,* vol. 28, 668.

50. Ibid., 680.

51. Memorandum from Aileen Lenk to Lloyd K. Garrison and Nathan P. Fein-singer, 17 Oct. 1945, 9, in Records of the U.S. Women's Bureau, National Archives, Record Group 86, box 1600.

52. *War Labor Reports*, vol. 28, 680.

53. Ibid., 686.

54. Ibid., 686.

55. Ibid., 683.

56. Like their counterparts in the UAW, the UE's female activists did not challenge the idiomatic definition of women's work. "We felt that there were certain jobs that couldn't be done by women because of the nature of the work," Margaret Darin Stasik recalled. "I think we would revise our thinking on that now. But at that time [the 1940s] we didn't." Cited in Linda Nyden, "Women Electrical Workers at Westinghouse Electric Corporation's East Pittsburgh Plant, 1907–1945" (M.A. thesis, University of Pittsburgh, 1975), 58–59.

57. Malm, "Local 201," 284n; Joseph Dermody to Mr. E. D. Spicer, 28 Dec. 1945, in *Exhibits*, 1222–23.

58. "Memorandum on Discrimination in Women's Rates of Pay by General Electric Company," June 1969, in *Exhibits*, 1356.

Chapter 6. The Women's Movement in the Wartime CIO

1. See Gladys Dickason, "Women in Labor Unions," *Annals of the American Academy of Political and Social Science* 251 (May 1947): 71.

2. These figures include Canadian as well as U.S. membership. The base of the percentages is the nonagricultural labor force. See Leo Troy, *Trade Union Membership, 1897–1962* (New York: National Bureau of Economic Research, Occasional Paper 92, 1965), 1–2.

3. Dickason, "Women in Labor Unions," 71–72. The most comprehensive overview of women and trade unions during the war period is Philip Foner's chapter on the subject in his *Women and the American Labor Movement: From World War I to the Present* (New York: Free Press, 1980), 360–93. See also the concise account in Susan M. Hartmann, *The Home Front and Beyond: American Women in the 1940s* (Boston: G. K. Hall, 1982), 64–70. There is also D'Ann Campbell's chapter, "Sisterhood versus the Brotherhoods: The War for the Unions," in her *Women at War with America: Private Lives in a Patriotic Era* (Cambridge: Harvard University Press, 1984), 139–61. Campbell provides a useful review of polling data on women's attitudes toward trade unions in this period, but her account is in other respects highly misleading and naive. For example, she fails to comprehend that growth in female membership in an individual union—especially in the 1940s—was largely an artifact of management's hiring policies rather than of union "hostility" or "friendliness" toward women. More generally, her account suffers from a failure to situate the problems of women unionists during the war period in the context of the twentieth century as a whole.

4. Dickason, "Women in Labor Unions," 71.

5. The 1939 figure comes from the mimeographed report of the UAW Fair Prac-

tices Department for 1946–47, 8, in the Walter Reuther Collection, Wayne State University Archives of Labor History and Urban Affairs [hereafter WSU Archives], box 21, folder: "Fair Practices Dept., 1946–47." Because the union was split into two groups in 1939, accurate total membership figures are not available. The 10 percent figure is based on the union's claim that "in 1940, there were 398,477 workers covered under UAW contracts," in R. J. Thomas, "Report to the Union," *UAW-CIO Ammunition* 1 (Oct. 1943): 8.

6. "Women Take Posts as Union Leaders," *New York Times,* 5 Feb. 1943; *Officers' Report* to the UE's 1944 Convention, 59.

7. U.S. Department of Labor, Women's Bureau, *Women Union Leaders Speak* (mimeo, 18–19 April 1945): 32.

8. Joel Seidman, *American Labor from Defense to Reconversion* (Chicago: University of Chicago Press, 1953), 91–108; Nelson Lichtenstein, *Labor's War at Home: The CIO in World War II* (New York: Cambridge University Press, 1982), 78–81.

9. U.S. Bureau of Labor Statistics, Bulletin no. 865, *Extent of Collective Bargaining and Union Recognition, 1945* (1946), 5.

10. James J. Matles and James Higgins, *Them and Us: Struggles of a Rank-and-File Union* (Boston: Beacon Press, 1974), 138.

11. "Women in Trade Unions during the War Period," in Records of the U.S. Women's Bureau, National Archives, Record Group 86, box 1352, p. 3.

12. "Work and Wage Experience of Willow Run Workers," *Monthly Labor Review* 61 (Dec. 1945): 1084. The lack of prior union experience may have been more common at Willow Run than at other plants, because it was a newly built plant with no prewar labor force at all. Unfortunately, however, no industry-wide data are available on this point.

13. Lichtenstein, *Labor's War,* 73, 101, 111–12. On anti-union bias among women, see Campbell, *Women at War,* 152–54. These data are not specific to women war workers, but are drawn from the entire female population, and so should be interpreted with caution.

14. Questionnaire response from Wade H. Edwards, UAW Local 674, (Norwood, Ohio—Delco and Chevrolet), in survey of locals, May-August 1944, in UAW War Policy Division—Women's Bureau Collection, WSU Archives, Series I, box 5, folder 5–11.

15. "Report of Conference on Women in War Industries," 11–12 March 1943, 14, in Records of the U.S. Women's Bureau, National Archives, box 1533, folder: "U.S. Conferences (Miscellaneous Reports)."

16. Ruth S. Coles, "Strikes and Lockouts in 1944," *Monthly Labor Review* 60 (May 1945): 965; Lichtenstein, *Labor's War,* 124; "Sweater Girl Row Up to Conciliator," *Detroit News,* 19 March 1943, in UAW Research Department Collection, WSU Archives, box 32, folder: "Women and the Labor Movement 1943–4 2 of 2"; "100 Women Stop Work in Bendix Plant on Plaint that Foreman Is 'Slave Driver'," *New York Times,* 23 April 1943.

17. "Minutes of Conference of District #3," 14 March 1942, 15, in Records of UE District 3, UE Archives, folder 115.

18. *Proceedings of UE Convention,* 1943, 92. For details on the growth of women's leadership in the UE and the policies designed to foster it, see the annual reports

of the "Committees on Women in the UE," in the *Proceedings of the UE Convention* over the war years.

19. "Women Take Posts as Union Leaders," *New York Times,* 5 Feb. 1943; Labor Research Association, *Labor Fact Book* no. 7 (1945), 71; *Proceedings of UE Convention,* 1944, 110.

20. Percentages compiled from Credentials Committee reports in the *Proceedings of UE Convention,* 1941 and 1944.

21. If by contemporary standards the CP's feminism seems underdeveloped, it did take unions as an important arena within which to pursue sexual equality. There has been no serious study of women and the CP in the war period. For a good critical account of the situation in the 1930s, see Robert Shaffer, "Women and the Communist Party, USA, 1930–1940," *Socialist Review* 9 (May-June 1979): 73–119. For interesting statistical data about women's leadership in the CP, which grew dramatically during the war years, see Harvey Klehr, "Female Leadership in the CP of the USA," *Studies in Comparative Communism* 10 (Winter 1977): 394–402. See also Maurice Isserman, *Which Side Were You On? The American Communist Party During the Second World War* (Middletown: Wesleyan University Press, 1982), especially pp. 140–41, and Roger Keeran's uncritical *The Communist Party and the Auto Workers Union* (Bloomington: Indiana University Press, 1980), chap. 10.

22. See "Women Take Posts as Union Leaders," *New York Times,* 5 Feb. 1943; *Labor Fact Book* no. 7, 70–71.

23. R. J. Thomas, "Your Rights and Your Responsibilities," *Women Work— Women Vote,* special supplemental edition to *UAW-CIO Ammunition* 2 (Aug. 1944): 28.

24. Twenty percent of the locals surveyed had no women members. All the figures cited here are based on the remaining 80 percent. The survey was conducted in August 1944. It should be borne in mind in evaluating this data that if a local had one shop steward who was female and one hundred who were male, it was counted among the 73 percent of the locals with female shop stewards—and similarly with the other categories. See "Sister Sue Says," *UAW-CIO Ammunition* 2 (Dec. 1944): 21.

The head of the UAW Women's Department reported to the U.S. Women's Bureau shortly after the end of the war that three hundred women were officers in local unions and that at least one thousand women served on various committees in local unions. See Mildred Jeffrey to Frieda Miller, 19 Nov. 1946, Records of the U.S. Women's Bureau, National Archives, Record Group 86, box 867, file: "Unions Auto Workers." Further confirmation of the wartime rise in women's representation in official UAW posts is offered in an untitled report written after the war by William Oliver, then Co-director of the UAW's Fair Practices and Anti-Discrimination Department (which included the Women's Department at this time), in which he states, "During the war years there was a steady increase in the number of elected positions women held in the union." Walter Reuther Collection, WSU Archives, box 21, folder: "Fair Practices Dept. 1946–47."

25. Figures compiled by the author by counting the names of delegates with unambiguously feminine names from the roll calls in the *Proceedings of the UAW*

Convention, 1940 and 1946. Because some delegates supplied only first initials, these figures may be slight underestimates.

26. *Proceedings of UE Convention,* 1943, 228.

27. Interview with Ruth Young Jandreau by author and Meredith Tax, Schenectady, N.Y., 29 Aug. 1985.

28. Oral history of Florence Peterson, *The Twentieth Century Trade Union Woman: Vehicle for Social Change,* Oral History Project of the Program on Women and Work, Institute of Labor and Industrial Relations, University of Michigan and Wayne State University (1978), 17 (copy in WSU Archives). See also Ruth Meyerowitz, "Women Unionists and World War II: New Opportunities for Leadership" (paper delivered at the meeting of the Organization of American Historians, San Francisco, April 1980).

29. The UAW held special women's conferences in 1942 (transcript in UAW War Policy Division—Victor Reuther Collection, WSU Archives, box 2, folder: "Conferences") and 1944 (report in UAW War Policy Division—Victor Reuther Collection, WSU Archives, box 27, folder: "War Policy Women's Bureau Nov. 1944-Jan. 1945"). The UE held many district women's conferences, accounts of which appeared frequently in the *UE News* during the war years.

30. See *UAW-CIO Ammunition,* various issues. The "Sister Sue Says" column appeared from the first issue of the magazine until August 1946. The special 1944 supplement, although designed primarily to mobilize the women's vote in the national elections, contains a great deal of material on other issues involving women at work.

31. Copies of the pamphlet are in the UAW War Policy Division—Women's Bureau Collection, WSU Archives, box 5, folder 5–15.

32. Copies in the PA Series, UE Archives. For example, see "UE Women Fight for Freedom," in folder 39. Unlike the UAW, the UE produced many women's pamphlets in the 1950s as well, which are in the PA Series as well.

33. *UE News* 4 (31 Jan. 1942, 28 March 1942); *Proceedings of UE Convention,* 1942, 28, 205; Finn Theodore Malm, "Local 201, UE-CIO: A Case Study of a Local Industrial Union" (Ph.D. diss., Massachusetts Institute of Technology, 1946), 204; Ruth Young to Mary Anderson, 10 March 1942, in Records of the U.S. Women's Bureau, National Archives, Record Group 86, box 865; "Leadership Education," p. 3f of "Preliminary Report—District 6 Membership Activities Report," in Records of UE District 6, UE Archives, folder 148; and leaflet, "Announcing Women Leaders Training School," in Records of UE District 6, UE Archives, folder 180.

34. Interview with Ruth Young Jandreau.

35. "Survey of Women in Labor Unions in a Mid-West War Industry Area," n.d., and accompanying summary sheet, "Women's Participation in Union Affairs," both in Records of the U.S. Women's Bureau, National Archives, Record Group 86, box 899.

36. Elizabeth Hawes, *Hurry Up Please Its Time* (New York: Reynal and Hitchcock, 1946), 42. Hawes worked in the UAW's Education Department for a short period, and this book is based on her own observations and experience.

37. Nina Pillard, "Perspectives of Difference: UE Women in Leadership During the 1940s" (M.A. thesis, Yale University, 1983), 26–27.

38. *Proceedings of the UE Convention,* 1942, 205.

39. These comments were on the questionnaire responses in the survey of locals, May-August 1944, in UAW War Policy Division—Women's Bureau Collection, WSU Archives, Series 1, box 5, folder 5–10. The great majority of the comments on the other questionnaires were similarly negative.

40. Marie J. Reed to James J. Matles, 21 Jan. 1943, in Records of UE District 6, UE Archives, folder 65. See also Pillard, "Perspectives of Difference."

41. Oral history of Mildred Jeffrey, *The Twentieth Century Trade Union Woman,* 50. See also Meyerowitz, "New Opportunities for Leadership," especially 26.

42. Oral history of Florence Peterson, 46. Regarding the power of the Regional Directors, see also oral history of Mildred Jeffrey, 63, and Hawes, *Hurry Up Please,* 47, 97, 102–3.

43. *Proceedings of the UE Convention,* 1943, 226–27.

44. "Women in Trade Unions during the War Period," 6.

45. Ruth Young to Women Staff Members, 20 May 1943, in Records of UE District 4, UE Archives, folder 93; "A Personal Service Plan for UE Locals," *UE News* 6 (19 Feb. 1944); *Proceedings of the UE Convention,* 1943, 222; interview with Ethel Shapiro Bertolini, The Life and Times of Rosie the Riveter Film Project, Series 4, Oral History of the American Left Collection, Tamiment Library, New York University; *Proceedings, First Annual Educational Conference,* International Union, United Automobile, Aircraft, and Agricultural Implement Workers of America, Chicago, 25–27 Feb. 1944, 94; "UAW Proposals for Union Counseling System," n.d., UAW War Policy Division—Women's Bureau Collection, WSU Archives, box 4, folder 9; "UAW-CIO Union Counseling System," n.d, UAW War Policy Division—Women's Bureau Collection, WSU Archives, box 27, folder: "War Policy— Women's Bureau October 1942-October 1944."

46. *Proceedings, First Annual Educational Conference,* 92–93. See also chapter 5, note 5, on this point.

47. "Women in Trade Unions during the War Period," 3.

48. Ibid., 6; Hawes, *Hurry Up Please,* 40.

49. In a different historical context, Alice Kessler-Harris has pursued this theme in an innovative and insightful way, making use of Frank Parkin's notion of "dual closure." As agents of social closure, according to Parkin, unions seek to usurp authority from those above them. Their effectiveness in doing so requires a strong and united membership. Applying this to male-dominated trade unions in the 1920s, Kessler-Harris writes: "labor leaders, eager to close ranks in the service of a militant fighting force, . . . often insisted that women accede to the prevailing male methods and goals, and interpreted women's attempts to find new paths to loyalty and participation as subversive." See Alice Kessler-Harris, "Problems of Coalition Building: Women and Trade Unions in the 1920s," in *Women, Work, and Protest: A Century of U.S. Women's Labor History,* ed. Ruth Milkman (Boston: Routledge and Kegan Paul, 1985), 110–38, and Frank Parkin, *Marxism and Class Theory: A Bourgeois Critique* (New York: Columbia University Press, 1979), 44–46, 79.

50. "Minutes of the Women to Win the War Conference," UE District Council

no. 7, Columbus, Ohio, 12 Dec. 1942, 4, copy in Records of the U.S. Women's Bureau, National Archives, Record Group 86, box 865; *Proceedings of the UE Convention,* 1942, 205.

51. "150 Delegates Discuss Labor Problems Here," *Michigan Chronicle,* 16 Dec. 1944, in UAW Research Department Collection, WSU Archives, box 32, folder: "Women and the Labor Movement 1943–4, 1 of 2"; "National UAW Women Spurn 'Special Favors,' " *Detroit Free Press,* 10 Dec. 1944, in UAW Public Relations Collection, WSU Archives, box 14, folder: "Women."

52. "Seniority Status of Women in Unions in War Plants," U.S. Women's Bureau pamphlet, Union Series, no. 1 (1945). The survey on which this pamphlet is based is the one referred to in note 33 above.

Chapter 7. Demobilization and Reconstruction

1. See U.S. Bureau of the Census, *Historical Statistics of the U.S.: Colonial Times to 1970* (1975), 131, 133. This claim is considerably more modest than William Chafe's controversial thesis that the wartime changes in female labor force participation make the 1940s a key "turning point in the history of American women." See William H. Chafe, *The American Woman: Her Changing Social, Economic, and Political Role, 1920–1970* (New York: Oxford University Press, 1972), 195. Indeed, many of Chafe's critics concede that the wartime transformation in female labor force participation was a permanent one, although they question the broader significance of this change. For a good review of the debate over Chafe's thesis, see Karen Anderson, *Wartime Women: Sex Roles, Family Relations, and the Status of Women during World War II* (Westport, Conn.: Greenwood Press, 1981), 3–11.

2. D'Ann Campbell, *Women at War with America: Private Lives in a Patriotic Era* (Cambridge: Harvard University Press, 1984), 224, 236.

3. U.S. Department of Labor, Women's Bureau, Bulletin no. 209, *Women Workers in Ten War Production Areas and Their Postwar Employment Plans* (1946), 4, 11, 42.

4. "Women's Postwar Plans," *UAW Research Report* 4 (March 1944): 3. This survey found that 74 percent of the women who had been factory workers two years earlier (in early 1942) and 49 percent of the others wanted to continue doing factory work after the war. (The women in the first group, that is, prewar factory workers, made up 26 percent of those surveyed.) Male workers were also surveyed by the UAW, and although it was assumed that they would want to remain in the work force after the war, only 76 percent indicated a preference for factory jobs, a figure not much greater than that for their female counterparts.

5. New York State Department of Labor, Division of Women in Industry, *Post-War Plans of Women Workers in New York State* (Aug. 1945), 12, 23.

6. Anderson, *Wartime Women,* 170–71.

7. U.S. Women's Bureau, *Women Workers in Ten War Production Areas,* 49; New York State, *Post-War Plans of Women Workers,* 6.

8. U.S. Women's Bureau, Special Bulletin no. 20, *Changes in Women's Employment during the War* (1944), 15.

9. New York State, *Post-War Plans of Women Workers*, 14.

10. Interview with Lola Weixel, The Life and Times of Rosie the Riveter Film Project, Series 4, Oral History of the American Left Collection, Tamiment Library, New York University.

11. This argument was first made by Betty Friedan in *The Feminine Mystique* (New York: W. W. Norton, 1963), especially chap. 8. The popular documentary film, *The Life and Times of Rosie the Riveter* (Franklin Lakes, N.J.: Clarity Educational Productions, 1980) also presents this view. See also Susan Hartmann, "Prescriptions for Penelope: Literature on Women's Obligations to Returning World War II Veterans," *Women's Studies* 5 (1978): 223–39. Recently, feminist scholars have developed more nuanced analyses of images of women in popular culture in the 1940s. Maureen Honey presents an interesting class analysis of popular wartime fiction in *Creating Rosie the Riveter: Class, Gender, and Propaganda during World War II* (Amherst: University of Massachusetts Press, 1984), and Andrea Walsh offers a sociological analysis of women and film in *Women's Film and Female Experience, 1940–1950* (New York: Praeger Publishers, 1984). See also Denise Riley's extremely sensitive discussion of the British case in "'The Free Mothers': Pronatalism and Working Women in Industry at the End of the Last War in Britain," *History Workshop* 11 (Spring 1981): 59–118.

12. Leila Rupp, *Mobilizing Women for War: German and American Propaganda, 1939–1945* (Princeton: Princeton University Press, 1978), chap. 6.

13. The literature has focused primarily on the case of the UAW. See Sheila Tobias and Lisa Anderson, "What Really Happened to Rosie the Riveter: Demobilization and the Female Labor Force, 1944–47," MMS Modular Publications, module 9 (1973), 1–36; Lyn Goldfarb, with Julie Boddy and Nancy Wiegersma, *Separated and Unequal: Discrimination against Women Workers after World War II (The U.A.W., 1944–1954)*, pamphlet (Washington, D.C.: The Union for Radical Political Economics' Women's Work Project [1976]); and Nancy Gabin, "Women Workers and the UAW in the Post World War II Period: 1945–1954," *Labor History* 21 (Winter 1979–80): 5–30.

14. New York State, *Post-War Plans of Women Workers*, 16.

15. "Policy on Women's Seniority Problems," *UAW-CIO Ammunition* 2 (March 1944): 13; "Women in Trade Unions during the War Period," draft report, 10, and memo from UE to U.S. Women's Bureau, 10 May 1945, both in Records of the U.S. Women's Bureau, National Archives, Record Group 86, box 1351.

16. *Proceedings of UE Convention*, 1943, 223

17. See Frank G. Pierson, "The Employment Act of 1946," in *Labor in Postwar America*, ed. Colston E. Warne (Brooklyn: Remsen Press, 1949), 283–300; and Stephen K. Bailey, *Congress Makes a Law; The Story Behind the Employment Act of 1946* (New York: Columbia University Press, 1964).

18. For a representative statement, see the National Women's Trade Union League pamphlet *Action Needed: Postwar Jobs for Women* (Washington, D.C.: NWTUL, 1944), 11–12. See also chapter 6 for discussion of the predominance of class interests over gender interests among female CIO activists.

19. The UAW had a "Model Veterans' Seniority Clause," which by 1946 was written into contracts with Chrysler, North American Aviation, and Mack

Truck, among others. See *UAW-CIO Ammunition* 4 (April 1946): 23. For the UE's contract provisions, see "GE, Wemco Locals Seek Equality for Veterans," *UE News* 7 (3 Feb. 1945): 1; and "Seniority and Jobs for Servicemen," *UE News* 6 (3 June 1944): 3.

20. NWTUL, *Action Needed*, 11–12; *Proceedings of UE Convention*, 1943, 223. For a similar statement by a female UAW activist, see *Proceedings of UAW Convention*, 1944, 120.

21. The Selective Service Act of 1940 guaranteed veterans seniority credit for the period for which they had been employed before the war, but beyond that the law was ambiguous. Lewis B. Hershey, director of the Selective Service, favored the "super-seniority" interpretation of the act and argued that the law's intention was to guarantee veterans an absolute right to reinstatement in their former or comparable positions and protection from layoffs for a year thereafter, *regardless* of the prewar seniority status of the veteran in comparison to that of a nonveteran whom he might displace. Under this interpretation, a veteran who had worked two years for a firm and then served four years in the military could displace a worker with twenty years' service. Organized labor strongly objected to this reading of the law, not only because it played havoc with the seniority principle, but also because it encouraged veterans to look to the government rather than to the unions for protection. Although supporting preferential treatment of a more limited sort for veterans, the unions viewed Hershey's reading of the law as an effort to divide the loyalties of veterans from those of other workers. The unions therefore urged veterans to reject the temporary, one-year guarantee proffered under the law in favor of permanent seniority protection that took the special situation of veterans into account. In 1946, the U.S. Supreme Court ruled against Hershey's "super-seniority" interpretation of the law. However, individual employers and unions remained free to enter into contractual agreements on the issue as they saw fit. For a full discussion of this controversy, see Robert P. Brecht, "Collective Bargaining and Re-employment of Veterans," *Annals of the American Academy of Political and Social Science* 227 (May 1943): 94–103; Joel Seidman, *American Labor from Defense to Reconversion* (Chicago: University of Chicago Press, 1953), 231–32.

22. "Sister Sue Says," *UAW-CIO Ammunition* 4 (Feb. 1946): 20. Emphasis in the original.

23. Interview with Ruth Glassman, Oral History of the American Left Collection, Tamiment Library, New York University.

24. Oral history of Mildred Jeffrey, *The Twentieth Century Trade Union Woman: Vehicle for Social Change*, Oral History Project of the Program on Women and Work, Institute of Labor and Industrial Relations, University of Michigan and Wayne State University (1978), 72, 75 (copy in Wayne State University Archives of Labor History and Urban Affairs [hereafter WSU Archives]).

25. *Proceedings of UE Convention*, 1944, 255–56.

26. "Report on Women in Our Industry," submitted by Ruth Young, Executive Secretary, District 4, to the General Executive Board, 16–17 March 1944, in United Electrical Workers, *Exhibits* in the case of the EEOC against General Electric (1976), 38 (copy in UE Archives, University of Pittsburgh).

27. Constance Green, "The Role of Women as Production Workers in War Plants

in the Connecticut Valley," *Smith College Studies in History* 28 (1946): 16; Albert Fitzgerald to Thomas Flanagan, 26 Aug. 1948, in *Exhibits,* 1050; and see chapter 8.

28. "Women in Trade Unions During the War Period"; UE memo, 10 May 1946 (see note 15); Finn Theodore Malm, "Local 201, UE-CIO: A Case Study of a Local Industrial Union," (Ph.D. diss., Massachusetts Institute of Technology, 1946), 372.

29. Ethel Erickson to Mrs. Hilton, 2 April 1951, with enclosed field reports, in Records of the U.S. Women's Bureau, National Archives, Record Group 86, box 1600, folder: "Equal Pay Study."

30. "Women in UE," (pamphlet) published by UE District 4, Newark, New Jersey, 1949, in *Exhibits,* 824.

31. Conrad Grimes [President, UE Local 804] to Dear Members, 11 Jan. 1946, in IUE Local 804 Records [unprocessed], Wright State University Archives, Fairborn, Ohio. A copy of the contract in effect at the time is also in this collection. It contains a seniority clause with no explicit sex discrimination but with seniority rights within job classifications.

32. Margaret Toy to Julius Emspak, 11 Oct. 1944, in Records of UE District 1, UE Archives, folder 146; Emspak to Toy, 26 Oct. 1944, in Records of UE District 1, UE Archives, folder 135. The memo from the UE to the U.S. Women's Bureau, cited in notes 15 and 28, claims that the union's efforts to narrow sex differentials in wages constituted its program for protecting women against downgradings.

33. "GE Seniority Clauses on Seniority in Layoffs," in *Exhibits,* 1411–14; Malm, "Local 201, UE-CIO," 374–75; Ronald W. Schatz, *The Electrical Workers: A History of Labor at General Electric and Westinghouse, 1923–60* (Urbana: University of Illinois Press, 1983), 113–14, 122–23.

34. This is discussed in detail in chapter 8. See also the sources cited in note 13.

35. Computed from U.S. Bureau of Labor Statistics, *Women in Factories* (mimeographed), 1947, 6–7.

36. The 47 percent figure is the mean of the percentages for each of the eight months from December 1945 to July 1946. See "Veterans Return to the Nation's Factories," *Monthly Labor Review* 63 (Dec. 1946): 924–34.

37. "Recent Trends Affecting the Employment of Women in Automobile Manufacturing in Detroit," 26 July 1946, in Records of the U.S. Women's Bureau, National Archives, Record Group 86, box 1290, folder: "247 Michigan Dept. of Labor."

38. Interview with Andrew Court, Detroit, Michigan, 25 June 1981.

39. This is Alan Clive's estimate in his *State of War: Michigan in World War II* (Ann Arbor: University of Michigan Press, 1979), 216. David Ross also stresses the limited reemployment rights of veterans in *Preparing for Ulysses: Politics and Veterans during World War II* (New York: Columbia University Press, 1969), especially 157.

40. "Veterans Return to the Nation's Factories."

41. Olga S. Halsey, "Women Workers and Unemployment Insurance since V-J Day," *Social Security Bulletin* 9 (June 1946): 4.

42. Unfortunately, detailed statistics on the long-term postwar employment sit-

uation of veterans are not available for individual industries. However, the aggregate data that do exist are suggestive. A special survey of veterans by the U.S. Census Bureau conducted in October 1955 found that ten years after the end of World War II, 28.5 percent of all veterans were employed in manufacturing jobs. Sixty percent of these veterans were less than thirty-five years old in 1955. (The survey included both Korean War and World War II veterans, but the latter comprised 85 percent of the total of twenty-one million veterans in the U.S. in 1955.)

Of the six million veterans employed in manufacturing jobs in 1955, five million were World War II veterans. About two million of these were thirty-five years old or more (in 1955). In 1947, the auto industry employed 5 percent of all manufacturing workers, so if we assume that auto also employed 5 percent of the veterans in manufacturing, we can estimate that one hundred thousand veterans over age twenty-five worked in auto in 1945. This is surely a maximum figure, because veterans' turnover was high, and auto firms were known to discriminate against older workers of both sexes. Also, Korean War veterans were probably disproportionately represented in the age group under thirty-five in the 1955 census. For the figures on veterans, see *Readjustment Benefits: General Survey and Appraisal. A Report on Veterans' Benefits in the United States by the President's Commission on Veterans' Pensions* (House Committee Print no. 289, for the use of the House Committee on Veterans Affairs, Staff Report no. 9, pt. A, 84th Cong., 2nd sess., Sept. 1956), 276. The 5 percent figure for auto employment is from the *1947 Census of Manufactures,* vol. 1, 70–77.

43. *Women in Factories,* 6–7.

44. Robert C. Weaver, *Negro Labor: A National Problem* (New York: Harcourt, Brace and World, 1946); August Meier and Elliot Rudwick, *Black Detroit and the Rise of the UAW* (New York: Oxford University Press, 1979), 213.

45. Ibid., 215.

46. The figures on Chrysler for 1945–46 are from Weaver, *Negro Labor,* 289. All the 1960 figures are from UAW documents submitted at the *Hearings before the U.S. Commission on Civil Rights,* held in Detroit on 14–15 Dec. 1960, 63–64.

47. U.S. Department of Labor, Women's Bureau, Bulletin no. 211, *Employment of Women in the Early Postwar Period, with Background of Prewar and War Data* (1947), 5; "Postwar Labor Turn-Over among Women Factory Workers," *Monthly Labor Review* 64 (March 1947): 411; *Women in Factories,* 6–7.

48. U.S. Senate Hearings, *Manpower Problems in Detroit,* 79th Cong., 1st sess., 9–13 March 1945, 13109–11; A. G. Mezerik, "Getting Rid of the Women," *Atlantic Monthly* 175 (June 1945): 81; and for employer complaints about unemployment insurance, see Walter F. Wright to John H. Middlekamp, 11 March 1944, memorandum on "Work Availability Michigan Area and Employees' Refusal to Work," in Records of the War Production Board, National Archives, Record Group 179, box 2106, folder: "631.044 Automotive Industry Labor #1."

49. "UAW Fights to Keep Women in Jobs Here," *Detroit News,* 19 July 1945, in UAW Public Relations Collection, WSU Archives, box 14, folder: "Women."

50. Oral history of Mildred Jeffrey, 63–64.

51. William Oliver, "Report on Employees Laid Off from the Bomber Project,

Highland Park Plant—(Johnson's Division): February 9, 1945," in UAW Ford Department Collection, WSU Archives, box 16, folder: "William Oliver Reports."

52. "Report of Women's Committee of Local 400—UAW-CIO," submitted to International Executive Board in Washington, D.C., 9 Nov. 1945, copy in Addes Collection, WSU Archives, box 69A, folder 69A–1: "400 (1) Highland Park, Mich. Ford Motor Company" (emphasis in the original).

53. *Women in Factories,* 7.

54. *Proceedings of the UAW Convention,* 1946, 53.

55. See Tobias and Anderson, "What Really Happened to Rosie the Riveter," 12–26; Gabin, "Women Workers and the UAW in the Post-World War II Period," 23f.

56. Oral history of Mildred Jeffrey, 70–71.

57. Jennie Lee Murphy and Minnie P. Sowell to Thomas J. Starling, 13 April 1946, in Walter Reuther Collection, WSU Archives, box 23, folder; "Ford Dept., 1946–47."

58. For example, see the case of Catherine Sulewski, in UAW Local 51 Collection, WSU Archives, box 25, folder 25–15: "Unemployment Compensation, Michigan, Corres. 1947," and the case of Sarah Strickland of Local 236 mentioned in "Summary of the Minutes—National UAW-CIO Advisory Council on Discrimination," Meeting of 2 April 1947, in UAW Fair Practices Department—Women's Bureau Collection, WSU Archives, box 2, folder 2–23: "National Advisory Council UAW-CIO, Statement and Minutes circa 1946," 5.

59. "Exodus from Auto," *UAW Research Report* 6 (April 1946).

60. "Employment: Cut-Backs of Women since VJ Day," in Records of the U.S. Women's Bureau, National Archives, Record Group 86, box 1536.

61. U.S. Women's Bureau, *Baltimore Women War Workers in the Postwar Period* (mimeo, 1948), 8, 19, 28.

62. New York State Department of Labor, Division of Women in Industry, *Employment of Women in the First Post-Reconversion Year in New York State, 1946–1947* (1947), 13–14.

63. U.S. Women's Bureau, Bulletin no. 216, *Women Workers after V-J Day in One Community—Bridgeport, Connecticut* (1947), 4.

64. *Baltimore Women War Workers,* 58, *Women Workers after V-J Day in Bridgeport,* 10; New York State Department of Labor, Division of Women in Industry, *Employers' Post-War Plans for Women Workers* (1945), 5.

65. *Unemployment Notes* 2 (3 Dec. 1945), issued by UE District 4—copy in Papers of the IUE, Rutgers University Library, New Brunswick, N.J., box A2.02, folder: "UE District 4—Council Meeting Minutes and District Exec. Board Meeting Minutes (1945–46)." This survey also included sixty-five men, fifteen of whom got new jobs at higher pay, sixteen at the same pay, and thirty-four with pay cuts (averaging 5 percent).

66. *Baltimore Women War Workers,* 42.

67. Ibid., 28; "Women in UE," published by UE District 4, Newark, 1949, in *Exhibits,* 825; Green, "Role of Women as Production Workers," 13. See chapter 8 for discussion of the internal controversy within the UE over this issue.

68. Interview with Lola Weixel.

69. William H. Chafe, *The American Woman: Her Changing Social, Economic, and Political Role, 1920–1970* (New York: Oxford University Press, 1972), 137; American Management Association, Special Research Report no. 2, *Supervision of Women on Production Jobs: A Study of Management's Problems and Practices in Handling Female Personnel* (1943), 8–10 (emphasis in the original).

70. "Meeting for Discussion on Labor Supply and Future Labor Requirements," 26 June 1942, Detroit, 30–31, transcript in Records of the War Production Board, National Archives, Record Group 179, box 1016, folder: "241.11R Labor—Women—Recruiting Drive."

71. *Factory Management and Maintenance* 101 (Feb. 1943): 94.

72. "Women Outdoing Men, Ford Survey Reveals," *Daily News,* 8 Sept. 1943.

73. *Employers' Post-War Plans,* 5; Green, "Role of Women as Production Workers," 65.

74. National Industrial Conference Board, "Wartime Pay of Women in Industry," *Studies in Personnel Policy,* no. 58 (1943): 27; "Woman's Place," *Business Week,* 16 May 1942, 20–22. For another example of this, see Katherine Glover, "Women as Manpower," *Survey Graphic* 32 (March 1943): 72. In interpreting these claims about women's greater productivity, it is important to note that women were new workers and often unfamiliar with established production norms. Indeed, male workers often expressed resentment of female rate-busters during the mobilization period. See, for examples of this, *Manpower Problems in Detroit,* 13345f, 13433, 13460, 13588, and 13593; and also *Proceedings, First Annual Educational Conference,* International Union, United Automobile, Aircraft, and Agricultural Implement Workers of America, Chicago, 25–27 Feb. 1944, 88–89. There is also some fragmentary evidence that women became accustomed to production norms as they gained experience in the plants. For an example of management accusations that women war workers were restricting output, see *Manpower Problems in Detroit,* 13559 and 13597–98.

75. *Modern Industry,* 15 July 1942, summarized in *Management Review* 31 (Sept. 1942): 303–4. Regarding the use of women as supervisors, see *Supervision of Women on Production Jobs,* 24–27. A more typical (and more skeptical) contemporary view of women's capabilities as supervisors is Donald A. Laird and Eleanor C. Laird, *The Psychology of Supervising the Working Woman* (New York: McGraw Hill, 1942), 118, 175–76. Rosabeth Moss Kanter provides an insightful analysis of the still-common view that women workers themselves prefer male supervisors in her *Men and Women of the Corporation* (New York: Basic Books, 1977), especially 186–95.

76. Computed from data in *The Management Almanac 1946* (New York: National Industrial Conference Board, 1946), 77.

77. U.S. Bureau of Labor Statistics, Bulletin no. 952, *Wage Structure—Metalworking Industries, 1945* (1949), 9, 78 has the 1945 figures. Strictly comparable data are not available, but women's average annual earnings in radio were only 58 percent of men's in 1936. See "Annual Earnings in the Radio Industry," *Monthly Labor Review* 49 (July 1939): 1690, and women's average hourly earnings in the part of the electrical industry making integral horsepower motors and generators

were 66 percent of men's in 1937. See "Earnings and Hours in the Manufacture of Electrical Products—Part 2," *Monthly Labor Review* 49 (July 1939): 195.

78. "Women's Rates Advance," *UAW Research Report* 4 (Oct.-Nov. 1944): 4.

79. "Wartime Pay of Women," 18–19. WLB policy permitted wage increases to eliminate sex differentials for "comparable work"; it did not mandate them. While there were many voluntary adjustments agreed to between management and unions, as well as many dispute cases, the differentials remained if the union did not raise the issue. For fuller discussion, see chapter 5.

80. New York State Department of Labor, Division of Women in Industry, *Women's Wages on Men's Jobs* (1944), 26.

81. See New York State Department of Labor, Division of Women in Industry, *Absenteeism in New York State War Production Plants* (1943); National Industrial Conference Board, "The Problem of Absenteeism," *Studies in Personnel Policy*, no. 53 (1943); "Women Workers on War Production," *UAW Research Report* 3 (March 1943): 3. This last item includes the following citation from *Wards Automotive Reports*, 20 Feb. 1943: "Some fears have been expressed that family ties, especially in the case of married women workers, would result in raising the absenteeism figure to an undesirable level. Such has not been the case so far. In fact, it is the other way around, the women workers appearing to be more dependable to a certain degree. In some of the larger plants, where as high as 4 percent of the total weekly factory operating rate is said to represent male absenteeism, the female worker shows only 1 percent."

82. *Manpower Problems in Detroit*, 13112–13.

83. See Howell John Harris, *The Right to Manage: Industrial Relations Policies of American Business in the 1940s* (Madison: University of Wisconsin Press, 1982), 66–67, 91–93.

84. Ibid. This is Harris's main thesis.

85. Recall the more general discussion of this problem as it arises within Marxist-feminist theories of job segregation by sex (chapter 1). Riley, " 'The Free Mothers,' " presents the most convincing case for this argument in regard to the postwar transition for the British case, but she relies on evidence about state policy with virtually none directly from employers.

86. Green, "Role of Women as Production Workers," 64–65 (emphasis added).

87. Meier and Rudwick, *Black Detroit*.

88. Ibid.; Weaver, *Negro Labor*.

89. Meier and Rudwick, *Black Detroit*, 113. See also Karen Anderson, "Last Hired, First Fired: Black Women Workers during World War II," *Journal of American History* 69 (June 1982), especially 86–87, where white male workers' attitudes toward women and blacks are compared.

90. Both the employment figures and the quote are cited in Herbert R. Northrup, Richard L. Rowan, et al., *Negro Employment in Basic Industry*, Industrial Research Unit, Wharton School of Finance and Commerce, University of Pennsylvania (1970), 65–75. The national employment figures are from the U.S. Census, and because (unlike the figures for Detroit) they include both production and nonproduction workers, they overstate the difference between Detroit and the nation as a

whole, for the vast majority of nonproduction workers were white in this period. The quote is from the *Wall Street Journal,* 24 Oct. 1957.

Chapter 8. Resistance to Management's Postwar Policies

1. For example, William H. Chafe's *The American Woman: Her Changing Social, Economic and Political Role, 1920–1970* (New York: Oxford University Press, 1972), while stressing the fact that women left their war jobs but not the labor force, makes no mention of such protests. More recent works have mentioned women's protests against sex discrimination within the unions but say virtually nothing about women's self-organization within the unions in opposition to management. See, for example, Alan Clive, *State of War: Michigan in World War II* (Ann Arbor: University of Michigan Press, 1979), 268, and D'Ann Campbell, *Women at War with America: Private Lives in a Patriotic Era* (Cambridge: Harvard University Press, 1984), 149–52. The major exception to this is Nancy Gabin's work on women auto workers, which documents in great detail both women's protests against discrimination within the UAW and their resistance to management. See her articles: "Women Workers and the UAW in the Post-World War II Period, 1945–1954," *Labor History* 21 (Winter 1979–80): 5–30; and "'They Have Placed a Penalty on Womanhood': The Protest Actions of Women Auto Workers in Detroit-area UAW Locals, 1945–1947," *Feminist Studies* 8 (Summer 1982): 373–98.

2. For accounts of the general management assault on labor in this period, see Clark Kerr, "Employer Policies in Industrial Relations, 1945 to 1947," in *Labor in Postwar America,* ed. Colston E. Warne (Brooklyn: Remsen Press, 1949), 43–76; and Howell John Harris, *The Right to Manage: Industrial Relations Policies of American Business in the 1940s* (Madison: University of Wisconsin Press, 1982), especially chapters 4 and 5. Union collusion with management is discussed in detail in chapter 7 as well as below.

3. "CIO Women Want Voice," *Detroit Times* 26 July 1945, in UAW Public Relations Collection, Wayne State University Archives of Labor History and Urban Affairs [hereafter WSU Archives], box 14, folder: "Women."

4. "Seniority," in R. J. Thomas, *Report of UAW-CIO Women's Conference* (Detroit: 8–9 Dec. 1944) to International Executive Board Meeting, 22 Jan. 1945 in UAW War Policy Division—Victor Reuther Collection, WSU Archives, box 27, folder: "War Policy Women's Bureau, Nov. 1944—Jan. 1945."

5. Mildred Jeffrey to Ruth Adlard, 5 July 1945, UAW War Policy Division—Women's Bureau Collection, WSU Archives, box 1, folder 1–1: "Absenteeism and Turnover—Correspondence."

6. The women delegates were from Locals 653 (Pontiac), 190 (Packard), 50 (Willow Run), 400 (Ford, Highland Park) and 600 (Ford, Rouge). See "Women Protest to WLB," *Detroit Times,* 19 July 1945, and "CIO Women Set to Revolt," *Detroit Times,* 21 July 1945, both in UAW Public Relations Collection, WSU Archives, box 14, folder: "Women."

7. "CIO Women Set to Revolt," *Detroit Times,* 21 July 1945; "Women Call UAW

Biased," *Detroit Times,* 30 July 1945; "Union Women Balk PAC Coup at Meeting," *Detroit Times,* 6 August 1945; all in UAW Public Relations Collection, WSU Archives, box 14, folder: "Women."

8. "CIO Women Want Voice," *Detroit Times,* 26 July 1945, in UAW Public Relations Collection, WSU Archives, box 14, folder: "Women."

9. Ibid.

10. R. J. Thomas to All Local Union Presidents, Regional Directors and International Representatives, 26 Sept. 1945, copy in Emil Mazey Collection, WSU Archives, Series 2, box 13, folder: "Women's Division, 1941–1947, 1." The letter was composed as if the Executive Board had independently adopted a concern with the women's seniority issue, in no way acknowledging the role of the women's delegation in urging it to act, but the letter's timing makes its actual origin obvious.

11. Ibid.

12. See Jonas Silver and Everett Kassalow, "Seniority in the Automobile Industry," U.S. Bureau of Labor Statistics, Industrial Relations Division (mimeo, April 1944), 5.

13. These comments accompanied questionnaires returned by Locals 72 and 172, in the UAW War Policy Division—Women's Bureau Collection, WSU Archives, Series 1, box 5, folder 5–12.

14. Harold J. Thompson to George F. Addes, received July 2, 1942, in Addes Collection, WSU Archives, box 100, folder 100–1: "WIM-WY (1 of 2)."

15. "Women Give Up Job Rights for 4 Weeks Severance Pay," *Detroit News,* 3 July 1945; and "Hit WLB Approval of MESA Pact to Fire Women First," *Daily Worker,* 25 July 1945; both in UAW Public Relations Collection, WSU Archives, box 14, folder: "Women."

16. "Women Protest to WLB" (see note 6).

17. Silver and Kassalow, "Seniority in the Automobile Industry," 26. A copy of the supplement to the UAW-GM contract covering this matter is in the UAW Research Department Collection, WSU Archives, box 13, folder 13–23: "GM Contract Negotiations, 1943–6."

18. "What Happens When 150 Women Are Fired," *UAW-CIO Ammunition* 5 (May 1947): 1–4; *UAW-CIO Fair Practices Fact Sheet* 1 (May 1947). The latter source mentions Della Rymer's activity in this dispute. (Her participation in the Women's Revolt is mentioned in "Women Call UAW Biased," cited in note 7). Regarding Pontiac's unsuccessful attempt "to secure approval from the union for special concessions to new women hires," see the *Report* of the UAW-CIO Fair Practices Committee and Anti-Discrimination Department to the International Executive Board, 10 Dec. 1946 (2nd Quarterly Report), 16.

19. "A Complaint from the Women," *New York Times,* 9 Nov. 1945, 12; "Report of Women's Committee on Local 400—UAW-CIO," submitted to International Executive Board Meeting in session in Washington, D.C., 9 Nov. 1945, copy in Addes Collection, WSU Archives, box 69A, folder 69A–1: "400 (1) Highland Park, Mich. Ford Motor Company."

20. "The Detroit West Side Local Stands Up for Its Women: An Incident in a Foundry," *UAW-CIO Ammunition* 5 (Jan. 1946): 30–31.

21. "31 Obscure Women vs. the Giant Chrysler Corporation: The Company Pays $55,000 in Amends for Pushing 31 Women Around," *UAW-CIO Ammunition* 6 (March 1948): 32–35.

22. "Report of Women's Committee of Local 400—UAW-CIO"; minutes of 20 May 1945 Local 400 meeting, section on "Discussion against Women under Interchangeable Group Agreement," 9–11, UAW Local 400 Collection, WSU Archives, pt. 1, box 1, folder: "Plant Wide Meetings, 1945"; "Report of Meeting on Women's Rehire Problem," 24 July 1946, and "Report of Lincoln Meet.," 28 July 1946, both in UAW Ford Department Collection, WSU Archives, box 16, folder: "Harry Ross—Reports."

23. "The Detroit West Side Local Stands Up," 31.

24. "31 Obscure Women vs. The Giant Chrysler Corporation."

25. "Report of Women's Committee of Local 400—UAW-CIO"; Local 400 Re: Discrimination against Women and Disabled Members," minutes of IEB meeting, 7–12 Nov. 1945, 41, in Addes Collection, WSU Archives, box 25, folder 25–6: "Minutes Sp. Board Meeting Nov. 7–12, 1945."

26. Minutes of 20 May 1945 Local 400 meeting, 9.

27. "Report of Women's Committee of Local 400—UAW-CIO."

28. *Proceedings of UAW Convention*, 1946, 51–52.

29. Ibid., 53; and regarding the threatened picket line, see "Report on Meeting on Women's Rehire Problem."

30. *Proceedings of UAW Convention*, 1946, 54.

31. A copy of the leaflet is in the Addes Collection, WSU Archives, box 69A, folder 69A–1: "400 (1) Highland Park, Mich. Ford Motor Company."

32. "Report of Women's Committee of Local 400—UAW-CIO."

33. For example, Alice Sowden of Local 125 complained to the International, "We were competent and skilled in our work, but were laid off for the stated reason 'that we were women' no other reason given. Excuse was that work was too heavy and that contracts for the same or similar products have been made since and we have not been called back to work. . . . Our steward has refused to represent us at union meetings. Our claims are disregarded and we are unable to get a hearing. (Addes Collection, WSU Archives, box 75, folder: "Appeal Case-A. Sowden v. Local 125") As Mildred Jeffrey recalled, "It happened, I think, in hundreds of cases. Grievances simply weren't processed." Oral history of Mildred Jeffrey, *The Twentieth Century Trade Union Woman: Vehicle for Social Change*, Oral History Project of the Program on Women and Work, Institute of Labor and Industrial Relations, University of Michigan and Wayne State University (1978), 70 (copy in WSU Archives).

34. A series of thirty-three letters from H. L. Lane, Jr. of Ford Labor Relations to Ken Bannon, dated September 18, 1946 to July 15, 1947, lists a total of 429 women "recalled for available work as per seniority." The letters are in the UAW Local 400 Collection, WSU Archives, pt. 1, box 9, folder: "Women Called Back, 1946–1947."

An indication of the extent to which the women so recalled were actually reintegrated into the Highland Park plant's work force is found in a memorandum sent on October 18, 1945 to Leon Pody of the UAW Ford Department from Joseph Bailey, a UAW International Representative, reporting on the situation at that time (UAW Ford Department Collection, WSU Archives, box 6, folder: "Female Employees"):

To date the results [of the Women's Agreement] have been as follows:

95 women have been notified to return to work.

12 refused to accept job offered to them.

32 failed to report as of October 16, 1946 (the Company has not enforced the five (5) day period referred to in the contract). Some of these women may return to work in the near future.

3 of these women have been given medical leaves of absence.

34 were actually reinstated and are working at the present time.

35. A copy of the leaflet is in the Addes Collection, WSU Archives, box 69A, folder 69A–1: "400 (1) Highland Park, Mich. Ford Motor Company."

36. See chapter 7.

37. Interview with Wanita Allen, Rosie the Riveter Film Project, Emeryville, California, p. 26 of transcript.

38. William H. Oliver to Richard T. Leonard, 21 Nov. 1945, UAW Ford Department Collection, WSU Archives, box 16, folder: "William Oliver Reports."

39. For another example of a situation where such a survey was conducted (at the Ford Rouge plant) see "Appeal Hearing—International Appeal Committee—Region 1A UAW-CIO, in the Matter of Anne Cooper and others versus Local 600 and Pressed Steel Unit, Local 600," transcript in Emil Mazey Collection, WSU Archives, box 29, folder 29–20: "Local 600—Appeal Hearing."

40. The decision went against the women because of a loophole in the Local 400 contract, signed in March 1945, which provided that workers could only bump others in their interchangeable occupational group with the least seniority (see discussion in text above of interchangeable groups). To eliminate the women, management would simply hire new male employees and place them on the heaviest jobs, so that women (as well as disabled or elderly men) laid off from other jobs could exercise their seniority bumping rights only on the jobs that were least desirable and most difficult to qualify for. "Thus thousands of female employees and elderly male employees were put thru a phoney process of purportedly exercising their seniority and were laid off because the company claimed they were physically unable to do the job to which their seniority entitled them," noted John Carney, president of Local 400 in a report to the UAW Executive Board. ("Local 400 Re: Discrimination against Women & Disabled Members.") Once the local, however unwittingly, had agreed to this arrangement, the Umpire Decision against the women was a foregone conclusion. It read in part:

The pertinent language of the contract is clear, and was purposely made clear, so as to limit the exercise of seniority against the employee with the least seniority in the group and against no one else. . . . The existence of legal limitations on the work which women can do was well known to the negotiators, as was the fact of physical incapacity of some employees for some jobs. But no exceptions were made to the general rule. . . . It can hardly be disputed that the Union's present position is not in accord with the local agreement . . . the local union, in its brief . . . fully recognized this and asked that the agreement "be renegotiated and revised . . . in the spirit and intent that it should have been done in the first instance." This, obviously, I have no power to require. (Opinion A–211, 30 Nov. 1945, "Lay-off of Female Employees Unable to Do Jobs Held by Youngest Seniority Employees in Labor Pool," in *UAW-Ford Umpire Decisions,* Harry Shulman, Opinions A1-A284, Decisions M1- M399, Issued by National Ford Department, UAW.)

41. "Departmental Communication," from Manton M. Cummins to All Building Superintendents, 30 Aug. 1946, in UAW Local 400 Collection, WSU Archives, pt. 1, box 9, folder: "Women Called Back, 1946–1947."

42. Ken Bannon to Edward Greenwald, 25 Feb. 1947, in UAW Local 400 Collection, WSU Archives, pt. 1, box 8, folder: "Seniority, 1946–1949." The same folder includes a handwritten note from Samuel Bitner, the District Committeeman in the department, also dated February 25, 1947, supplying him with this information. How the complaint originated, however, is unclear—it was probably called to the committeeman's attention by some of the workers in the immediate vicinity of the three positions involved, but there is no record of this, or of the gender of the original complainants. See also H. Doran, for E. M. Baker, Director, Hourly Personnel Department, Industrial Relations Division, Ford Motor Company, to Ken Bannon, 28 Feb. 1947; and Ken Bannon to H. Doran, 6 March 1947, both in UAW Local 400 Collection, WSU Archives, pt. 1, box 8, folder: "Seniority, 1946–1949."

43. "UE Fights for Women Workers" (UE pamphlet, 1952), 35, reproduced in United Electrical Workers, *Exhibits* in the case of the EEOC against General Electric (1976), 863 (copy in UE Archives, University of Pittsburgh).

44. Ronald W. Schatz, *The Electrical Workers: A History of Labor at General Electric and Westinghouse* (Urbana: University of Illinois Press, 1983), 121–22.

45. See chapter 7.

46. See chapter 3.

47. See the materials from this case reproduced in *Exhibits,* 1218A-K; and "Report of the Investigating Committee on the Married Women's Appeal in Sharon," in Records of UE District 6, UE Archives, folder 545; the case is also discussed in Schatz, *The Electrical Workers,* 125–27.

48. Sally McGrath, et al. to Stanley Loney [President, UE District Council 6], 25 June 1948, in *Exhibits,* 1218F-G.

49. Ibid., regarding the threat see pp. 1218F-G and regarding the settlement pp. 1218J-K.

50. Marie Sutton to Albert Fitzgerald, 2 March 1948 [1949], in Records of UE District 2, UE Archives, folder 181.

51. Albert Fitzgerald to William Lieberman and Leo Benoit, 29 March 1949, in Records of UE District 2, UE Archives, folder 174.

52. See the news clippings in Records of UE District 2, UE Archives, folder 198; and leaflet, "UE Says Fire Married Women," 27 Feb. 1950, in IUE Local 755 Collection, Wright State University Archives, Fairborn, Ohio, box 69, file 8: "Leaflets on Union Politics, 1950." Ronald Schatz points out that the Communist Party was beginning to question the principle of strict seniority by 1949–50, with a view to altering the status of blacks in the electrical industry (a subordinate status re-

produced by straight seniority), foreshadowing the concept of "affirmative action" that emerged in the 1960s (*The Electrical Workers,* 127f). It is striking that such arguments were not advanced by the Communists in the UE in relation to women workers—although because the CP position in regard to blacks won little support, the absence of such a position regarding women was of little practical consequence.

53. Memorandum from David Scribner and Peter Agbondi to Albert Fitzgerald, 18 Aug. 1948, re: "Westinghouse, Sharon Married Women," reproduced in *Exhibits,* 1218B-D.

54. In both auto and electrical manufacturing, the change in the composition of the female labor force by age and marital status was dramatic in this period. In 1930, 80 percent of women auto workers and 87 percent of women electrical workers had been thirty-four years old or less. By 1950, the *median* age of women auto workers was thirty-six, and that of women electrical workers was thirty-two. The change in regard to marital status was also drastic: While in 1930, only 40 percent of women auto workers and 23 percent of women electrical workers had been married, by 1950, 67 percent of women auto workers and 62 percent of women electrical workers were married. Data compiled from the U.S. Bureau of the Census, *1930 Census of Population,* vol. 5, 267–78, 469, 533; and U.S. Bureau of the Census, *1950 Census of Population,* Special Report P-E, no. 1B: *Occupational Characteristics,* 72–80, 96, 98.

55. "Interview: Comparable Worth in the Forties: Reflections by Sylvia Scribner," *Women's Rights Law Reporter* 8 (Winter 1984): 106.

56. "Terms UE Proposal 'Miserable Package'," *UE News* 8 (5 Jan. 1946): 3.

57. "Against the Mainstream: Interview with James Matles of the UE," in *Studies on the Left* 5 (Winter 1965): 45; "GE Settles for 18 1/2 . . .," *UE News* 8 (23 March 1946): 1; "$56 Million Profit not Enough for GE," *UE News* 8 (11 May 1946): 12.

58. "WH Agrees to 18 Plus 1, Union Security and Full Contract," *UE News* 8 (11 May 1946): 5.

59. Statistics for the immediate postwar period on sex differentials in wages for these industries are sparse, and strictly comparable data for the war and postwar periods are not available. The closest approximation is in the 1950 census, which has figures by sex on the median annual income of operatives in auto and electrical manufacturing who worked fifty or more weeks in 1949. According to this data, women auto operatives earned 80 percent of the annual income of male operatives in 1949, compared to the 90 percent figure cited above for 1944. Similarly, in electrical manufacturing, women operatives earned 72 percent of the annual income of male operatives in 1949, compared to the 75 percent figure cited above for 1945. (The wartime figures are based on hourly earnings—see pp. 121–22.) For the 1949 data, see U.S. Bureau of the Census *1950 Census of Population,* Special Report P-E, no. 1B: *Occupational Characteristics,* 251, 254, 259, 262. Note, however, that the trend was in the opposite direction at General Electric, where according to UE records there was a significant narrowing of sex differentials between 1945 and 1951. (See p. 149 and note 62 below.) The discrepancy may be because of the fact that the 1949 data are for annual earnings, as opposed to the hourly earnings in the 1944 and 1945 data as well as the GE data. If men worked more overtime than

women in 1949, the 72 percent figure would be distorted in a downward direction
in terms of its comparability to the 75 percent figure for hourly earnings in 1945.

60. "Women in UE," issued by District 4, Newark, 1949, reproduced in *Exhibits*,
822.

61. "Minutes of UE National Fair Practices Committee," 12 Dec. 1950, reproduced in *Exhibits*, 399.

62. *Exhibits*, 1357. See also "UE Strike Victory at Tung-Sol Narrows Women's
Differential," in UE District 4 Fair Practices Bulletin, no. 1, 12 June 1953, reproduced in *Exhibits*, 1020B; for other evidence (grievances and records of collective
bargaining) of continuing UE efforts to narrow differentials, see *Exhibits*, 1230–
33, 1241–42, 1258–59, 1261–62, 1264–65.

63. "UE Fights for Women Workers," 33.

64. Ibid., 9. (Emphasis in the original.)

65. In recent years, the IUE has brought up the issue of comparable worth again.
See for example *IUE* v. *Westinghouse Electric Corp*. 23 FEP Cases 588 (3rd Circuit,
1980), and for a fascinating analysis of the emergence of the issue in an IUE local
(Local 201, at the Lynn, Massachusetts General Electric plant) in the 1980s, see
Marcia Hamms, "Women Taking Leadership in Male Dominated Locals," *Women's
Rights Law Reporter* 8 (Winter 1984): 71–82.

Chapter 9. Epilogue and Conclusion

1. See Janet L. Norwood, *The Female-Male Earnings Gap: A Review of Employment and Earnings Issues*, U.S. Department of Labor, Bureau of Labor Statistics,
Report 673, September 1982, and James P. Smith and Michael P. Ward, *Women's
Wages and Work in the Twentieth Century* (Santa Monica: Rand Corporation, 1984).
Smith and Ward find a significant decline in the wage gap in the 1980s (although
virtually no change in the 1960s and 1970s) and extrapolate from this to predict
future improvement in women's economic status relative to men's over the next
twenty years. While they attribute the change to improvement in "women's market
skills," they do not consider the important fact that real male wages have been
declining in the 1980s, because of employment contraction and union concessions
in high-wage male jobs in basic industry. This alone may account for the reduction
in the wage gap. If so, the result does not represent any true improvement in women's
situation.

2. There have been a number of studies of occupational segregation by sex that
rely upon the methodology pioneered by Edward Gross in his classic article, "Plus
Ca Change. . . The Sexual Structure of Occupations over Time," *Social Problems*
16 (Fall 1968): 198–208. Gross demonstrated that the extent of segregation by sex
had remained virtually unchanged over the decennial censuses from 1900 to 1960.
Francine D. Blau and Wallace E. Hendriks found a slight diminution in the extent
of segregation over the 1960s, reported in their article, "Occupational Segregation
by Sex: Trends and Prospects," *The Journal of Human Resources* 14 (Spring 1979):
197–210. Refuting earlier studies that claimed that no change in the extent of seg-

regation by sex occurred in the 1970s, Andrea H. Beller argues that there was a greater decline during that decade than in the 1960s, although in both cases the change is quite modest. Andrea H. Beller, "Trends in Occupational Segregation by Sex and Race, 1960–1981," in *Sex Segregation in the Workplace: Trends, Explanations, Remedies,* ed. Barbara F. Reskin (Washington, D.C.: National Academy Press, 1984), 11–26.

3. See Victor R. Fuchs, "A Note on Sex Segregation in Professional Occupations," *Explorations in Economic Research* 2 (Winter 1975): 105–11; Janice N. Hedges and Stephen E. Bemis, "Sex Stereotyping: Its Decline in Skilled Trades," *Monthly Labor Review* 97 (May 1974): 14–22; and Beller, "Trends in Occupational Segregation."

4. These data are drawn from U.S. Department of Labor, Women's Bureau, Bulletin no. 298, *Time of Change: 1983 Handbook on Women Workers* (1983), 55–60.

5. On changing attitudes, see Andrew Cherlin and Pamela B. Walters, "Trends in United States Men's and Women's Sex Role Attitudes: 1972 to 1978," *American Sociological Review* 46 (Aug. 1981): 453–60; and Frank L. Mott, ed., *The Employment Revolution: Young American Women in the 1970s* (Cambridge: MIT Press, 1982). For a useful historical discussion of the decline of the family wage ideology, see Barbara Ehrenreich, *The Hearts of Men: American Dreams and the Flight from Commitment* (New York: Anchor Press, 1983).

6. In 1980, 60 percent of women and 64 percent of men polled by the Roper Organization indicated that they supported efforts to strengthen the status of women, while in 1970 40 percent of women and 44 percent of men were found to support such efforts. See *Virginia Slims American Women's Opinion Poll* (The Roper Organization, 1980).

7. For summaries of these laws, see U.S. Women's Bureau, *Time of Change,* 144–49, and for discussion of the enforcement mechanisms, see U.S. Commission on Civil Rights, Clearinghouse Publication 70, *Affirmative Action in the 1980s: Dismantling the Process of Discrimination* (Nov. 1981), especially 15–29.

8. On the 1970s, a good overview is Brigid O'Farrell and Sharon L. Harlan, "Job Integration Strategies: Today's Programs and Tomorrow's Needs," *Sex Segregation in the Workplace,* 267–91. On the 1980s, see Clarice Stasz, "Room at the Bottom," *Working Papers* 9 (Jan.-Feb. 1982): 28–41; "Damage Report: The Decline of Equal Employment Opportunity Enforcement Under Reagan," *Women Employed Advocates Bulletin* 3 (Dec. 1982): 1–5; "U.S. Plans to Ease Rules for Hiring Women and Blacks," *New York Times,* 3 April 1983, 1, 17; and "Changes Weighed in Federal Rules on Discrimination," *New York Times,* 3 Dec. 1984, A1, B10.

9. Total employment in "Electronic Components and Accessories" (Standard Industrial Classification 367) grew from 16 percent of the total employment of the "Electric and Electronic Equipment" industry (SIC 36) in 1960 to 19 percent in 1965, and from 20 percent in 1975 to 27 percent in 1980. More than half of the employees in SIC 367 were female in all four years. Comparing this data to that in Table 7, the correlation to the expansion of female employment as a proportion of all employment in SIC 36 is clear. Data for SIC 367 are from U.S. Bureau of Labor Statistics, Bulletin 1312–11, *Employment and Earnings, United States 1909–78*

(1979), 333; U.S. Bureau of Labor Statistics, *Supplement to Employment and Earnings* (July 1983), 105.

10. In 1973, the U.S. Equal Employment Opportunity Commission charged both the Ford Motor Company and General Motors with employment discrimination. Both charges were settled via conciliation agreements. See "Ford Motor to Spend $23 Million to Settle Bias Case," *New York Times,* 26 Nov. 1980, 1, 11. "GM Agrees to Pay $42 Million to End Case on Job Bias," *New York Times,* 19 Oct. 1983, A1, A21.

11. The current campaign for pay equity has changed this somewhat, as discussed on p. 159.

12. See chapter 1.

13. See U.S. Commission on Civil Rights, *Affirmative Action in the 1980s,* 33–37.

14. There is now a vast literature on comparable worth. Good overviews include Bureau of National Affairs, *Pay Equity and Comparable Worth* (Washington: BNA, 1984); and Roslyn L. Feldberg, "Comparable Worth: Toward Theory and Practice in the United States," *Signs* 10 (Winter 1984): 311–28. In late 1984, Reagan administration officials repeatedly denounced the idea of comparable worth: "Reagan Aide Assails Comparable Worth Idea," *New York Times,* 19 Oct. 1984, A14; "Speakes Criticizes Pay Equity Plan," *New York Times,* 26 Oct. 1984, 9; "Concept of Pay Based on Worth is the 'Looniest,' Rights Chief Says," *New York Times,* 17 Nov. 1984, 15.

15. In 1984, women were 33.7 percent of all union members in the United States, the highest proportion ever. See "Changing Employment Patterns of Organized Workers," *Monthly Labor Review* 108 (Feb., 1985): 29. For an overview of the relationship of women to the labor movement in recent years, see Ruth Milkman, "Women Workers, Feminism and the Labor Movement since the 1960s," *Women, Work and Protest: A Century of U.S. Women's Labor History,* ed. Ruth Milkman (Boston: Routledge and Kegan Paul, 1985), 300–22.

Index

A Note on the Author

Ruth Milkman holds degrees from Brown University and the University of California at Berkeley. She is currently associate professor of sociology at Queens College, City University of New York. Her articles on women, work, and unions in the past and present have appeared in such publications as *Feminist Studies, Politics & Society, The Nation, Socialist Review,* and *The Review of Radical Political Economics,* and in several anthologies. She is the editor of *Women, Work, and Protest: A Century of Women's Labor History* (Routledge and Kegan Paul, 1985).

A Generation of Boomers: The Pattern of Railroad Labor Conflict in Nineteenth-Century America
SHELTON STROMQUIST

The New England Working Class and the New Labor History
EDITED BY HERBERT G. GUTMAN AND DONALD H. BELL

Labor Leaders in America
EDITED BY MELVYN DUBOFSKY AND WARREN VAN TINE

Barons of Labor: The San Francisco Building Trades and Union Power in the Progressive Era
MICHAEL KAZIN

Once a Cigar Maker: Men, Women, and Work Culture in American Cigar Factories, 1900-1919
PATRICIA COOPER

Gender at Work: The Dynamics of Job Segregation by Sex during World War II
RUTH MILKMAN